Advances in Contemporary Educational Thought Series
Jonas F. Soltis, editor

Beyond Liberal Democracy in Schools

The Power of Pluralism

Barbara J. Thayer-Bacon

Foreword by Maxine Greene

TEACHERS
COLLEGE
PRESS

Teachers College, Columbia University
New York and London

Portions of the text have been reprinted and adapted from the following sources:

Thayer-Bacon, B. (2006). Beyond liberal democracy: Dewey's renascent liberalism. *Education and Culture, 22*(2), 19–30.

Thayer-Bacon, B. (2006). Shared authority in democratic classroom communities-always-in-the-making. In K. Cooper and R. White (Eds.), *The practical critical educator: Critical inquiry and educational practice* (pp. 95–109). Amsterdam: Springer.

Published by Teachers College Press, 1234 Amsterdam Avenue, New York, NY 10027
Copyright © 2008 by Teachers College, Columbia University

Library of Congress Cataloging-in-Publication Data

Thayer-Bacon, Barbara J., 1953–
    Beyond liberal democracy in schools : the power of pluralism / Barbara J. Thayer-Bacon.
        p. cm. — (Advances in contemporary educational thought)
    Includes bibliographical references and index.
    ISBN 978-0-8077-4865-7 (hardcover : alk. paper)
        1. Education—Philosophy. 2. Democracy and education. 3. Pluralism (Social sciences). I. Title.
    LB14.7.T525   2008
    370.11'5—dc22   2007050684

ISBN 978-0-8077-4865-7 (hardcover)

Printed on acid-free paper
Manufactured in the United States of America

15 14 13 12 11 10 09 08   8   7   6   5   4   3   2   1

*This book is dedicated to the
students, teachers, principals, and parents
of the schools I visited, as well as the hosts
who helped me get in the doors and gave me
a place to stay while there.*

Contents

Series Foreword

This is a very unusual and engaging book. While its major grounding and themes are highly theoretical, its forceful argument comes out of Thayer-Bacon's five real-world immersions in and observations of schools in five different cultures: Mexican, Native American, African, Chinese, and Japanese. It is a masterful, in-depth blend of theory and practice rendered in the personal and compassionate voice of the author while still remaining scholarly and academic in tone and purpose.

In this book, Thayer-Bacon seeks to find a way to go beyond the dominant Euro-Western political-social philosophy of classical liberalism whose basic values are individualism, rationalism, and universalism. She arrives at a theory of social life and schooling that she calls "transactional," one that should be viewed basically as "individuals-in-relation-to-others" whose basic values are "fraternity, equality, sharing, and cooperation." To arrive at this theory, she examines a number of theoretical works that critique classical liberalism, offers her own critique, and then draws from her observations of other cultures' ideas, values, and themes that ground her developing theory of a "democracy-in-the-making."

Also unique to her approach is that, for each foreign culture she observes (Mexican, African, Japanese, and Chinese), she presents a parallel observation of an American school whose students are fully or mainly from the same cultural background (i.e., African American, Mexican American, Chinese American, and Japanese American). This not only helps her develop her theory, but also makes it quite relevant to her critique of and recommendations for American education.

Her work not only offers a solid philosophical argument regarding political-social theory for our society and its schools, but also provides a new paradigm for doing philosophical work in education and connecting the real world to theory. It is truly an Advance in Contemporary Educational Thought.

—Jonas F. Soltis,
Series Editor

Foreword

This is a wise, lively, and enticing book studded with personal observations and revealing interviews. The author is a professor of history and philosophy of education, and what she writes is grounded in her knowledge of theory and her teaching experiences in a Montessori school, in public schools, and in a graduate school of teacher education. Her distinctive responses to diverse schools in this country—schools with majority populations of Native Americans, African Americans, Mexican Americans, as well as the Highlander Folk School—add concreteness and splashes of color to each account. Yet, the accounts go much further than the supplying of information.

Dr. Thayer-Bacon's work becomes particularly interesting when her inquiries begin to lead her to an ethnographic approach. Her brief engagements with a Ghanian and a Japanese family in their home countries make her comparison of their schools with ours particularly enlightening. She provides cameo shots of discipline and authority at work in classrooms that cannot but help to break stereotypes of schooling in Ghana and Japan, as well as other countries of interest in an increasingly globalized world.

All these particulars are discussed in a historical and philosophical context having to do with transformations of the theory and practice of democracy since the end of the 19th century. The author uses John Dewey's phrase "a community in the making" from his book *Philosophy and Civilization* to intensify her central point: the crucial departure from the liberal, rationalist, individualist understanding of democracy. She points to the Enlightenment-era roots of what democracy signified in human lives and then—calling on the literature of critical theory, feminism, post-modernism, and contemporary descriptions of an unsettled world—she explicates as well as any of today's educational theorists and historians the significance of "shared identities," transactionalism, and the great range of human relationships. This is an exciting book that will expand readers' perspectives while adding color and light to what they already know.

—Maxine Greene

Acknowledgments

I am daunted by the impossibility of thanking all who have contributed to a project that has spanned 7 years of my life and has taken me to 23 schools in four different states in the United States and four other countries (five, if I include the Navajo Reservation as a nation, which is certainly how the Diné view it). Many of the people to whom I owe so much must remain nameless to protect the confidentiality of the schools and those who attend and work there. If I could, I would name every student, teacher, parent, and principal I talked to; I would like them to know how very grateful I am for their generosity and kindness, and I would like to thank them for welcoming me to their schools and sharing their experiences with me.

The teachers, librarians, counselors, and principals I *can* thank include: Joe Lucente and Irene Sumida, Mike Weinstead, Jeff Castlebury, Carol Grant-Allen, Ms. Brice, Ms. Malaika and Elijah, Mike Masters, Ms. McDuffey, Mr. Whipple, Glenda Davis, Daphane Odom, Ann Thorton, Mr. Shelby, Vivian, Comfort, Happy, Elizabeth, Eric, Beatrice, Lawrence, Selena, Ophelia, Lidia, Joseph, Suzanne, Ruth, Joan Delgai, Lefel and Kathryn Vann, Joe, Leandra Begaye, Sharon Begaye, Carrie Barstad, Ann, Carol Sample, Jason, Sean, Rachel, Ben and Laura Bearclaw, Liz, Jenni, Natalie, Noah, Justin, Mr. Fukunaga, Kay, Mr. Mio and Motoko Mito, Ms. Katayama, Jennifer Waller and Jack, Mr. Tani, Ms. Hirano, Mr. Kakizaki, Mr. Yasuda, Mr. Koyama, Mr. Nakamura, Mr. Sataka, Gina Ferrante, Stacey Revitz, Helen Cheung, Margaret Ames, Annie, Lloyd Schine, Yvette Nash, Monica, Ms. B., Sharon Yow, Annie Won, Kat, Dorothy Williams, Mr. Tam, Doug Rich, Dave Philpot, and Eva Lee.

I offer special thanks to the wonderful people who hosted me, several of whom gave me a place to stay and fed me, some who extended their invitations to include my family: Caroline, Magdalena and Juan, Bernard Woma and Fortune, and their family—especially Julius and Michael, Jane Wolfle, the nuns and priest at the Catholic Mission in Klagetoh, Ian Harris and Sarah—and especially Sophie, Kikue Yamada and her family—especially Takashi and Buba, Joel and Michelle Brown, and Hongmei Peng and her family—especially

Qing Qing. I also thank two of my former colleagues at Bowling Green State University, Steve Cornelius and Karen Kakas, who put me in contact with Bernard Woma and Terrell Piechowski, both of whom helped me receive invitations into the local schools.

I started this project upon arriving at the University of Tennessee to work in the Cultural Studies program from 2000 to 2001. I am very grateful for the support I received in 2001 to 2006 from three department heads: Joy DeSensi, Michael Waugh, and Russ French. I also received support from my college during this time frame, particularly from three college deans: Glennon Rowell, John Koontz, and Bob Rider. Early on in the beginning of the project I also received support from the university in the form of a faculty development grant, and I must thank Anne Mayhew, academic provost (now retired), for that boost that helped me get going.

I have had several very talented graduate students help me along the way with hunting down sources in the library and online, finding schools to contact, and coming with me to some of the sites and serving as my translator/guide. Adam Renner helped me with research on Mexico and Mexican American education as well as African American education; he also helped me narrow down my possibilities for places where I could observe schools, and made the arrangements to travel to Ghana, West Africa—which was no easy feat. So Young Kang helped me with Native American research and contacts and Japanese American school observations. During the time she was helping me, I had a visiting scholar from Korea, Dr. Jeong Bong Cho,who shared his thoughts with us about the project. Asami Segi helped me get into the Japanese Saturday School and a nearby Japanese boarding school, and accompanied me to Japan to serve as my translator and guide in the Japanese school we visited. Yan Cao and Hongmei Peng helped me find research on Chinese Americans and education in China, and Yan accompanied me to the Chinese Sunday school while Hongmei accompanied me to China to serve as my translator and guide in the Chinese school we visited. Hongmei Peng and Scott Ellison also served as manuscript editors, reading the manuscript for errors and checking all the quotes and citations for accuracy. I engaged in many conversations with all of these students about the project, and am deeply indebted to them for sharing their insights along the way.

I shared the manuscript of this project in two stages with two different Cultural Studies seminars in the spring of 2006 and 2007, and the students who read the material gave me feedback on drafts of this material. We also talked much about the ideas within. I shared all the chapters concerning the schools with key teachers, counselors, and principals whose stories I tell and offered them the chance to make corrections. Whatever changes they suggested, I honored. I also shared the philosophical side of this work with key colleagues: Heesoon Bai, Karen Cooper, Bernardo Gallegos, Jim Garrison, Gert Biesta, Frank Margonis, A. G. Rud, Lynda Stone, Sharon Todd, Steve Tozer, Robert White, and Maxine Greene, and benefited from their work, insights, and feedback.

I presented various sections of this work at conferences that date back to 2001, and cite these conference papers at the end of each chapter. I thank the participants of these various conference sessions who responded to my papers through questions and conversations. Their questions helped me to clarify my thinking and further the development of this theory, and their enthusiastic responses encouraged me to continue with the work.

I have not only spent endless hours talking to my family about this project, but have taken my "mini-family" along with me on my travels as much as I was able (funding being our only limitation). Sam (my son) and Charles (my life partner) Bacon were as excited about traveling to other countries as I was, and while I spent time observing in local schools they took West African drumming lessons, explored the local communities, haggled for gifts in the arts bazaar, found the local bakeries and vegetable and fruit stands, caused riots with pre-schoolers who had never seen a White person before, explored the latest technology and fancy malls in China, tried the food at the American franchises, and tried to adapt to the very hot climates. I learned as much or more from staying with local people with my family and watching the children and adults interact as I learned in the schools. Sam turned 12 in Ghana and 15 in China. All of the families we stayed with came to the United States and stayed with us as well; I think their comfort and willingness to do so was because they came to know me as not only a scholar or teacher, but also as a mother and wife. Thank you, Charles and Sam, for your wonderful spirits that span cultural differences so easily; you have added more to the success of this research than I can say.

Finally, thank you's need to go to the people at Teachers College Press: to the two reviewers who gave me careful, thoughtful responses to a draft of the book; to the series editor, Jonas Soltis, for wanting to include this book in his series and for his insightful feedback and encouragement; to Christian Anderson for editing assistance and advice; to Shannon Waite for her careful production editing; and to Brian Ellerbeck, senior acquisitions editor, for listening to me talk about this project over the years at AERA conferences, and waiting patiently as I completed the manuscript. Brian worked to help take a 589-page manuscript down to a manageable, publishable size. Cutting stories I love has been a slow, painful process, for I see the faces of the people in the stories and hear their voices, and I smell the smells of the classrooms, buildings, towns, and homes that I stayed in. Thank you, Brian, for helping me get to the end and see the final product in print.

Chapter 1

Current Democratic Theories

I teach philosophy of education to graduate students in education seeking to obtain teaching credentials and master's and doctoral degrees. I teach future teachers about the history and philosophy of education in the United States, and I teach cultural studies students about the development of educational thought through a look at the influences of classical Euro-Western philosophy on today's educational thinking. Every year that I teach these courses I am reminded that the United States was founded on a concept of democracy that has philosophical roots in the Euro-Western classical liberal theory of Locke (1632–1704) and Rousseau (1712–1778). I also spend a great deal of time in K–12 schools in America, and am continually reminded in my visits of how much influence classical liberal theory still holds on the daily practice and design of schools in America. I see this influence in the individual grading system that is almost universally embraced and in the competition that such grading encourages. I see it in the typical structure of American classrooms, with a solitary teacher in front of a room full of students arranged in rows of individual desks and in the individual seatwork and assignments students do on a daily basis. I see it in the teaching of a curriculum that is presented as generic, neutral, and universal, giving students the skills they need to be rational, autonomous individuals in a free society.

For classical liberal political philosophers such as Locke (1823/1960) and Rousseau (1762/1968), the role of government/the state is to protect individuals from others and otherwise stay out of their lives and allow them to live as they freely choose. The goal of liberalism is to secure opportunities for individuals to realize their full potential. Classical liberal democracy emphasizes a negative view of freedom as being "freedom from." "Freedom from" focuses on individual rights as natural rights and emphasizes the need to protect these natural rights, for they belonged to individuals prior to the formation of political governments and social relations. It is an argument for the primacy of the individual over the state. Arguments are made that individuals need protection from invasion, criminals, legal contracts that are not honored, and so on, as well as protection from others trying to take away their rights to free speech, to carry arms, and so forth. Individuals need freedom from restrictions. Such a view of democracy is based on a strong assumption that individuals develop atomistically on their own. This view is also based on a strong assumption of rationalism, on freed intelligence, that individuals can learn to think for themselves and use their reasoning capacity to critique their government's actions and change the government if it is not meeting their individual needs. Liberal democratic theories, even in relatively recent forms such as Dewey's (1935) *renascent liberal democracy* or Rorty's (1998) *social hope*, are vulnerable to criticism that they continue to focus on individual freedom and autonomy. They are also vulnerable to charges that they continue to use an Enlightenment type of rationalism as their method of critique, even in Dewey's (1916/1996) later scientific method, in Habermas's (1984) ideal speech acts, and in Rawls's (1993) veil of ignorance. I will be addressing the vulnerabilities exposed by these charges.

Great changes have occurred in political philosophy and in societies at large since Locke and Rousseau were writing. We live in times that Nancy Fraser (1997) describes as "postsocialist." Today, key underlying assumptions of liberal democratic theory are being questioned and dismissed. Enlightenment rationalism and the idea of a unitary subject have come under serious criticism by postmodernists, feminists, and critical theorists. Rationalism is criticized for focusing exclusively on Reason as the ultimate source for finding Truth at the expense of other important tools we could use, such as emotions, intuition, and imagination (Boler, 1999; Greene, 1995; Thayer-Bacon, 2000). Rationalism is also criticized for its assumption of the existence of absolute Truth and for its lack of attention to power issues (Foucault, 1980; Lyotard, 1984; Rorty, 1979; Thayer-Bacon, 2003). Individualism is criticized for its assumption that we develop into selves on our own, naturally, without the help of others (Noddings, 1984; Ruddick, 1989), thus ignoring the impact of social forces and the context within which we develop (Grimshaw, 1986; Smith, 1987, 1990). Individualism is also criticized for its assumption that our selves are unified and whole, rather than multifarious and fractured, and are certainly not completely understood by ourselves, let alone by others (Flax, 1990; Irigaray, 1974; Levinas, 1987).

Fraser (1997) says we live in times when group identity has supplanted class interests and when the need for recognition overshadows the need for redistribution. She suggests that we live in times when no credible vision of an alternative to the present order is available, that the visions we have lack the power to convince because they bracket questions of political economy. The visions she refers to include radical democracy, multiculturalism, political liberalism, and communitarianism. Given these great changes in political philosophy and in societies at large, we still find the influence of liberal democratic theory in U.S. schools. Even more radical and more recent educational theorists talk about the goal of education in terms of autonomy, self-awareness, and self-actualization, reaching one's full potential, and becoming an empowered change agent (Freire, 1970, 1985; Giroux, 1981, 1983, 1988, 1992; hooks, 1994, 2003; McLaren, 2003; West, 1994). When will we ever get beyond Locke's and Rousseau's influence? My project aims to develop a relational, pluralistic social political theory that moves beyond liberal democracy. As a scholar, my theoretical background is in philosophy of education, and my interests include pragmatism, feminist theory and pedagogy, and cultural studies in education. My perspective is a pragmatic, social feminist one.[1]

I want to follow Fraser's advice of not bracketing questions of equality and distribution, which Jonathan Kozol (1991, 2005) so vividly reminds us of with his description of current American schooling in *Savage Inequalities* and *The Shame of the Nation*. However, I also want to be careful not to take a distribution focus only, for this tends to place our focus back on *individual* rights, opportunities, and issues of self-respect, which leads us again into the trap of thinking there is a unitary subject. Surprisingly, given the time that has passed since Dewey was writing, I find that he is still a key source to help us find our way out of liberal democracy's assumptions and show us how to move on. Even though Dewey's liberal democratic theory focused on individual freedom and autonomy, he offered us the possibility of moving beyond individualism with his theory of social transaction (Dewey & Bentley, 1949/1960). Even though he assumed an Enlightenment type of rationalism, he showed us in *Logic: The Theory of Inquiry* how to move beyond this rationalism in his arguments for truths as warranted assertions (Dewey, 1938/1965). I will follow Dewey's social transactional lead and describe our world as one that is pluralistic, relational, and in process as we continually contribute to the ongoing construction of knowing.

I will address Iris Young's (1990b, 2000) concern for more focus on differences, and emphasize social differences as resources without falling into the trap that Young does of embracing a wholesale, undifferentiated, uncritical version of the politics of difference. Like Chantal Mouffe (1993), I refrain from embracing extreme pluralism that emphasizes heterogeneity and incommensurability, which leads us to what I call *naive relativism*, or the sense that anything goes (2003). Instead, I will argue that certain differences should be challenged and even eliminated (such as extreme levels of classism) while others should be enjoyed (see Fraser, 1997). We need a differentiated politics of difference that represents a more *qualified relativist* view of truths, moving further in the direction to which Dewey pointed in *Logic*. Such a view argues that we make decisions based on the best criteria and standards we can agree upon, with the full understanding that these criteria and standards are fallible and subject to change. Our criteria and standards must be submitted to continual critique and reevaluation, even criteria that we cherish, such as individuality and freedom.

Through my project I intend not only to develop a relational, pluralistic social political theory that moves beyond liberal democracy, but also to consider how such a theory translates into our public school settings. As a pragmatist and scholar in cultural studies, it is vital that my theory writing be informed by practice in order to keep it grounded in the historical, local, contingent, everyday world. If I do not turn to the everyday world of schooling practice in various cultures, I risk writing a theory that assumes a universal, abstract perspective and imposes it upon everyone's reality. A theory that is separated from everyday practice will be unable to address anyone's particular reality. Consequently, when I began working on this project, prior to writing any philosophical political theory that moves us beyond liberal democracy, I immersed myself in particular school cultures and communities, observing in accordance with a phenomenological methodology. I realized that I was raised in an American culture that embraces classical liberal values of individualism, universalism, and rationalism. As a child I was taken to John Wayne, Steve McQueen, and Clint Eastwood movies and watched *The Lone Ranger, Gunsmoke, Maverick,* and *Bonanza* on television; as a teenager I read Ayn Rand's *The Fountainhead* and *Atlas Shrugged.* In school I was taught the pioneer stories of the taming of the Wild West with heroes such as Davy Crockett and Daniel Boone, and I was told the Horatio Alger "rags to riches" stories. I was taught the American merit myth that if I worked hard I could become successful and rich like the tycoons of the Industrial Revolution, or like today's sports heroes and pop singers. I sat at my individual desk quietly working by myself, completing my seatwork and homework, and receiving high grades and the rewards that came with them.

In order to help me address my own cultural limitations and better understand the tough questions and issues that a relational, pluralistic political theory must contend with in our pubic schools, I designed a study that required me to spend time in U.S. schools where the majority of the students historically have been disenfranchised from the country's "democracy." It occurred to me that the students who were struggling the most in U.S. schools—the ones with the highest drop-out rates and the lowest proficiency exam scores—were also the students whose cultural backgrounds had a more collective focus in which the family, not the individual, was the heart of the community, abiding by the notion that "it takes a village to raise a child." These students were Native American, Mexican American, and African American (Ladson-Billings, 1994; Nieto, 1992). Collective, communitarian values of cooperation, sharing, and fraternity, based on a belief in the interconnectedness of the self to others and to nature, are in direct contrast to the individualistic values that shaped America's government as well as its schools. I suspected that if I studied Native American (Indian), Mexican, and African cultures in depth, I would gain a greater appreciation of the values and beliefs that support a collective socio-political focus and a greater understanding of how these values and beliefs function in contrast to individualistic ones. However, I certainly do not argue that Mexican, African, and Native American students do not "succeed" in U.S. schools (based on Euro-Western standards of what counts as success) solely because of their contrasting sociopolitical values from the "norm" of individualism, for these cultural groups have also faced tremendous racist barriers in America for extended periods of time. Rather, I suggest that the individualism that informs most classrooms in the United States makes it *even more difficult* for students from communitarian cultures to succeed, not that it is the only factor.

There are students who come from cultural groups with a communitarian focus, such as Jewish, Chinese, and Japanese students, who do have higher success rates in the U.S. schools in terms of grade point averages, graduation rates, test scores, and continuation on to college graduation. Asian Americans and Jewish Americans have been stereotyped as "model minorities" who are assumed to be very successful in U.S. schools (Nieto, 1992). Why do these students succeed? I suspected that closer agreement and comfort with individualism corelates with higher success rates, but this was something I wanted to explore further. Thus, I included Chinese and Japanese cultures in my study of collective sociopolitical views, as these students have a high success rate in American individualistic schools while also having experienced significant racism. These cultures are different from one other as well as distinct from the White, European American culture.

My plan was to immerse myself for one year per culture in the literature on each cultural group, examining basic cultural beliefs and how they translate into lifestyles as well as basic school curriculum designs and pedagogical methodologies. There are reports of students from communitarian cultural backgrounds who are succeeding in U.S. schools that have been redesigned to reflect more community-based cultural values (Abowitz, 1999, 2000; Ladson-Billings, 1994). When we remove failing students from schools with an individualistic focus and place them in schools that emphasize cooperation, fraternity, and connectedness to one another as well as to their larger social community, the students' success rates improve significantly. I planned to spend time in communities where students from these five cultures were succeeding in American schools, as well as travel to the origin countries to see how their collective focus translated into their school curriculum and instruction.

I knew at the start of this project, which I called "The C.A.R.E. project" (Culturally aware, Anti-racist, Relationally focused, Educational communities), that a researcher could spend a lifetime studying each of these cultures and that I was spending only one year on each. I also knew that an anthropologist could spend years in each of the school sites that I was only planning to visit for a week. However, I still believed there was much I could learn from these five collective cultures in the 5 years I was devoting to studying them and the 10 weeks, minimum, I was planning to spend in their schools. I believed that it was very important for me to make the effort to open myself up to what they could teach me, using a phenomenological approach that is intuitive and receptive, to make sure my theory was grounded in the actual experiences of real people. I spent 5 years arranging visits, traveling great distances, and making new friends.

All 17 of the schools I wrote to asking for permission to visit graciously opened their doors to me and invited me in. For *all* of them, including the schools in the United States, I was the first researcher to come spend a week in their schools. For most of the schools, I had to meet with someone closely connected to the school who could speak on my behalf and introduce me before I was able to contact the school directly and receive a letter of invitation. In my contact letters I explained that I was not a qualitative or quantitative researcher seeking to do an ethnographic field study but rather a philosopher of education and that my project was educational political theory writing. I explained further that my goal was to write an original philosophical political theory that applied directly to schools in America, in an effort to address concerns for students disenfranchised in U.S. schools today. I explained that my role would be strictly one of observer, taking field notes of what I observed. I promised to protect the identities of the school, the people who worked there, and the students, and said that I did not seek to see student files or conduct formal interviews.

I wanted to be as unobtrusive as possible and cause the least amount of work for the schools that I could. I tried to become like a fly on the wall so I could see "the norm" as much as possible. I wanted to see how various cultural values and beliefs spilled into the school and affected students' relations to one another and to their teachers, as well as how the teachers related to one another and to their students' family members. I knew I was being successful when the students and teachers would often forget that I was even there. Usually it took a day or two before that occurred. Always, the teachers and students honored my efforts by trying to go on with "business as usual." I now have a large amount of rich field notes concerning these five cultural perspectives to inform my theory writing. For the two schools where I did not know the language of the country (Japan and China), I took field notes of everything I saw and my interpreters (graduate students from my program) wrote down what the children and teachers said, leaving me with two sets of field notes that I could later comibine into one.

I went into these schools not knowing what I would find and what themes would emerge. In each case I tried to be open to what I saw and experienced, write rich notes, as well as take pictures and collect school handouts and maps to help me remember the school. Then I let the experience "sit with me" for a while as I transcribed my notes and continued to read and reflect on my experience. For each culture I studied a major theme that emerged while I was at the school. These were not subtle themes I had to dig for; they were vivid physical experiences I could not ignore.

In the following chapters I share my observations and experiences as anecdotal stories, using a narrative style of philosophical argumentation as impressionistic accounts of practices that illuminate the relational and pluralistic democratic theory I seek to develop. I also use the stories to help me translate my sociopolitical theory into educational theory and recommendations for school reform in U.S. public schools. This project has implications for schools beyond the boundaries of the United States, as classical liberalism has been imposed or embraced by the educational systems of all countries colonized by England, France, and, more recently, the United States. Students from community-based cultural backgrounds, which include the majority of indigenous peoples, have struggled to succeed in individualized classrooms worldwide. It is my hope to contribute a relational, pluralistic educational theory that will help *all* students have a chance of actively participating in a democratic-society-always-in-the-making.

The democratic theory I develop in this text is not one that is based on classical liberal or communitarian values alone but is informed by both. It is a radical democratic theory that represents feminist and multicultural concerns. It is radical because I present an antiracist theory that critiques basic foundational-level assumptions embedded within both individualism and collectivism. The theory I develop moves beyond modernism and critical theory as it seeks to address postmodern concerns of power and exclusionary practice without appealing to grand narratives such as Reason, the Scientific Method, or Dialogue. I argue that the world we live in is a transactional world that is continually in process; it is an interactive, interrelational world where individuals affect their social groups and social groups affect individuals (Dewey, 1916/1996).[2] Dynamic changes take place with the self and the community because of their interaction with one another in which all are affected. I argue that the more we can understand how connected we all are to one another, the closer we will come to living in a world we may someday call a democracy.[3]

I begin by considering various current philosophical democratic theories and how successful they are at moving beyond classical liberal democratic theory. I show that these current descriptions do in fact still cling to the assumptions embedded within classical liberal democratic theory. Once having established classical liberal's influence in current theories, we can more readily understand the assumptions that I argue need to be discarded if we hope to move beyond liberal democracy. I do not offer an in-depth discussion of classical liberal democratic theory as there are many sources available to the reader that offer detailed discussions of classical liberal theory.[4] However, since I wish to show how classical liberal assumptions are still embedded within current democratic theoretical work, it is necessary for me to begin by sketching out what these assumptions are. I also create a conversation with the current theorists to establish what the problems are with classical liberal democracy. In this way we will be positioned to move beyond liberal democracy to the pluralistic, relational direction I want to point us.

I begin my discussion of current philosophical democratic theories with John Dewey's *renascent liberal democracy*. I do so for several reasons. Since Dewey's work has strongly influenced current democratic theories, such as Benjamin Barber's *strong democracy*, a return to his work will help us better understand the theories of those that followed. In addition, Dewey has influenced my own theory, for he offers us direction for how to move beyond liberal democracy, even though he wasn't able to completely move beyond it himself. I begin with the neat summation Dewey offers of liberal democratic theoretical assumptions and their pros and cons in a key work titled *Liberalism and Social Action* (1935). Then I consider two other key political pieces he wrote about democracy, *The Public and its Problems* (1927) and *Freedom and Culture* (1939).

From here, I transition from the discussion of Dewey's liberal democratic theory to Barber's strong democracy. Then I consider in depth Young's *deliberative democracy* and Laclau and Mouffe's *radical democracy*. These political philosophers expose problems with one another's work that we will examine as well as contributions from other critical voices. In this way, a conversation will evolve about democratic theory that is enriched by the diverse perspectives and critiques presented.

RENASCENT LIBERAL DEMOCRACY (JOHN DEWEY)

John Dewey's concept of democracy as a mode of associated living, which is much broader than any particular view of political democracy, as well as his concept of transaction, are the cornerstone of the relational view of democracy I describe. Dewey recognizes that we start out as members of communities, in associated living, and that our first community is our family, which nurtures us and with whom we experience face-to-face relationships. Dewey (1916/1996) begins his classic work, *Democracy and Education,* with a discussion of social communities and how individuals develop out of those communities. In many of his writings we can find Dewey discussing infants and their relationships to their mothers as well as to their extended families. Unlike classical liberal philosophers, Dewey does not treat individuals as if they sprout out of the ground without mothers who nurse them and fathers who bathe them. He does not ever lose sight of the fact that we all begin our lives in someone else's loving arms. Dewey developed a sense of self that begins in-relation-with-others, a social self that develops and grows to become more autonomous and rational as it continues to interact with others.

It is not until late in Dewey's career, in his work coauthored with Arthur Bentley (1960), *Knowing and the Known,* that he introduces the term *transactional,* but one can find the seeds for this idea in many of his earlier writings, including *Democracy and Education.* Earlier, Dewey used the term *interaction* to describe relationships that affect one another, but later he amended the term to *transaction* because he realized that individuals can interact with one another without necessarily being affected by the interaction in significant ways, like billiard balls that hit each other on a pool table and bounce off of each other but still maintain their original form. For Dewey, the result of selves interacting with one another is that both are changed, and, thus, their relationship is more accurately described as a "transaction." Communities help shape the individual into who she or he becomes, but individual selves, when they are young and immature, also help shape and change the community because of their immaturity, which allows them to be flexible, open, adaptive, and growing. In order to explore how Dewey's concept of transaction affected his own view of democracy, I turn to the three key later works of his I named above. I begin with *Liberalism and Social Action,* in which Dewey offers an excellent analysis of classical liberal political theory and its development.

Liberalism and Social Action is from Dewey's Page-Barbour Lectures delivered at the University of Virginia and published in 1935. He begins this series of lectures by laying out the history of liberalism as he seeks to find the permanent values in liberalism and how to maintain these values in the 1930s world of his time. In typical Deweyian style, his method of philosophical argumentation is a historical approach. After pointing to the fact that liberalism can be traced back to ancient Greece and the idea of "free play of intelligence," Dewey begins his historical analysis in earnest with John Locke in 1688 and his vision that governments exist to protect the rights of individuals. He shows us how Locke's philosophy focuses on the individual, where individualism is opposed to organized social order. For Locke there is a natural opposition between an individual and organized society. Locke was seeking to find a way to escape the constraints of society that had developed by his lifetime. He solved this problem by beginning with the assumption that individuals develop on their own, as self-made men, and have the freedom to decide whether or not to join with others to form a society. The decision to join with others is always at the expense of the individual's freedom. Locke described democratic governments as offering individuals the service of safeguard and protection to ensure that their individual rights are honored and that others do not harm them. However, this is always a precarious governmental service that must be kept in check to ensure that the government does not infringe on individual rights any more than is necessary to protect the society. The relationship between individuals and the government is one of distrust and suspicion; the individual must always be alert to make sure the government is powerful enough to protect individual rights but not so powerful that it tramples individual rights. Key values of Locke's classical liberalism are that every individual has the right to "the full development of his capacities" and that liberty is "the most precious trait and very seal of individuality" (Dewey, 1935, p. 24).

Dewey's insightful criticism of early liberalism is that it assumes a conception of individuality "as something ready-made, already possessed, and needing only the removal of certain legal restrictions to come into full play" (p. 39). Dewey tells us the "Achilles heel of early liberalism" is the idea of separate individuals, "each of whom is bent on personal private advantage" (p. 54). Early liberalism did not conceive of individualism "as a moving thing, something that is attained only by continuous growth" (p. 39). Dewey offers us his description of the individual as not starting out in a state of nature prior to entering a social state, but rather as a human infant connected to and cared for by family members. He warns: "liberalism that takes its profession of the importance of individuality with sincerity must be deeply concerned with the structure of human association. For the latter operates to affect negatively and positively, the development of individuals" (p. 41). From Dewey's criticism of early liberalism, we can see that it is clearly the case that he did not begin his own democratic theory with an assumption of atomistic individualism.

Apparently, Locke was not able to see social arrangements as positive forces but rather as external limitations. According to Dewey (1935), it is not until the second half of the 19th century that the idea arises that the state should be instrumental in securing and extending the liberties of individuals (pp. 5–6). Slowly we see a shift from the idea of using government action only for protection and safeguarding to arguing that we can use governmental action to aid and alleviate the suffering of those who are economically disadvantaged. During the 19th century there is a movement in liberal thinking from seeing society as only a hindrance to individuals to beginning to see society as offering assistance and help toward individual development. During the second half of the 19th century in American history we find arguments for the value of public education for children whose parents cannot afford to give their children private education. Horace Mann and others suggest that the government (federal and state) should pay for public education out of public funds raised through individual taxes. Today in political discussions in the United States, Libertarians and conservative Republicans represent the early classical liberal's view of democracy as one where the least government is the best, and Democrats and moderate Republicans represent the new liberals of the 19th century who are committed to using society and the state to help individuals develop to their full capacity.

Dewey (1935) recognizes the important battles that were won by early liberalism in terms of freedom of thought, conscience, expression, and communication. These qualities are what he sees as essential for us to have "freed intelligence." For Dewey, the enduring values of early liberalism are "liberty; the development of the inherent capacities of individuals made possible through liberty, and the central role of free intelligence in inquiry, discussion and expression" (p. 32). However, Dewey does not regard "intelligence as an individual possession and its exercise as an individual right" as classical liberalism does (p. 65). Intelligence depends on "a social organization that will make possible effective liberty and opportunity for personal growth in mind and spirit for all individuals" (pp. 56–57). Again we find evidence that Dewey does not rely on an atomistic view of individualism.

Freed intelligence is a social method that Dewey wants to be identified with the scientific method of investigation. Importantly, because he describes freed intelligence as a social method of inquiry, he recognizes that intelligence is not a ready-made possession; it must be secured. He is very aware that oppressions in terms of slavery, serfdom, and material insecurity are harmful to freed intelligence. He gave the Page-Barbour Lectures during the Great Depression and was worried about fascism and communism at the time. Dewey argues for a "renascent liberalism" that recognizes that democracies must establish material security as a prerequisite for individual freedom.

We do find evidence that Dewey's democratic theory relies on an assumption of rationalism in his concept of freed intelligence. Dewey trusted that the scientific method of inquiry would replace brute force as the method of cooperative intelligence. He was greatly influenced by Darwin's *Origin of Species*, as were other classic pragmatists such as Peirce and James, and he references Darwin's contribution to scientific thinking in many of his writings, including *Liberalism and Social Action*. In *Democracy and Education*, Dewey (1996) emphasizes freed intelligence through his discussion of reflective thinking that begins in doubt, where one is stirred to move to action, to generate possible hypotheses and test these out in order to arrive at a conclusion that ends the doubt. Reflective thinking is the scientific method, which, by 1935, Dewey describes as "freed intelligence." Predictably, he ends *Liberalism and Social Action* by pointing to education as the first object of a renascent liberalism to aid the production of habits of mind and character that are necessary for freed intelligence.

In Dewey's (1927/1954) *The Public and Its Problems*, which is based on lectures he gave in 1926 at Kenyon College, Ohio, prior to the Great Depression, we find him worrying about the problem of loss of a public and how this loss affects democracies. Interestingly, he does not begin his talks by looking at political philosophy and the public but rather begins by looking at individuals. He wants to emphasize "that all deliberative choices and plans are finally the work of single individuals" (p. 21). However, just when we think we have caught Dewey assuming individualism, he goes on to criticize individualism and say that individuals exist and operate in association. Again he talks about how we are born infants, "immature, helpless, dependent upon the activities of others" (p. 24). What we believe is the outcome of association and intercourse. For Dewey, conjoined, combined, associated action is a universal trait of the behavior of things. A society is individuals in their connections with one another, whereas a political state is a distinctive and secondary form of association.

Dewey (1927/1954) then turns to examining the democratic state, and as in *Liberalism and Social Action*, we find that he again takes a historical look at what formed democracy. It was not theory that formed democracy but rather a convergence of a great number of social movements. Again we are reminded of the fear of government and the desire to reduce its power that motivated Locke. Dewey shows us again that Locke took the route of individualism, "a theory which endows singular persons in isolation from any associations," "a doctrine of independence of any and all associations," to diminish the government's power (pp. 86–87). Locke's route was to go back to the naked individual and sweep away all associations as foreign to his nature and rights. Other forces that contributed to this concept of individualism (also discussed in *Liberalism and Social Action*) include Adam Smith's *laissez-faire* capitalism, the Millses' (father and son) utilitarian economic theory, and science's development of machines (which today I think we would describe more generally as Newton's atomistic and mechanistic scientific description of the universe).

Dewey (1927/1954) argues that there was no need for Locke to take the individualism route he took in order to limit the role of government. It would have been enough to assert that some primary groupings have claims that the state should not legitimately encroach upon. These primary groupings include families and neighbors. Our roots for democracy began in the false roots of individualism. Again, Dewey shows how we start out our lives in association with others, with our earliest associations being face-to-face interactions with families and neighbors. They are our "chief agencies of nurturance" and they are "bred only in intimacy" (p. 211). According to Dewey, "There is no substitute for the vitality and depth of close and direct intercourse and attachment" (p. 213).

In *The Public and Its Problems*, Dewey (1927/1954) discusses how in the United States we are losing face-to-face interactions in the small community life and town meetings that were the cornerstone of American democratic polity. He describes the printing press, railways, telegraphs, mass manufacturing, and urban centers (basically, the Industrial Revolution) as well as the large influx of immigrants, as leading to a loss of the public. In 1926 he was worried that the American public is becoming too large, too diffused and scattered, and too intricate in composition. What is his solution to this problem of loss of the public and the apathy and indifference to democracy that it breeds? We come back to Dewey's key idea that democracy is a social idea as well as a system of government, and the second form of democracy (political) depends on the first (social). A democracy is shared interests established through interaction; it is associated joint activity that is dependent on community to exist. For Dewey, we are born in associations, but not necessarily in communities. We have to initiate our young into communities by teaching them our language and customs through education. For Dewey, democracy is an ideal always-in-the-making, never to be achieved, and so is community. (pp. 148–149). His solution to the problem of loss of a public is to restore our local communities, for they are the medium for democracy. "Democracy must begin at home, and its home is the neighborly community" (p. 213). Dewey wants communities restored that are alive and flexible as well as stable, that "manifest a fullness, variety and freedom of possession and enjoyment of meanings and goods," that are responsive to the complex world in which we are enmeshed, local but not isolated (p. 216). We find below that Benjamin Barber also turns to similar solutions to help strengthen democracy, while Iris Young offers us a startling contrasting view.

Dewey's *Freedom and Culture* was published in 1939, during the outbreak of World War II, when there was great fear as to whether or not democracy would survive. This time Dewey decides to look at democracy in the United States and its development with the help of Jefferson, rather than Locke, since he argues that conditions in the United States are different from those in Britain. He starts with a cultural focus (to enumerate the terms under which human beings associate and live together), suggesting that we cannot isolate any one factor such as the relations of industry, communication, science, art, or religion. For Dewey, all of these terms are intrinsic parts of the culture that affects politics, with no single factor being dominant over all others. Dewey

criticizes Marxism because it isolates one factor, economics, as being dominant in its discussion of human associations. He tells us that the full conditions
for a complete democratic experience do not yet exist.

Using his historical approach again, Dewey (1939) reminds us in *Freedom
and Culture* that America began with an economic focus (rebellion over taxa-
tion, restrictions on industry and trade). As in *The Public and Its Problems*, we
again find Dewey taking a romantic view of early theory and practice in the
United States, presuming a harmony between liberty and equality in farming
times that changed with the advent of industry. Again, Dewey warns us that we
are not going to have democracy until *all* our institutions are run democrati-
cally (church, business, schools, family, law, government, etc.).

In *Freedom and Culture*, Dewey (1939) connects the future of democracy to
the spread of the scientific attitude, as in his "freed intelligence" in *Liberalism
and Social Action*. Here he argues that the scientific attitude is our sole guarantee against widespread propaganda. Dewey recognizes that democracy needs
free speech, free press, free assembly, and an education system that encourages
inquiry—a scientific attitude. We can secure democracy with all the resources
provided by collective intelligence operating in cooperative action (p. 176).
Dewey ends *Freedom and Culture* by returning to Jefferson, emphasizing that
Jefferson was not afraid of change. Jefferson referred to the U.S. government
as "an experiment." Dewey encourages us to have the same attitude. As in *The
Public and Its Problems*, he again points to the need for face-to-face interaction, political organization in small units, and direct communication in order
for democracy to thrive (p. 159). Again, he recommends, "Democracy must
begin at home, and its home is the neighborhood community," (p. 213). And
again, as in *Liberalism and Social Action*, he recognizes the need for equaliza-
tion of economic conditions so free choice and free action can be maintained.
Dewey tells us that democratic ends demand democratic methods. His central
claim is that "The struggle for democracy has to be maintained on as many
fronts as culture has aspects: political, economic, international, educational,
scientific and artistic, religious" (p. 173).

What distinguishes the pluralistic, relational democratic theory that I
present in this text from Dewey's liberal democracy are the assumptions of
rationalism and universalism that form the basis of his renascent liberalism.
We find the assumption of universalism in his romantic view of agrarian U.S.
society prior to the Industrial Revolution and in the influx of immigrants at
the turn of the 19th/20th centuries. We also find universalism in his romantic
view of face-to-face interactions in small communities prior to the Industrial
Revolution and in his recommendation that we get back to face-to-face interactions through such methods as town meetings. We discover his assumption
of rationalism in his naive view that the scientific method is what will lead us

beyond the powerful influence of culture and fears of social determinism and indoctrination.[5]

A pluralistic, relational view of democracy insists that we need to look at America's past from the perspective of African Americans, Native Americans, Mexican Americans (nonvoluntary immigrants and conquered people indigenous to this land), and women and children (viewed as property of males). The wealth of the United States was built on the free, slave, and indentured labor of these people, who were not recognized as citizens until the 20th and 21st centuries (children still are viewed as the wards of their parents). The radical view of democracy presented in this text insists that we consider power issues involved in face-to-face interactions in small communities and the kinds of homogenizing and silencing effects these communities have on diverse opinions and perspectives. The voices of people from the dominant culture who acquired fluency in the dominant language and practiced oral skills and styles of relating valued by the dominant culture were the only ones heard in the town meetings that Dewey and Barber want to go back to today. People living in the communities who were not considered citizens were not allowed to attend the meetings, or, if they were, they were seated in the balconies or the back of the hall and were not allowed to speak.

The view I offer in this text recognizes the limitations of the scientific method and its biases and prejudices, which are disguised as neutral and universal, relying on rationality and valuing reason. Science has been used to argue racist and sexist biological deterministic views of inferiority for non-Anglos and women. Due to feminist theory and critical theory, we now recognize that even science is embedded within paradigms that shift over time, and that what we take to be neutral criteria, standards, and principles are negotiated and influenced by the scientists doing the investigating (Harding, 1991; Haraway, 1988; Keller, 1985). With the introduction of the views of minorities and women, we have exposed the limits of reason and can now recognize other tools we can use in our inquiries, including intuition, emotions, and imagination (Thayer-Bacon, 2000).

By now we should have a solid understanding of classical liberalism's foundational beliefs as well as the problems these beliefs present for democratic theories. By considering Dewey's renascent liberalism in contrast to classical liberalism, we uncover his powerful criticisms of classical liberalism. We also learn the limits of Dewey's ability to move beyond his own embeddedness within a liberal culture and discover the biases that affected his criticisms and recommended solutions. Now we will be able to recognize Dewey's influence on current democratic theories. One political philosopher who is influenced by Dewey in particular and pragmatism in general is Benjamin Barber, whose concept of *strong democracy* we will now discuss.

STRONG DEMOCRACY (BENJAMIN BARBER)

In *Strong Democracy*, Benjamin Barber (1984) argues that democracy's central values are participation, citizenship, and political activity. He is very critical of liberal democracy's description of man as alone, separate, hedonistic, and aggressive.[6] Modern versions of man describe him as a "privatized client-consumer who demands his rights, sells his services, contracts his relationships, votes his interests, and cost-analyzes his life-plan" (p. 71). Barber shows us how liberal democracy defines man in a way that undermines democratic practices. He describes three views of liberalism: anarchists who distrust all governments (Hobbes, Locke, Rousseau), realists who argue for the need for political coercion and legal sanctions in order to prompt hedonists to honor the needs and rights of others (Machiavelli, early Mills), and minimalists who distrust individuals and the state and promote a politics of tolerance (later Mills, Rawls). Barber shows that all three views of liberalism begin with an assumption of the value of individuals and a view of groups as hindrances. He calls liberalism "politics as zookeeping," for it argues that we should be admired for our proud individuality but also must be caged for our untrustworthiness and antisocial orneriness (pp. 20–25). The paradox of liberalism is that our natural condition jeopardizes our potential freedom while the state endangers our actual freedom. Liberalism abstracts human beings from their social settings and tries to reconstruct them as being in "a state of nature" as "absolutely autonomous individuals." Liberalism's private, asocial individuals lead us to solipsism. Man is defined in a way that deprives him of the potential strength of mutuality, cooperation, and common being. He is in permanent exile. For Barber, liberalism lacks a theory of citizenship.

What kind of theory of citizenship does Barber (1984) offer? Interestingly, he defines man as a social being capable of citizenship, but he places this social being within a private, dependent realm, as someone who must be transformed into a free citizen. Man is a social being who is capable of citizenship that is based on common action as neighbors, not on law or blood ties. But apparently we don't start out as citizens; we must become citizens. For Barber, a citizen is a political actor only if he is able to choose freely, autonomously, with deliberation and responsibility. Free choosers are by definition reasonable, able to make choices that are not random or coerced, but deliberative. He says, "We are born in chains—slaves of dependency and insufficiency—and acquire autonomy only as we learn the difficult art of governing ourselves in common" (p. xv). Thus, we discover that Barber relies on a strong concept of "autonomy" in his definition of citizenship, which returns us to individualism and rationalism.

Barber (1984) defines his citizenship democracy as *strong democracy*, to distinguish it as a form of participatory democracy from representative democracy (authoritative, juridical, pluralist) as well as from unitary democracy (communitarians). Strong democracy is *"politics in the participatory mode where conflict is resolved in the absence of an independent ground through a participatory process of ongoing, proximate self-legislation and the creation of a political community capable of transforming dependent, private individuals into free citizens and partial and private interests into public goods"* (p. 132; emphasis added).

Barber's (1984) solution to liberalism is the cultivation of community judgment, or what he refers to as "politics." His concept of politics is based on rejecting the assumption of universalism while still embracing the value of rationalism in the form of deliberation. For Barber, politics are "conditions that impose a *necessity for public action, and thus for reasonable public choice, in the presence of conflict and in the absence of private or independent grounds for judgment*" (p. 120, emphasis added). "To be political is to *have* to choose," and to have to choose without reference to grounds that are a priori. To be political is to be "without guiding standards or determining norms" yet under the pressure to have "to act, and to act with deliberation and responsibility as well" (p. 121). Barber seeks to sever politics from Truth, arguing that "politics is not the application of Truth to the problem of human relations but the application of principle in a world of action where absolute principles are irrelevant" (pp. 64–65). He defines *political truth* as something that is "made in the course of experience" and links this definition to James (p. 65). He embraces a view of "fallibilism" (belief in the impossibility of attaining knowledge that is certain) that leads to "a world in which truth has no warrant."

This is a problematic reading of fallibilism, which leads to fears of vulgar relativism. Neither Peirce, James, nor Dewey argued for a world in which truths have no warrant. For Peirce (1958), Truth is something we will arrive at in the future, it will be something upon which we all agree, and it is based on scientific and logical testing. For James (1909/1975), truth is that which satisfies our inquiries, and is based on the whole body of truths from the past as well as on the coercions of our senses today. For Dewey (1938/1965), truth is warranted assertability, and is based on our best efforts to consider all options and solve all doubts. Since I wrote about this topic at length in 2003, I will not go into it in depth here. Suffice it to say, Barber's view of fallibilism is problematic, and he cannot turn to Peirce, James, or Dewey for support of a vulgar relativist position such as the one he wants to present. James and Dewey can help him with a qualified relativist argument that acknowledges that our criteria and standards are fallible and corrigible, and Peirce can help him with his view of knowers as situated, limited human beings in need of educated others to help them develop deeper understanding. However, Barber is in trouble in trying to place his politics in the realm of action without any way of solving problems except by way of brute force, or falling back on assumptions of rationalism and autonomy.

Barber's (1984) model of strong democracy stirs up fears of anarchy and despotism. He thinks he can solve these community dangers through civic education that occurs through practice. He wants to achieve a creative consensus, which arises out of common talk, decisions, and work. He wants people to experience direct political participation in face-to-face communities by relying on direct communication. He wants weekly neighborhood assemblies and televised town meetings. He wants a Civics Communications Cooperative, local volunteer programs, and a rotating lottery system for citizens to take their turn in political positions at the local level. Problems that he grapples with in this model of strong democracy include scale, for his model is dependent on direct communication (he thinks he solves this problem through district-area town meetings); inequality of capitalism, which he tries to solve by splitting politics from economics and arguing that politics precedes economics; and global markets and large corporations, which Barber argues are an enemy to democracy—they are incompatible with freedom and equality and obliterate the distinction between public and private (another split Barber seeks to maintain).

We will find below that Iris Young's (2000) democratic theory emphasizes diversity and qualitative differences. She worries that Barber's strong democracy retains the features of the universalistic ideal of the civic public and the "common good" that lead to exclusions, the silencing of some points of view, and the narrowing of the agenda for deliberation. An emphasis on the civic public "can incline some or all to advocate removing difficult issues from discussion for the sake of agreement and preservation of the common good" (p. 44). Young also worries about Barber's insistence on face-to-face discussions and the silencing of voices that occurs in these discussions. I share Young's concerns.

I agree with the criticisms Barber offers for liberal democratic theory; they are sharp and to the point, and humorously point out the paradox of a theory that begins with individuals, while at the same time distrusting and fearing individuals. However, Barber's strong democracy and the pluralistic, relational democracy I present in this text part ways right at the start with their basic concepts, for strong democracy is based on hidden Enlightenment assumptions of individuality in his concept of autonomy, and rationality in his concept of deliberation. Although he does not fall into the trap of assuming universalism, he defends his politics severed from Truth solely on the basis of action. In contrast, a pluralistic, relational democratic theory defends its politics on a pragmatic view of truths as pluralistic, in process, and continually qualified. Barber also builds into his theory of democracy dualistic splits between the private and public as well as splits between the political and economic that cannot hold up from a relational perspective. Let me explain further.

The transactional relational perspective I present here is based on Dewey's concept of a transactional, as we discovered above, as well as a relational ontology, developed by several feminist scholars.[8] Barber and I are in agreement that human beings are social beings. But we are not in agreement that we are "born in chains—slaves of dependency and insufficiency." For Barber, this social quality is one we must break free of; it binds us and contains us, and limits our ability to choose freely, autonomously. For me, the fact that we are social beings means that we are always in-relation-with-others. We become individuals out of our social settings and we continually affect the social settings we live in; it is a give-and-take that works both ways. We never choose freely, autonomously, without the influence of others. The myth of autonomy is a dangerous and deceptive myth that is a holdover from the classical liberal assumption of individualism. We are always influenced by the cultural and natural contexts of our lives, so deeply that it is even difficult for us to become conscious of these influences, without the help of others not like us. Others, as strangers who can never be completely known to us any more than we can ever be completely known to ourselves, help us gain greater awareness and understanding of our situatedness. Others bind us and help us become free at the same time.

The relational perspective I present here is also based on a feminist view of relationality that argues we cannot split the private world of the home from the public world of the political. The private world of the home is political, too. Barber is not only concerned with "transforming dependent, private individuals into free citizens," he is also concerned with transforming "partial and private interests into public goods." Barber's partial and private interests seem to be based on a view of power as public, separate from private interests. For Barber, private interests are relegated to the home and citizenship interests are positioned in the public world of goods. From a pluralistic perspective of lower economic classes, ethnically underprivileged minorities, women, and children, there is no need to remind them or us that the private world of the home is a very political world. For those who lack authority and power, it is a dangerous world that must continually be negotiated with one's survival in mind. Private interests are greatly influenced, allowed, and even dictated by those who maintain power in the public world. The boundary between the public and private is not nearly as sharply defined as Barber assumes it is. It is a boundary established by social norms and standards based on those in positions of authority and power able to exert their will over others.

Like Dewey with his concept of "freed intelligence," Barber introduces an assumption of rationalism with his concept of deliberation that ignores or devalues other tools besides reason to help us decide on courses of action. And like Dewey, Barber seeks to re-create town meetings and face-to-face relations that leave us with the same concerns expressed above about homogenization and the silencing of differences. Barber's move to separate the political from the economic and to declare that the political precedes economics allows him to ignore material needs. A pluralistic, relational view of democracy must contend with issues of power, access, and material need, and point to the many people who will not have the time or means to attend neighborhood town meetings, let alone the language skills necessary to express their views and have them be understood. Not all people will be able to take their turn in the lottery system and participate in local governance, which leads to concerns of exclusion and elitism. Barber's recommendations end up sounding romantic and naive. Capitalism and global markets run by large corporations are realities today that directly affect people's daily lives. Economics must be addressed in current political theory in order for that theory to have any chance of impacting people's lives. Material needs cannot be brushed aside as secondary to political concerns.

It is time to bring a woman's voice into this conversation. A pluralistic view of democracy such as the one I present here must place power issues in the foreground in order to ensure the valuing of cultural diversity. I turn to postmodern and critical theory to help in those efforts, as illuminated by the works of Iris Marion Young.

DELIBERATIVE DEMOCRACY (IRIS MARION YOUNG)

In *Justice and the Politics of Difference* (1990b), Young values pluralism and the critical role of conflict. She makes a solid case that democracy cannot aim for consensus, harmony, and reconciliation, for these goals lead too easily to domination and oppression of "people not like us." Her methodology is situated analysis as a critical theorist, using reflection that is historically and socially contextualized. She relates that feminist and postmodern analysis inform her use of theories as "tools" she "takes up." Young defines *social justice* as "the elimination of institutionalized domination and oppression" (p. 15). She recognizes that distribution is important but she does not want our focus to be only on material goods, while ignoring the institutional context that determines material distributions. According to Young, a distributive focus fails to bring social structures and institutional contexts under evaluation. It ignores decision-making issues and division-of-labor issues. Young points out that a distributive focus on justice, such as John Rawls takes, places the focus on individual rights, opportunity, and self-respect. Distributive justice takes an individual focus, inherited from classical liberalism.

Young (1990b) tells us she has a relational focus, but what she means by this is that her focus is on processes, not things that are static. She argues that rights are relationships, not things, just as power is a relation, an ongoing process, not a thing. In terms of individuals, Young's relational focus means that individuals act in relation to one another. She seeks to enhance two values: (1) developing and exercising one's capacities and expressing one's experience, and (2) participating in determining one's action and the conditions of one's action (p. 37). Young tells us she assumes the equal worth of all persons, by which she means that each person has the right to self-development and self-determination. Thus, we find that Young wants to preserve the liberal commitment to individual freedom and autonomy, as well as embrace plural definitions of the good.

We can see Young's (1990b) liberal commitment to individualism as well as her commitment to plurality in the metaphorical city she develops to describe her view. Young does not seek town meetings and a public square, like Dewey and Barber. She wants an *unoppressive city,* one with a population large enough that people can find freedom in anonymity. She does not want to know everybody, nor does she want everybody to know her; she wants to be able to come and go unnoticed unless she chooses to be noticed. She wants a city where people can form coalitions to solve problems if they need to, and then dissolve these coalitions and reclaim anonymity if they so desire. She wants a place that is open to unassimilated otherness, a place that offers social differentiation without exclusion, a place that offers variety, erotic attraction, and publicity.

Of course, Young (1990b) knows that her unoppressive city is a social ideal that does not exist. For her, it offers a description that underscores individual autonomy and freedom as well as cultural diversity. Unfortunately, Young does not consider at length the problems, inequalities, and oppressions that exist in real cities that make it so difficult to find much hope in her unoppressive city ideal, thus making it seem highly romanticized. A quick glance at any real city points us to oppressive conditions where some people live in beautiful apartments, condominiums, even homes with exquisite views of the ocean, lake, river, and/or mountains, while others live in inner-city ghettos behind barred windows and locked doors to protect themselves from criminal activity. Some people have doormen, maids, and drivers who pick them up to take them where they want to go, while others commute great distances on public transportation, and still others huddle in the subway stations, trying to stay warm as they seek a handout for a cup of coffee.

The very conditions that offer Young (1990b) the anonymity she seeks—being unnoticed in a highly populated city—also create dangerous conditions where a person can lie on the sidewalk dying while people walk by. The very conditions that allow people who do not know each other well to form highly diverse coalitions to solve problems, then disperse when their problem is solved, are the same conditions that allow people to decide *not* to form coalitions because they don't know the other people very well and don't care about their problems enough to act upon them. Therefore, their problems are never solved because not enough people decide to act. In a large city, people are bombarded with other people's needs and find it necessary to develop a protective shield of indifference. People in large cities learn how to insulate themselves from the overstimulation of so many others, and are thus in danger of becoming callous and indifferent to issues and concerns that in small towns would be cause for action by most of the people.

It is true that cities offer a much greater possibility for diversity in a democracy. We can even point to Dewey as an example of someone who sought the city life, for, while it is often pointed out that he grew up in rural New England, he chose to work in Chicago as a professor and then move to New York City to finish out his career and life. New York City is a symbol of cultural diversity because it was the port of entry to the United States for most immigrants during Dewey's lifetime. However, Young is guilty of embracing a wholesale, undifferentiated, uncritical version of politics of difference that leads other political philosophers, such as Nancy Fraser (1997), to fear that Young's unoppressive city will lead to a vulgar relativism where anything goes. Fraser recognizes that, while there is much value in the cultural diversity of a city, there is also great harm in the differences in material wealth as well as differences such as quality of care and the extent to which one experiences indifference or even hatred. Fraser convincingly recommends a more unequivocal politics of difference, one that recognizes that there are multiple kinds of differences that need to be critiqued rather then embraced wholesale, as Young is inclined to do. Fraser recommends that some differences, such as economic class, should be eliminated through redistribution of wealth and the abolishment of class distinctions (a Marxist kind of argument); other differences, such as those in care for the young and elderly and healthcare, should be universalized; and still others, such as diverse cultures, should be enjoyed by recognizing and valuing the rich heritages of a range of cultures (in agreement with Young).

In Young's (2000) *Inclusion and Democracy*, we again find her calling for widening and deepening democracy through inclusion. Her key assumption is that democracy promotes justice. Again, she uses critical theory, socially and historically situated normative analysis, to make her case. She addresses a heterogeneous public engaged in transforming institutions to make them more effective in justly solving shared problems. Her public has differences and conflicts. Her polity is not just the state but also other social institutions such as family, schools, and religions. Her key concerns are political exclusion and marginalization. She assumes a causal connection between social and economic inequality and political equality, but she does not theorize this connection in any detail, which makes her position vulnerable to Fraser's (1997) criticism that she does not attend enough to material needs.

In *Inclusion and Democracy,* Young (2000) refines theories of deliberative democracy, such as Habermas's, by adding strong inclusion and political equality to the deliberative democratic ideals of inclusion, political equality, reasonableness, and publicity (p. 17). Young does not assume face-to-face deliberation and a focus on argument as the primary form of political communication (as Dewey and Barber do); nor does she claim that democratic commitment requires privileging unity and the common good (as Barber does); nor does she assume norms of orderliness that can be exclusionary. She argues for *differentiated solidarity* to combat exclusion and affirm the freedom of association. Differentiation solidarity allows for the freedom to voluntarily cluster, to form temporary coalitions in any effort to solve common problems, and then disband (her unoppressive city metaphor). It expands conceptions of political communication beyond assumptions of rationalism. However, we find that differentiated solidarity is also meant to foster individual freedom. Young is concerned with the institutional conditions necessary for promoting self-development and self-determination (her definition of justice, p. 33). Young seeks a "relational autonomy" that consists in "the structuring of relationships so that they support the maximal pursuit of all individual ends" (p. 231). Again, we run into an underlying valuing of individualism in democratic theory. Young argues that oppression and domination are institutional constraints on self-determination and self-autonomy.

Communitarians, such as Judith Green (1999), have criticized Young's politics of difference for destroying the common good, weakening national identity, and undermining class solidarity. Young's (2000) response to these criticisms is that social difference (group) cannot be reduced to identity. Those who use a logic of substance to conceptualize "groups" (a set of essential attributes = the group) set up a rigid inside/outside distinction that denies differences within and across groups. Everyone in a group does not share the same attributes. To conceptualize "groups" based on a set of essential attributes is to essentialize groups, reducing the many to one identity. Young wants to emphasize that many people deny that group positioning is significant for their identity. She also emphasizes the variety of differences within groups and the shared attributes across groups.

In the end, I agree with Young that there is a third alternative to either private interest competition (liberal democracy) or difference bracketing public discussion of the common good (strong democracy). I describe this third alternative as pluralistic, relational democracy-always-in-the-making. We both agree that all of us, as individuals, are limited in our knowledge due to our situatedness, and we both agree that we can overcome our own limitations by attempting to expand our thinking through transactions with others not like us. But Young (2000) arrives at this third alternative, which for her is deliberative democracy, by a different path from mine. She uses a "relational logic" to show that social groups are not explicitly constituted by their social conditions, but rather emerge from the way people interact. This relational logic seems similar to Dewey's description of transactional relations, for Young emphasizes that individuals are not aggregates with separate boundaries that have no relation to one another. However, at the same time Young argues that individuals are agents, in the sense that "we constitute our own identities, and each person's identity is unique" (p. 101).

Here is where I part company with Young. Young views individualism in the form of individual autonomy and agency, and I argue that we do not choose our identities under conditions of our own choosing. I develop my identity as a girl/woman in a society that is sexist and homophobic. Others develop their identities as Navajos or Hopis in a society that has sought to destroy their identity group through various acts of genocide over the past 500-plus years. We actively appropriate our own multiple group positionalities, but we don't have complete control over this.

Young (2000) separates the personal from the political, and worries about structural differences in her politics of difference, not cultural differences, which she says are more personal. She leaves cultural differences alone. I argue that separating the personal from the political is impossible. Euro-Western cultural groups—the Spanish, French, and British for example—arrived in North America with assumptions of cultural superiority to the indigenous people already living in North America. These assumptions of superiority allowed them not to see the "Indians" as even having cultures and to describe them as "primitive savages." Once labeling the indigenous people of the Americas as "primitive savages," the colonizers' cultural views allowed them to kill these people and not judge their acts as murder. Their cultural views then allowed them to claim to "discover" a land already long inhabited, and to rule as theirs a land where people already lived with various forms of political governance. With the example of the colonization of the Americas, we are reminded that racism simultaneously exists at personal, social, and institutional levels, and that these levels interact with one another, feed on one another, and affect one another (they are transactional relationships). It is not only impossible but dangerously deceptive to think we can separate political differences from cultural differences, for we rely on our cultural values and beliefs to establish the norms and standards we use to develop our political institutions.

Young offers a significant contribution to the current conversation of democratic theory with her efforts to affirm diversity and plurality. She is sensitive to issues of power and shows this in the prominence of various forms of exclusion, marginalization, and segregation in her discussions of inclusion. Unfortunately, she embraces a wholesale acceptance of cultural differences and pushes culture into a private realm that is separate from the public realm of politics. Her wholesale acceptance of cultural differences prohibits her from addressing oppressive conduct that develops in cultures that view themselves as superior to others and strive for forced assimilation and/or elimination of diverse "inferior" cultures. Her split between public and private and culture and politics does not hold up, and the effort to maintain these splits masks how power works to exclude rather than affirm diversity and plurality, thus undermining her efforts to develop a democratic theory that is more inclusive. Young also does not "go far enough" in her efforts to debunk classical liberalism, for she clings to key concepts of liberal democracy in the form of self-determination and self-autonomy that point us right back to individualism.

I turn now to Chantel Mouffe, and her collaborative author, Ernest Laclau, for one last example of current democratic theory that addresses issues of power and may lead us beyond classical liberal assumptions of individualism, universalism, and rationalism. Laclau and Mouffe contribute an important postmodern critique of classical liberalism and Marxism to our conversation on democratic theories.

RADICAL DEMOCRACY (LACLAU AND MOUFFE)

Ernesto Laclau and Chantel Mouffe's (1985) radical democratic theory does not fit neatly into either liberal or communitarian camps, and, therefore, has drawn criticism from both camps. Laclau and Mouffe caution that classical liberals tend to polarize individual rights over the common good and the role of citizens. Yet they also caution that communitarians such as Michael Sandel represent the "common good" as derived from political debate that is peaceful and benevolent conversation and harmonious dialogue, thus ignoring the ubiquity of domination and resistance in *all* discursive situations. In *Hegemony and Socialist Strategy: Towards a Radical Democratic Politics*, Laclau and Mouffe offer an antiessentialist intervention to liberalism, communitarianism, and Marxism that underscores acts of power, a dimension of coercion and undecidability. They eliminate structural relations of oppression by recognizing that oppression and exploitation are deeply rooted in social relations (Smith, 1998).

Laclau and Mouffe (1985) recognize the dangers of liberal democracy's idea of an "unencumbered self" and a "unitary self." They show that liberal democracy (Locke's contract theory and Smith's *laissez-faire* bourgeois economics) is based on "possessive individualism." Liberalism begins with equality and freedom but tolerates the formation of a highly unequal social order. Laclau and Mouffe (1985) also critique Marxism for essentialist presupposing of the existence of "universal" subjects and for conceptualizing the social as "rational, transparent order." Smith (1998) describes Laclau and Mouffe's critique of Marxism as "post-Marxism," not anti-Marxism. They develop a democratic theory that is antifoundational of politics based on antifoundational epistemological and ontological presuppositions. Laclau and Mouffe do not reject the Marxist critique of capitalism, but they call for a decentering of class. They argue, contrary to Marxism, that there is a difference between class as structural position and class as subjective position. Class structural positioning does not lead directly and immediately to class-defined subject position. Just as class can be distinguished as structural and subject positions, so, too, can race, gender, and sexual orientation. What is needed for subject position formation is the development of a shared interpretation of a common structural position. Smith (1998) describes Laclau and Mouffe's theory of identity formation as a constructivist theory. Every floating signifier bears the traces of past articulations. Yet every relationship between a sign and the signifier is arbitrary. A language is a system of social conventions that facilitates communication between individuals. For Laclau and Mouffe, every social formation remains an incomplete totality, and identity formation always remains incomplete. That incompleteness always leaves room for subversive resistance.

Laclau and Mouffe (1985) soundly critique Marxist claims that democratic demands are bourgeois, making the case that we cannot know democratic demands in advance. We need context-specific analysis, a mobile approach that we can get by promoting vigorous debate and critique from within. Laclau and Mouffe use a logic of contingency that they insist is incompatible with the logic of necessity. Their logic of contingency does not lead to naive relativism, for it is qualified; it has finite possibilities. Like James's (1976, 1977) radical empiricism and pluralism and Dewey's (1955) warranted assertability, Laclau and Mouffe's logic of contingency carries the weight of the past in its present, it is historical. They insist that all traditions are open to new articulations, but they do not argue that all arguments are equally valid. Clearly, they do not develop a theory that assumes universalism. Their radical democratic theory requires a fallibilist approach. It is nonessentialistic. It preserves plurality of the social (as does Young). However, unlike Young, they do not assume a radical pluralism that threatens to lead to naive relativism. For Laclau and Mouffe, like Fraser (1997), difference is celebrated as long as it does not promote domination and inequality.

What about an assumption of individualism? Smith (1998) argues that Laclau and Mouffe's radical democracy does not fit into either liberal or communitarian camps, but rather breaks new ground. Yet I wonder how new the ground is that they break. Laclau and Mouffe question, like communitarians, the classical liberal prioritization of individual rights over the common good. They worry about the role of citizens for individuals who seem to be mere sums of desire. They fear the classical liberal detachment of "I" from her political community. Laclau and Mouffe agree with communitarians that the political subject is a socially positioned self with multiple subject positions inscribed within diverse social relations. However, like classical liberals, Laclau and Mouffe also caution the imposition of a substantial conception of the common good. They worry about overdetermination of the group over the individual. They invoke the classical liberal principle of autonomy to avoid the logic of assimilation, and thus, hopefully preserve genuine multicultural pluralism. They agree with Rawls that plurality of individual conceptions of goods is a good in itself. Laclau and Mouffe are also concerned that communitarians tend to represent the political debate of the "common good" as a peaceful and benevolent conversation through harmonious dialogue, when historically we know that these debates over the "common good" have led to lynching, slavery, and genocide. Laclau and Mouffe argue convincingly that both liberals and communitarians ignore the impact of power relations. I believe this is Laclau and Mouffe's significant contribution to current democratic theory. They invoke Foucault's principle of the ubiquity of domination and resistance in *all* forms of discursive situations. They do not think we can get rid of power, that we can ever occupy a space beyond power, but that we can transform power when it is oppressive. Radical democracy aims to transform the prevailing oppressive forms of power. The details of any kind of substantial alternative to placing our hopes on institutional solutions, however, are not offered by Laclau and Mouffe. This lack of substantial alternatives draws Fraser's (1997) criticism, and it is a criticism that Smith (1998) agrees is founded. My question of how new the ground is that Laclau and Mouffe break can be further explored by looking at the direction Chantal Mouffe has moved in her continued work.

In Chantal Mouffe's (1993)*The Return of the Political,* we can find further development of the radical democratic theory on which she collaborated with Ernesto Laclau. It is here that we get a clearer understanding of the principle of autonomy and the role of the individual that is alluded to in *Hegemony and Socialist Strategy.* In *The Return of the Political,* Mouffe points out that the current conception of the political that informs democratic thinking is rationalist, universalist, and individualist. She does not reject rationality, individuality, or universality, but she affirms that they are necessarily plural, discursively constructed, and entangled with power relations. She argues that (1) every identity is relational, (2) every identity is the affirmation of difference, (3) the political is not a certain type of institution but a dimension inherent in every human society that determines our very ontological condition, and (4) a world without antagonism is an impossibility.

Like Young, Mouffe (1993) argues that communitarians sacrifice the individual to the citizen. She agrees with Young that the "common good" is incompatible with pluralism, although she criticizes Young for ultimately essentializing the notion of "group." Mouffe describes as a positive of liberal democracy its focus on individual freedom and personal autonomy, which she argues leads to plurality. Mouffe tries to make the case that liberal democracy and radical democracy share a common starting point: the individual. However, she reframes individuality so as to restore its social nature without reducing it to being just a component of the whole. Her fear is that without a starting point of the individual, we are faced with the threat of social determinism. Mouffe suggests that individualism is needed for pluralism, and, thus, is needed for democracy. Yet she also rushes to clarify that she is not talking about an essential individual, a unitary subject. She defines *individual* "as constituted by the intersection of a multiplicity of identifications and collective identities that constantly subvert each other" (p. 97). Mouffe recognizes that the "liberal individualism is unable to understand the formation of collective identities and it cannot grasp the collective aspect of social life as being constitutive" (pp. 110–111).

In *The Democratic Paradox*, Mouffe (2000) highlights the paradoxical nature of modern liberal democracy, with liberalism's focus on individual freedom and democracy's focus on equality (which Laclau and Mouffe earlier labeled as communitarianism's focus on equality). Mouffe shows how liberal democracy rests on two logics that are incompatible and irreconcilable, but this does not cause her to conclude that we need to move beyond liberal democracy, as I claim. Instead, she thinks the tension is good between the logic of democracy that seeks homogeneity as a condition of its possibility and entails inclusion-exclusion, and the logic of liberalism that stresses "humanity." Mouffe recommends that we find value in this paradoxical tension. For her, liberal democratic politics consists of the constant process of negotiation and renegotiation (p. 45). Mouffe worries that our more recent efforts to build a consensual politics of the center—Bill Clinton's presidency is her example of this—jeopardizes the future of democracy. Why? Because, for Mouffe, conflict and confrontation are good for democracy. Consensus in a liberal-democratic society is always the expression of hegemony and the crystallization of power relations. She advocates open confrontation, for then power relations are always put into question and no victory can be final (p. 15). "To imagine that pluralist democracy could ever be perfectly instantiated is to transform it into a self-refuting ideal, since the condition of possibility of a pluralist democracy is at the same time the condition of impossibility of its perfect implementation. Hence, the importance of acknowledging its paradoxical nature" (p. 16). Unfortunately, if we apply Mouffe's example to the first 6 years of George W. Bush's presidency and to current politics in the United States, we find a country not in agreement but very much split along party lines. Instead of healthy debate and expression of diversity, we find a strong expression of hegemony in George W. Bush's presidency that verges on fascism from the perspective of those whose votes were ignored and who found themselves excluded from the conversation and ridiculed as "liberals" who are unpatriotic in the country's time of need, according to Bush's logic of fear.

In *The Democratic Paradox*, we find that Mouffe (2000) embraces the value of liberal democracy instead of pushing beyond its paradoxical logic. Her faith in the appeal of contradiction cannot hold in times when one form of power relations wins the upper hand, for if that winning power does not share her value of diversity, those that disagree with the winning power will find themselves excluded from the democratic process. There are too many examples of times in history when this has happened and democracy has not thrived as a result to counter Mouffe's faith in the value of paradox. What Mouffe needs is a transactional view of individuals-in-relation-to-others in order to get her out of the bind of having to refer back to individualism in order to maintain a pluralistic view of democracy-always-in-the-making. Laclau and Mouffe realize that democracy cannot aim for consensus, harmony, and reconciliation, for every consensus involves exclusion. Every consensus is the result of provisional hegemony. They appreciate the critical role of conflict in democracy and that democracy will always be "to come," and can never be. However, they fall back on the classical liberal assumption of individual freedom and personal autonomy in order to counter the power of social groups over the individual, even as they make the case that classical liberals are blind to power (Laclau and Mouffe equate power with the political). A transactional view of relations helps us understand that individuals develop within social groups while at the same time they continually affect and change their social groups through the unique qualities they contribute to the group. The development of an identity always involves a dimension of coercion, which the classical liberal makes invisible. But the individual developing an identity is also always in relation to others, and always brings to the social group a dimension of contingency and undecidability, which communitarians make invisible. In the tension between stability and chaos, equality and liberty, rationality and emotions, diversity and commonality, this is the place where a transactional democracy-always-in-the-making exists.

In Mouffe's (2005) latest work, *On the Political*, she challenges a "post-political" vision of globalization as a consensual form of democracy. Here, she recognizes the dangers I point to with the antagonistic dimension of the political, as well as the need to move beyond the uncontested hegemony of liberalism. Her vision of a world beyond liberalism is a multipolar world that is a plurality of hegemonic powers, since there is no hope of ever getting beyond hegemony. She recognizes that our task is

> to envision the creation of a vibrant "agonistic" public sphere of contestation where different hegemonic political projects can be confronted [for while] it is not in our power to eliminate conflicts and escape our human condition, . . . it is in our power to create the practices, discourses and institutions that would allow those conflicts to take an agonistic form. (pp. 3, 130)

Agonistic forms of conflict are we/they relationships "where the conflicting parties recognize the legitimacy of their opponents" (p. 20). Mouffe recognizes the dangers I point to in the current political world of the United States as an example of democratic confrontation being replaced by confrontation based on identification with non-negotiable moral values. Unfortunately, in the post 9/11 world of the United States, as viewed from President Bush's perspective, there is no possibility of separating his view of the political from his fundamentalist Christian values, just as the Taliban are unable to separate their fundamentalist Islamic values from their view of the political. It will take tremendous negotiation on the part of others who do value a multipolar world, and removal from positions of power of those who seek a unitary vision of globalization, for the seriousness of our current antagonistic condition to dissipate.

CONCLUSION

I began this chapter by sharing what has motivated me to work on this project and how I set about working on it. I offered a description of my overall C.A.R.E. project and the study of five collective cultures I developed as a way of informing my thinking and making sure my theory was connected to the daily practice of schooling. I then turned to an examination of various current philosophical democratic theories and how successful they are at moving beyond classical liberal democratic theory. I demonstrated that, in fact, these current descriptions still cling to assumptions embedded within classical liberal democratic theory. I began this examination with John Dewey's renascent liberal democracy to help us understand the need to move beyond classical liberal democracy. Dewey offered his astute criticisms of liberalism, as well as a key to help us move beyond liberalism with his transactional view of relations. Yet he also modeled for us how difficult it is to let go of liberalism's assumptions of rationality and universalism.

I then turned to Benjamin Barber to consider a contemporary democratic theory that is greatly influenced by Dewey's ideas, developing them further in a communitarian direction. Barber helped us further explore liberalism's lack of a theory of citizenship. Still, we found that Barber's strong democracy retains assumptions of universalism, individualism, and rationalism. We worried about exclusion and the narrowing of the agenda for deliberation as a result of their universalistic ideal of the civic public and the common good. We worried about the silencing of voices in face-to-face discussions. We found the assumption of individuality lingering in Barber's concept of autonomy and rationality in his concept of deliberation. Barber's separation of the political from truths caused us to worry about anarchy and despotism, and his splits between the public and private as well as the political and economic were found to be problematic as well, for they fail to address concerns of power, access, and material need.

I then turned to two examples of political philosophers who specifically address concerns of power in their democratic theory: Iris Young's deliberative democracy and Lacalu and Mouffe's radical democracy. Young seeks to develop a politics of difference in which power issues and access are underscored, although she does not focus on material need. Laclau and Mouffe, as post-Marxists, do a better job of addressing class issues. Neither example embraces liberalism's assumptions of universality and rationalism, but both theories still cling to a liberal commitment to individualism. We found with Young's metaphor of the unoppressive city that she wants to preserve the liberal commitment to individual freedom and autonomy, as well as embrace plural definitions of the good. She is concerned with the institutional conditions necessary for promoting self-development and self-determination. Laclau and Mouffe dance between liberalism and communitarianism on the issue of individualism as well, but they fall back on the classical liberal assumption of individual freedom and personal autonomy in order to counter the power of social groups upon the individual. We also learned that Young embraces plural definitions of the good wholesale, without offering any critique of various definitions and how some may lead to exclusion and exploitation of others, thus making her unoppressive city vulnerable to fears of vulgar relativism. She achieves this wholesale acceptance of cultural differences by maintaining a separation between the personal and the political and delegating culture into the personal realm, beyond critique, while placing structural differences in the public realm of politics open to critique. Her public/private and culture/politics splits end up undermining her efforts to develop a democratic theory that is more inclusive. Laclau and Mouffe's radical democratic theory is also nonessentialistic and fallibilistic in its approach. Like Young, they also seek to preserve plurality; however, unlike Young, Laclau and Mouffe do not assume a radical pluralism that threatens to lead to naive relativism. For them, difference is celebrated as long as it does not promote domination and inequality.

Now that we have explored several examples of current democratic theories and brought out their strengths and weaknesses, I hope the reader is convinced that there is more work to be done to help us get beyond classical liberalism and its assumptions of universality, rationality, and individualism. Even democratic theories that have benefited from critical, feminist, and postmodern arguments and let go of assumptions of universality and rationality still cling to individualism. And, in democratic theories that seem to have let go of individualism for the common good, we still find individualism, as well as universality and rationality, lurking.

In this chapter, I established that there is a need for what I have to offer, while at the same time highlighting the work of other political theorists who contribute to my own project. In the next five chapters, I expand upon a pluralistic, relational democratic theory by developing key themes for a transactional view of democracy-always-in-the-making and how these translate into the daily practice of schooling, with the help of the five collectivist cultures I studied in contrast to the individualistic culture of White, middle- and upper-class America, with which I am so familiar. The concluding chapter, Chapter 7, sums up the examples from the C.A.R.E. project as illustrations of a democracy-always-in-the-making that moves beyond liberal democracy, and seeks to emphasize questions of equality and distribution as well as a differentiated politics of difference. It is my sincere hope that this text will help all students have a chance to actively participate in a democratic society-always-in-the-making.[9]

Chapter 2

Shared Responsibilities

As I described at the outset of Chapter 1, I am a pragmatist and a scholar in cultural studies. This means that I believe it is vital that my theory writing be informed by practice in order to keep it grounded in the historical, local, contingent, everyday world. I am not a qualitative researcher or anthropologist; I am a philosopher of education developing a theoretical argument with the help of narrative stories from the field to illustrate the theory I seek to develop. I am not trying to make empirical claims about the schools I visited, nor do I claim expertise in the cultures I am studying. The cultures I am studying are complex, multiple, diverse, and continually in the process of changing.

I am also a former elementary school teacher who has taught in lower elementary school in Pennsylvania (aged 6–9), upper elementary Montessori classrooms in California (aged 9–12), and K–12 public school classrooms in Indiana as a substitute teacher. For 7 years, I taught elementary children and loved every moment of it, even the hard moments; I do not know of a job that is more challenging, stimulating, and rewarding. I am also the mother of four children, three of whom have gone through school from preschool to or through graduate education, and one of whom is still in a K–12 classroom. I approach my visitations to schools as a friend and colleague of the teachers and principals, not as someone trying to pass judgment on their teaching and administrating abilities. I deeply respect the work that teachers do, having been one myself for a good while; I know how difficult and important their jobs are. I approach my visitations to schools with a deep love of children as well, and a strong belief that they can teach us so much if we only listen. I also approach my visitations to schools with a deep sense of humility in recognition of what I do not know about their particular sites and the people who work there and, as a White, Euro-Western American, what I don't know about their cultures. I spent the vast majority of my time in the schools I visited with the children, watching and listening to what they had to say and trying to learn as much as I could from them. I went through their school days with them. Before and after school, I talked to their teachers and principals and parents when I could.

My original focus for this project was Mexico and Mexican Americans because of their disenfranchisment in U.S. schools, misunderstandings in the public consciousness (Portales, 2000), and my familiarity with the culture and the Spanish language, having lived and taught in California for many years. The values of family and community are celebrated in the work of Mexican American scholars, writers, and artists, thus making Mexico and Mexican Americans serve very well as an example of a collective culture (Valdès, 1996). From my research I learned that there are 13 million Latinos in the United States, one out of nine citizens are Latino according to the 2000 consensus (Portales, 2000), and that by 2010, Latinos are predicted to be the largest minority group in the United States, surpassing African Americans (Slavin & Calderòn, 2001). From another source (Suàrez-Orozco & Suàrez-Orozco, 1995), I learned that 60% of Latinos living in the United States are Mexican Americans.[1] I also learned that Mexican American students have a 35.3% drop-out rate for people aged 16–24, while others say it is as high as 38% (Slavin & Calderòn, 2001). For first-generation Mexicans the drop-out rate is 17%, but for second-generation students it rises to 24% (Slavin & Calderòn, 2001), For all of these reasons, Mexico and Mexican Americans rose to the top of my list as a good place to start my school visitations and my year of immersion in the research on their culture and schools.

I observed a Mexican school in central Mexico (*La Escuela*), and a charter school in the southwest United States with a population more than 80% Mexican American (*Los Estados Unidos*).[2] Both *La Escuela* and *Los Estados Unidos* describe their mission statements using democratic language. *La Escuela* is an award-winning educational program that has helped more than 2,500 children and adults from indigenous communities in a central state of Mexico for 18 years. They say in their publications that they seek to empower disadvantaged children and youth who live in remote areas, and create a sense of cultural belonging and commitment toward their own communities. The founders of *La Escuela* are deeply concerned about the mass migration of people from their communities to larger cities and abroad (the United States) because of a lack of opportunities in their communities. They estimate that 50,000 people migrate from their state each year. *La Escuela* has won several national and international awards for its excellent educational programs. It was founded by a married couple and several parents who could not afford to send their children to public school in Mexico because of the cost of instruction fees and supplies. *La Escuela* began by meeting in parents' homes until the money could be raised to build a school. It is not a public or a private school but a nonprofit school existing on donations, sponsorships, and grants. The parents supplied the labor and much of the materials to build the school. They built one school in town and three in remote indigenous villages, and they have a bus to help with transportation needs. I visited the school in town that had 500 students enrolled from ages 3 to 16.[3] They also offer vocational training for parents during the day and Saturday school for parents so they can receive an education along with their children.

Los Estados Unidos is a charter school, one of the oldest in the United States, and also one of the largest with an enrollment of 1,400 preschoolers to 5th graders. The school is located in an old, well-established Mexican American community with a population that is over 80% Mexican American. The school operates on a year-round schedule in order to accommodate the number of students enrolled. It is clear that its enrollment has grown over the years, for there are 6 permanent buildings and 17 modular buildings on campus. There are three teams (A, B, C) that rotate attendance, with two of them in school while one is off. Students attend school year-round for 3 months on and 1 month off. *Los Estados Unidos* was founded by a group of teachers, a dynamic Asian American principal, Arlene, and a Mexican American director, Michel, specifically to target the needs of Mexican American students and their families in the area. The school was originally bilingual, with a teacher or aide in each classroom who spoke Spanish fluently, but they voted to discontinue Spanish instruction because of their state's decision to discontinue bilingual education and offer only English. They tried continuing Spanish instruction in spite of the state's decision, but found that, because of their lower test scores (which resulted from the few years spent immersed in English), the students were disfavored and placed in lower tracks and ESL (English as a second language) programs when they entered middle school. *Los Estados Unidos* is also an award-winning school, with "Distinguished School" proudly painted above the main entrance as well as on the auditorium wall. It has received significant grant support, as can be seen from the number of computers in the school. Every 4th and 5th grader has a Macintosh computer, half of the 3rd graders have their own, and every classroom has at least five computers.[4] The school also offers an adult education program for parents as well as Saturday art programs for the community at large.

In this chapter, I share some stories from my visit to *La Escuela* and *Los Estados Unidos* in an effort to better understand how we can encourage citizens to contribute to their school communities and develop a sense of *shared responsibility*. Following the lead of Myles Horton, founder of Highlander Folk School, I begin each section with stories, which I then analyze in terms of what they represent for a relational, pluralistic democratic theory. Horton (1990) always said you must begin with practice and move to theory, after having tried the reverse and finding it didn't work with his students.[5] In the "Arrival and Departure" and "Parental Relations with the Schools" sections, I focus on the interactions of outsider adults, parents, and myself with the school staff. These stories elucidate two key concepts in democratic theory—respect and human dignity and their role in encouraging contributions by citizens. Through the stories we see the importance of welcoming others and valuing their input, and we discover how these two key concepts translate differently in the two schools I visited. I discuss these two concepts further with help from Iris Marion Young (2000), for in *Inclusion and Democracy*, she focuses specifically on issues of inclusion and exclusion. I show how respect and human dignity change in a relational, pluralistic political theory to become "shared responsibility" based on expressions of care.

In the section titled "Student Roles in the Schools Visited," I consider citizenship roles in terms of students' roles only. I examine the various assumptions upon which differing citizenship roles depend as these assumptions became vividly apparent through my field observations. I again begin with stories from my visits to *La Escuela* and *Los Estados Unidos*, to help us discover how the concepts of democratic citizen and empowerment translate differently in the two schools I visited. I discuss the concepts of democratic citizen and empowerment further in this section with the help of Angela Valenzuela (1999). Again, I show how the emphasis on *individual development* changes in a relational and pluralistic political theory to *shared responsibilities*, or what Valenzuela refers to as *reciprocal relations*. Recommendations for school reform in the United States, based on what we learn here, are more fully developed in the final chapter.

ARRIVAL AND DEPARTURE

I wrote the same basic letter to the two schools sharing what my research was about. As I said in the outset of Chapter 1, I acknowledged that the staff were very busy and promised that I would try to stay out of their way and not create any work for them. I stated that I only wanted to observe as much as I could of the school culture while disturbing it as little as possible (recognizing, of course, that just being there would disturb the school to some degree). However, I soon learned that in Mexico it is considered very rude to ignore a visitor, and I was greeted warmly and embraced and brought into the school community. When I arrived in Mexico on Sunday I was picked up by the school curriculum director/principal, Maria, and taken to my hotel, then to dinner, and showed around the market square (with Maria greeting students from the school and their parents as we walked around). In the morning I was picked up by Maria and taken to the school. Being picked up by Maria was no simple ride, for Maria's car (a five-seater from Texas) became a bus for the school as we drove along. Any student or teacher she saw along the way was offered a ride until the car could hold no more. Only the first day did she save me from having a child on my lap. The rest of the week I arrived at the school with a shy child on my lap and four to five more children and adults in the back seat.

The first day, we arrived later than Maria would have wished. On Monday mornings, the school always has an opening ceremony, which Maria presides over. She was late because she had picked me up, but when we arrived at the school she did not get out of the car and rush to the opening ceremony. Instead, she greeted students and parents who were in the courtyard, many of whom had waited to see her. It takes time for Maria to get to her office on any day of the week, and that Monday was no exception. I was not left out of this greeting process but was introduced to many people as she slowly made her way to the opening ceremony. And I was not allowed to fade into the background at the opening ceremony, but was brought forward and introduced to the entire school population as a visitor from the United States who would be studying their school all week and whom Maria hoped the school would make welcome. Later I was told by the school director, José, "Maestra, mi escuela es su casa" (Teacher, my school is your home). Maria also sent her secretary around to the teachers to let them know I would be coming to their classrooms and to please welcome me. This same secretary escorted me to the first room I visited, and then left me to find my way around. After introductions, Maria and the rest of the school staff went about their work and left me to my observations. However, if there was a staff meeting or staff celebration (birthday party on Friday), a student was sent to find me and make sure I attended as well. Because of the way I was first introduced, I was able to slide in and out of classrooms easily all week without having teachers stop and inquire who I was. The teachers and students went on with business as usual and often they did not notice I had entered the room until I was there for some time.

Mexico is a large, diverse nation, yet it is typical of the people to make sure visitors are warmly greeted and introduced to everyone, so the people will feel comfortable approaching the newcomer and the newcomer will feel comfortable approaching the people. It is considered rude to approach someone you have not been introduced to. Not only do the people of Mexico greet one another warmly and seek to make visitors feel at home, but they also are very expressive and kind in their goodbyes. Goodbyes are long and drawn out, with a great deal of thank you's and hugs. On the final day I was in Mexico, I was invited to dinner at José and Rosa's home, the two founders of the school. Maria was also invited. Grandma was also included, as well as the mother of a school pupil who worked as their housekeeper and her two children and one grandchild. There was also one of *La Escuela*'s first students, Juan, who had started school at the age of 9, and now, at the age of 27, was working for the school, keeping their accounting books. I spent 6 hours in this beautiful home discussing my research and having the chance to have any questions I had answered. I also served as a consultant for them while I was wined and dined. They apologized for not doing more, wanting to take me for coffee and dessert on the way back to my hotel. I bowed out as graciously as I could.

In contrast, my arrival at *Los Estados Unidos* began at the airport on Sunday where I rented a car and drove to the hotel and the school using directions from MapQuest, as I had never been sent any directions. I explored the community on Sunday and discovered roosters crowing right across the street from the school and a ranch with horses two blocks away. There were several mercados and vendors within walking distance of the school; it felt like I was back in Mexico, except that I had yet to receive a greeting. The feeling of similarity ended as soon as school started on Monday.

I arrived on the first day of school at 8 A.M., only to find that school starts at 7:50 A.M. and that, consequently, I was late. No one had communicated to me when school started, and they also neglected to tell me I would be arriving for the first week of school. Neither Michel, the director, nor Arlene, the principal, came out to greet me when I arrived. I found their offices and introduced myself, and gave them each gifts I had brought for them as well as the school. I was never approached by either of them all week. What little conversation I had with them I initiated. I was introduced to the administrative assistant by Arlene, and told the secretaries could help me with signing in, giving me a map, and so forth. There were no other introductions. The teachers were never informed of my arrival, who I was, or why I was there. Even if Arlene and Michel had forgotten about my visit, which they admitted they had on Friday at my exit interview, they did nothing to inform the teachers after I arrived. No note in their mailboxes, nothing. Consequently, all week long, I walked into classrooms where I had to introduce myself, apologize to teachers for interrupting their classes, explain what I was doing there, and ask that they please ignore me. As the week went on and I had more opportunities to talk to teachers, or at least see them and be seen by them, I was able to slide in and out of classrooms more easily. As the end of the week approached, I requested an exit interview with Arlene and Michel and was offered 20 minutes on Friday afternoon. Fortunately, that time extended to 45 minutes. Still, they did not ask me anything about my research or ask me to share any of my observations with them. They did not see me as a possible consultant or contributor to their work.

A cynic might say, "Well, the people in Mexico were just being kind to you and courting you because they need your help, they need your money, and so forth." But that wasn't the case. What I experienced was a way of being courteous and respectful and a display of manners that made me feel as if my contributions were valued and welcomed. I watched Maria treat the teachers, children, and their parents in the same warm, friendly, embracing way, and I watched her and other teachers do the same thing with one another in other settings. There was a curiosity and interest and respect accorded me in Mexico that I only received from a few of the teaching assistants in *Los Estados Unidos* and a few teachers who were Mexican American. Could it be that the one school was not used to having visitors and that the U.S. school was overrun by too many visitors? Both schools receive outside visitors who come to see them. It's true that *Los Estados Unidos* has many visitors because of its technology and its status as a charter school. However, since *La Escuela* is a school that survives on grants and donations, it also has many visitors; it has students from universities in the United States who visit and conduct research, as well as other contributors from Mexico and other countries such as Canada.

The way I was greeted and welcomed in the two schools was sharply contrasting. The difference caused me to look closely at how parents were greeted as well as spoken about by the teachers and administrators in both schools.

PARENTAL RELATIONS WITH THE SCHOOL

Initially, I had a hard time recognizing the parents at *La Escuela*. At first, I just saw many parents dropping their children at school and picking them up. Soon I realized that many of the women who worked in the school's vocational training shop during the day sewing had children in the school. Later in the week, I realized that many of the adults who worked in the school also had children in the school. Parents came to the school for several reasons. Many would line up at the office each morning to pay their child's fees (they pay what they can), with the longest line being on Friday when it was teachers' pay day. Many came in to talk to Maria, the school principal, about issues and concerns they had.[6]

The administration and teachers in *La Escuela* welcomed and very much appreciated the parents' contributions, which they depended on for survival. They treated the parents like friends, being warm, friendly, and affectionate with them. They were compassionate, listened to their problems, and admired them for what they do. They were well aware of the parents' lives and their issues, where they live, children who are born, people that are ill, and many times, these situations affected school programs. The week I was there, the computer teacher was absent having eye surgery and the dance teacher was in the hospital giving birth. Fewer parents were there for the Saturday adult education class because the former week had been an exam week, and they now had pressing family needs that needed to be taken care of. I seldom heard the parents talked about in a disrespectful way. There were one or two stories:

the mother who sent her children to school on the public bus without an adult or older child to escort them when they were very young, and the child who was about to drop out because her family didn't value education. I heard more stories about the children who were orphaned and adopted by the staff and families at the school to help them have a good start in life, and I met several of these children. At *La Escuela,* the parents are treated with respect and dignity, are welcomed warmly to the school, and are encouraged to contribute and help in whatever way they can. Many of these families are extremely poor. Many parents are illiterate but value the education their children receive. The school also opens up its space to the parents and lets them use the office equipment, computer equipment, and meeting spaces when they work on projects for the school. The parents in turn help raise the money for the teachers' salaries and buy or contribute supplies their children need.

At *Los Estados Unidos,* Arlene and Michel arrive to school at 6 A.M. They are at their desks busily working when the first parents arrive to drop off their children for breakfast before school begins, and are at their desks long after the last parents have picked up their children from after-school care. They work very hard for their school, and the teachers admire them and appreciate their hard work. But the parents stand outside the gate and don't dare to enter the grounds.

Los Estados Unidos says in its mission statement that it includes families and the community in the school structure and curriculum, which was one of the reasons I chose this school to observe. I thought that a statement of inclusion would demonstrate a valuing of the local families' Mexican culture and a desire to encourage democratic participation. I was wrong. At *Los Estados Unidos,* the staff share responsibility for the school but the relationship with the parents is patriarchal. I noticed from the start that parents didn't come onto the school grounds. They came before school to drop off their children and after school to pick them up, but they would stand outside the gate, away from the school grounds. I wondered if they were not allowed in, but that was apparently not so. The security guard said they could come on the grounds if they asked for permission to do so. By witnessing the Pre-school Parent Orientation on Wednesday, the whole school's Parents Orientation on Friday, and having the chance to talk to Arlene (school principal) and Michel (school director) on Friday, I began to get a better sense of the school's relationship with the parents. (Please note that I did not get to talk to the parents about this issue).

It seemed from my observations that parents were not greeted and welcomed at *Los Estados Unidos* beyond a superficial level. The parents were viewed by Arlene, and some of the teachers, as being lazy, ignorant, naive, and unaware, and as devaluing education. These sentiments were expressed to me in various conversations with the staff during the week and at my exit interview. The relationship between the parents and the staff is neither warm, trusting, nor respectful; rather, it is distant and patronizing. There is discrimination based on social economic status, if not out-and-out racism. Thus, the parents stay away for the most part. They come for Parents Orientation, but the staff feel they have to make it mandatory and bribe the parents with free school supplies in order to get them to come. The staff of *Los Estados Unidos* set up a strict schedule for the meetings, saying that if the parents do not show up for Parents Orientation on time, they will not be allowed into their child's classroom. They treat the parents like children, threatening them with the loss of their child's place in school and making them fill out all the enrollment forms again if their children miss more than 5 days of school. They must reapply for the track they want for their children (A, B, or C), with the threat that siblings could end up in different tracks.

The way the staff of *Los Estados Unidos* spoke of the parents and treated them would not be tolerated in an upper-middle-class public school in the United States, such as the one my child attended at the time. Nor was such behavior tolerated at *La Escuela*. Maria, principal and curriculum director at *La Escuela*, told me a story about young adults who were in the Mexican military and working at the school on Saturdays for their military service. She eventually sent them away because they treated the parents with disdain and disrespect, even though it might have meant that the school would no longer receive help from other soldiers doing their military service. Fortunately, the military sent a new group of soldiers who were respectful to the parents and willing to help. And they were greeted and welcomed to the school.

CONNECTING THEORY WITH PRACTICE, PART I

I want to further explore the idea of how we greet and welcome people into school communities. When I went to observe in *La Escuela* and *Los Estados Unidos*, I did not know this theme would become a focus for further consideration. However, I experienced the same kind of treatment as the parents did in the two schools, and so it was vividly brought to my attention. The one school went out of its way to welcome me and inform me "Maestra, mi escuela es su casa," while the other school forgot I was coming. *La Escuela* sent for me to attend their staff meetings and asked me to share my research project with them and give them feedback from my observations. I spent 6 hours in discussion with the school founders on my last day, Saturday. *Los Estados Unidos* had staff meetings I stumbled upon accidentally and they had no questions for me at the end of my week at the exit interview I requested.

They scheduled me for 20 minutes on Friday. Of course, they were very busy; after all, it was the first week of the new school year, and yes, I had promised not to create work for them.

In *Inclusion and Democracy*, Iris Young (2000) offers a model of deliberative democracy that she describes as a process of communication among citizens and public officials. In her chapter "Inclusive Political Communication," she focuses specifically on issues of exclusion and inclusion, as she makes the case that democracy is a call for inclusion and political equality. Young explores some of the ways citizens are kept from participating in communication, such as by being kept outside of the process of discussion and decision making (she calls this external exclusion), as well as by being dismissed, ignored, or patronized (she calls this internal exclusion). Certainly what I witnessed and experienced at *Los Estados Unidos* involved internal exclusion (patronizing relations) as well as external exclusion (not being allowed in classrooms, on school grounds, or to attend meetings). Young goes on to consider everyday modes of communication that aid communication, and one of these is "greeting, or public agreement."

When people are greeted, they are publicly acknowledged for the unique people they are. They are called by their name. They are hugged, kissed, have their hands shaken, and drinks and food offered, depending on the cultural rituals for greetings. Greetings open up the opportunity for the other to contribute. They are acts of caring. The greeter makes the first move, exposing herself and making herself vulnerable and risking rejection. However, such an act of exposure acknowledges the other's vulnerability as well, for if the other is not greeted, she will be excluded from the communication process. So we can see how a greeting establishes respect for the other and makes it possible for a bond of trust to be formed. As Young (2000) points out: "The gestures of greeting function to acknowledge relations of discursive equality and mutual respect among the parties to discussion, as well as to establish trust and forge connection based on the previous relationships among the parties" (p. 59). Of course, greetings can be forced and superficial or fake. Still, without the moment of greeting, no discussion can take place.

I (re)learned in my visits to *La Escuela* and *Los Estados Unidos* that greetings help people feel welcome and confident that they can contribute to the place where they are visiting and that their contributions will be valued. Being greeted does not mean that one's contributions will be agreed with and accepted, but if the greeting is sincere, it does mean that the one being greeted will be treated with generosity and that what they have to say will be attended to with care. Without greetings, people are excluded, even if they are already members of the community, as with the parents at *Los Estados Unidos* (internal exclusion), and especially if they are not already members, as with my visit (external exclusion).

The staff at *Los Estados Unidos* would no doubt disagree with my description of their school. They would protest that while they may be frustrated with their lack of parental participation, they are certainly kind and respectful to the children enrolled in their school. This seems to be true, based on my observations. I saw no signs of overt child abuse or neglect, although I did hear examples of psychological harm through belittlement and the use of fear tactics. Overall, though, this is considered a fine school—indeed, an award-winning, distinguished school—and many teachers expressed to me their pleasure in working at *Los Estados Unidos.* The children in the school are treated with dignity and respect, although they are not allowed to act without permission or they will get in trouble. However, the children were the ones asked to give their parents the school's patronizing message that if they did not show up on time for Parents Orientation they would be turned away.

The staff at *Los Estados Unidos* argues that they are teaching their students to be democratic citizens. They teach them to be responsible, and by this, they mean showing up at school on time with their homework completed and the necessary materials for the day's lesson, and ready to obey the rules. They are teaching the students to be respectful in terms of not interrupting teachers when they are talking, keeping their hands to themselves, and not bothering their neighbors. They are trying to teach the parents the same values: to attend parent orientation meetings and show up on time prepared to listen attentively to the teacher and school principal or director. The staff at *Los Estados Unidos* does not see what role they play in creating a school where parents are disengaged and detached. As with many schools in the United States, it is easier for the staff to blame the parents for being lazy, ignorant, too busy, or not valuing education than to take a hard, critical look at what they are doing that makes parents feel that their contributions are not welcome or valued (Romo & Falbo, 1996; Valdès, 1996).

However, the staff at *La Escuela* would have no trouble seeing the role the staff at *Los Estados Unidos* plays in excluding parents. They would view the way the staff relates to the parents as rude and disrespectful. They would find their manner brisk and dismissive. They would be impressed with their efficiency and punctuality, but they would not find the staff very responsive to parents' needs or their children's needs. They would be sad to see what little the school is doing to help the parents feel empowered by acting to make changes in their society so their children will have a chance to grow up in a more just society. *La Escuela*'s parents work hard and have little in the way of resources to give to the school. Yet they give the school so much. They built it and made it what it is, and they continue to work to maintain it. They feel a strong sense of shared responsibility and pride in their work. The staff and parents at *La Escuela* remind us that the development of shared responsibility begins with a greeting.

La Escuela and *Los Estados Unidos* represent different models of democracy, with *Los Estados Unidos* emphasizing individualism as expressed in a liberal democracy and *La Escuela* focusing on students and their parents in relation to larger community needs. *Los Estados Unidos* is succeeding in raising individual students' test scores and placing some of their students in higher tracks in middle schools, hopefully opening up chances for more opportunities for these students. *La Escuela* is succeeding in creating in students and their parents a sense of cultural belonging and commitment toward their own communities. I was very fortunate to have the opportunity to observe *La Escuela,* for I had no idea I would find a school that so nicely models a democracy-in-the-making with a pluralistic and relational focus, one where the boundaries between individuals and others blur and dynamic changes take place as a result of their transactions with one another. The staff at *La Escuela* understand that a democracy-in-the-making depends on members who feel that they have a shared responsibility to contribute and participate in discussions. The staff make their school decisions in ways that include the participation of others, particularly the parents. Those who teach at *La Escuela* and discover that they don't feel comfortable with a shared responsibility model based on political equality soon leave, usually after one year. Those who remain appreciate the energy of the school and value the many contributions various people make. They understand the importance of greeting people and welcoming them into the school community as a means of establishing equality and mutual respect so that people will contribute to the school's success. It is how they were treated when they were hired and why they decided to work in a school that pays them less than others and is pressed every month to make payroll. They understand that such a democracy-in-the-making must make the valuing of difference and diversity central to their school mission.

We can learn from *La Escuela* and *Los Estados Unidos* that parents only feel a sense of shared responsibility when they are treated with respect and dignity, and are viewed as important and valued contributors to the school community. A relational focus teaches us to pay attention to our priorities and values, and place people at the top of our list, ahead of technology, punctuality, and control. We begin to pay attention to relationality by noticing how we greet and welcome others, for when we offer a warm, friendly, respectful greeting, we start to build trust and bonds and we open up an inclusive space for conversation to begin. "Hola, maestra, mi escuela es su casa."

STUDENTS' ROLES IN THE SCHOOLS VISITED

I now turn to some stories that portray the difference between the two schools in their treatment of the children. The sharp contrast between the two schools that I found in the treatment of adults is equally apparent in the treatment of students. The students at *La Escuela* interacted freely with one another, their teachers, and with me, while the students at *Los Estados Unidos* were strictly forbidden from any interaction unless under direct teacher supervision, even at their assigned playground areas during recess and lunch. I ended each day at *La Escuela* exhausted from the amount of conversing I did in a second language, mainly with students but also the teachers. I ended each day at *Los Estados Unidos* having had next to no conversation with students and staff who were fluent in English, my first language.

When I arrived at *La Escuela,* the students were sweeping the courtyard and getting rid of puddles that had formed from the rain that fell the night before. The students take turns cleaning their own classrooms, the bathrooms, and the courtyard/playground area. The only part of the school that is not cleaned by students is the central office where the school director, José; Maria, the principal; and the secretaries and other administrators work, and where the teachers maintain their desks. An elderly woman cleans their two floors every afternoon. On Monday mornings the school holds a schoolwide opening ceremony, and all the students go to the back courtyard and stand with their classrooms and teachers, organized with the classes arranged from youngest to oldest and forming a circle around the courtyard. Here, the older students lead the school in a pledge and the singing of patriotic songs. There is also a different class each week that has the responsibility for presenting a lesson for the school. The Monday I was there, a class of 9-year-olds put on a skit about recycling and proudly displayed posters they had made to teach us about the need to recycle. The same students then went from class to class during the week distributing recycling containers and later collecting what the students had managed to recycle that week.

While at *La Escuela*, I learned that several of the high school students are responsible for designing the curriculum and teaching the Saturday school for adult education. I also learned that the high school students have a print shop for one of their afternoon vocational skills classes and they make all the brochures and flyers the school uses to advertise itself. And on Friday, I observed the high school students leading the elementary students in a 3-hour social activist community-building activity that *La Escuela* calls *Commando Blanco.* It was clear from various activities occurring during the week that the students at *La Escuela* played an active role in their school and that their participation is counted upon.

Los Estados Unidos is a different story. Students have jobs in their classrooms handing out books and materials and are responsible for keeping their desk areas clean, as is seen in most schools across the United States. Beyond that, I didn't observe them being responsible for more than their own behavior. There are many young adults attending college and mothers needing part-time jobs who work as classroom aides, supervise recess and lunch periods, provide before- and after-school care, and teach gym. There are also adults who teach the adult education classes on campus during the day. It is very clear at *Los Estados Unidos* that the adults who work for the school are in charge, and not the students or their parents.

At both schools, I was on my own at lunchtime and brought my own lunch, which I ate while observing the students at lunchtime. At *La Escuela,* teachers dismissed the class one table at a time and the students would line up at the door waiting for the teacher's instruction to leave; alternatively, they would leave the room only after the teacher finished teaching and left the room for lunch. The students would escort themselves to the lunchroom and either line up to pay for lunch or sit at a table to eat the lunch they brought from home. The tables in the lunch area are covered, but the students are free to eat anywhere in the open courtyard area, which is at the center of the school and to the back of it. Students are also allowed to eat in their classrooms, where the teacher doesn't supervise the kids but eats her lunch and attends to paperwork; sometimes there is no teacher in the classroom and the students eat and play or just talk with one another. When it is time for class, they return to the room or line up outside the room, getting ready to return to work.

While students play outside at *La Escuela,* other students work in class or take their final exams, as was the case during the week I was there. Within the rooms you can hear the kids outside playing even if the doors and windows are closed. Still, the students and teachers ignore the noise and work undisturbed on their lessons. During the first 2 days I was at *La Escuela,* I found the open courtyard space and the unsupervised eating and playing in the classrooms very confusing. I couldn't figure out what was going on and who was in charge. I couldn't see a pattern, for it seemed so loose and chaotic. By the third day, I recognized the children by their size (an indication of their age) and had gotten to know many of them somewhat through my talks with them. I also knew who the teachers were because I had visited their rooms and observed their staff meeting. Eventually, I was able to identify the primary kids who stayed in their playground area and ate in their own rooms or courtyard area with one or two adults loosely observing. The lower elementary students were dismissed with the primary kids, and the upper elementary students were dismissed with the junior high and high school students. This meant that they weren't playing directly by the classrooms in session, even though the children's play could still be heard. I also noticed a few teachers playing with the older students at lunchtime, functioning as supervisors, but again, very loosely. When the kids were dismissed for recess, they were just let go to play in the open play areas until it was time to return to class.

During recess or lunchtime, I was continually approached by children of all ages who wanted to talk to me and hear me talk in English. We worked hard to communicate with one another, me in my sketchy Spanish and rapid English and they in their rapid Spanish and sketchy English. At first, they were a little shy and embarrassed, but after I assured them I needed their help with Spanish and they realized I could help them practice their English, they overcame their shyness and often approached. I talked to many students at *La Escuela* during the week, and we learned a lot from one another about families, customs, popular culture (music, films, stars, sports), and so forth. To their great delight, I also translated almost every child's name—or, at least, it sure felt that way to me—into English for them.

In contrast to my visit to Mexico, the school *Los Estados Unidos* felt incredibly controlling. The children are escorted by an adult, usually the classroom aide, to the play area for recess. The kids line up to be dismissed, and, in some rooms, they even line up in a particular order (one room was organized in alphabetical order and the students were told they would re-main in that order all year). Each classroom is assigned play areas on the playground and are allowed to play only in those areas. Each classroom is given two numbers, and each week those numbers change. The numbers are painted on the blacktop, defining for the students the area where they can play; for example, in the baseball area or the jungle gym or the four-square area. When the bell rings or a whistle blows, they run to line up at another numbered spot on the blacktop, and the classroom aide or teacher escorts them back to their classrooms. They are taught how to walk in line, how to hold their hands behind their backs, what speed to walk, how quiet they should be, and so forth.

At *Los Estados Unidos,* a few children would wave or smile at me, but next to none talked to me; most of them ignored me altogether. I didn't have a con-versation of any length with any of the students. There was no way for that to happen while I was in their rooms without them getting in trouble for talking, and outside the rooms, they played with one another, trying to avoid relating to the adults. Lunchtime is the only time the children are allowed to mix with those from other classrooms and play spontaneously with one another, but even those encounters are allowed only within strict boundaries. First, they are escorted to the lunchroom, where they line up on painted lines, and are then dismissed, line by line, to get their food. A lunchroom monitor dismisses the students individually or by table to leave the lunch area and go line up to play. Next, they are dismissed by groups to go to the play area until a bell rings and a whistle blows. The students then line up again at their designated locations numbered on the blacktop, where a teacher picks them up and escorts them to the bathrooms and then back to their rooms. They have lunch together with one other grade: kindergarten with 1st grade, 2nd with 3rd grade, and 4th with 5th grade.

The fairness of this comparison can be questioned by pointing to the different sizes of the two schools: *La Escuela* was smaller than *Los Estados Unidos*, with 500 and 1,400 students, respectively (around 870 are at *Los Estados Unidos* at a time due to the year-round schooling schedule). One can argue that, because of the size of its population, *Los Estados Unidos* has to be more controlling to make sure the kids are safe and no one gets hurt. From my observation, both schools seemed very safe. I never saw a child hurt another child at *La Escuela* in the entire week. At *Los Estados Unidos,* I did see a child get hurt on the basketball court on Friday morning during Parents Orientation. One can counterargue that *Los Estados Unidos* should have less to worry about in terms of safety because of its smaller age range—it has children aged 3 to 11—while *La Escuela's* children should be at more risk of harm because of its much wider age range—it has children aged 3 to 16. There are certainly plenty of adults in the United States who fear placing teenagers with primary-age children because of the big difference in their developmental levels. In fact, at *La Escuela,* there was less risk for the younger children because the older children looked out for the younger ones or did not interact with them at all. I saw many older children escorting younger ones to school and home. In both settings, it was clear that the children were respectful of one another and well disciplined and courteous. However, there was a vibrancy and aliveness at *La Escuela* that was missing at *Los Estados Unidos*, except at lunchtime and before and after school. Overall, the students at *Los Estados Unidos* were very docile and passive, and I saw them get into trouble with the adults if they tried to be anything but docile and passive. In contrast, the children at *La Escuela* were treated as if they had self-discipline and could monitor themselves, and they did. They were also treated as if they shared responsibility for one another's well-being.

CONNECTING THEORY WITH PRACTICE, PART II

The mission statements at both *La Escuela* and *Los Estados Unidos* say they teach their students how to be good democratic citizens, but they mean very different things by this. The founders of *La Escuela* told me they consciously designed their school in a way that makes sure the students are actively involved in the school and share responsibility for the school's success. They want the students to experience what it is like to be decision makers, and to know that they can act to make changes in their lives. They designed many curriculum activities and placed into the very structure of the school ways to encourage students to develop their voices and become empowered, socially responsible, citizen activists. For example, in Commando Blanco, they learn that what they contribute to the family and home is an important example of citizenship, and that they can do the same for their community. They learn how to research topics of concern such as recycling and organize letter-writing campaigns to get the city and state to pave their residential streets so that their garbage will be picked up. They learn to notice, as well as question and critique, the government's policy of paving only certain streets and not others. They learn responsibility in terms of taking care of one another, their school, and their community, and they work to change and improve conditions. *La Escuela* does not base its conception of democratic citizenship on assumptions of individual rights and autonomy. Instead, it starts with a transactional view of individuals in relation to others that clearly recognizes how interconnected and associated we are to one another. The staff teaches the children to be socially active, democratic citizens who understand that they must work not just for their own needs but also for the needs of others, for both kinds of needs are very much intertwined.

The founders and staff at *La Escuela* have learned the same lessons Myles Horton (1990) and the staff at Highlander learned about how to teach students to be empowered democratic citizens: that people learn how to make decisions by doing it, that they have the capacity to govern themselves but they need to exercise that capacity. The people working at *La Escuela* learned this by letting students contribute to running the school and learn leadership skills and how to think and act for themselves. However, unlike Highlander, *La Escuela*'s staff did not have to overcome what their culture taught them about the value of individualism in order to learn how to teach students to become empowered citizens. Instead, they had to overcome the opposite, for they come from a culture that teaches that the meaning of self is derived from their family and community. According to the research I have read, the Mexican culture (recognizing that it is complex, diverse, and fluid) in general has more of a communitarian emphasis on family and the common good over individual goods, as well as a patriarchal emphasis that elders, especially the elder males, have the highest authority in terms of knowing what is best for the family and community (Griswold, 1984).

At *Los Estados Unidos,* students learn that responsibility means being on time, following directions, getting one's homework done, and not causing problems or disturbances in school. Being a good citizen means obeying the rules and following adult directives. It means toeing the line. The stress at *Los Estados Unidos* is on external control and adult authority. The students are afraid to make decisions for themselves because they are afraid they will make the wrong decision and lose their privileges. If they do not turn their computer on or off promptly when the teacher says to, they lose the privilege of working on the computer. If they stray from the exact program the teacher wants them to work on, they lose computer privileges. If they do not get their work done on time, they lose recess time. If they are caught talking to their neighbor, they are moved to an isolated location and handed a textbook with assigned reading.

The teachers at *La Escuela* also want their students to be on time, get their work done, and come to school clean and ready to work, and the principal does worry about efficiency and having the students "on task" more. Maria does worry about things like how efficient the passing between classes is, but she does not solve these problems by insisting that the teachers exercise more control and authority. She asks the teachers to think about how they can help the students learn to be more responsible for themselves and one another; her focus is on teaching the students to develop internal control and self-discipline. At *La Escuela*, the teachers and administrators take a transactional relational view on how to teach students internal control, so the students feel empowered as democratic citizens who have control over their destiny. The teachers are comrades, friends, adults who are there to help the students; they are to be respected for sure, but not feared. Teachers who are uncomfortable with this approach choose not to stay and continue employment at *La Escuela*. These are teachers, as elders, who are more traditional and wish to exert more authority, and *La Escuela* is not the school for them.

What I saw at *Los Estados Unidos* was a good, solid school full of children who are treated like they are in jail and in need of constant adult monitoring. The children are treated kindly, and respectfully, and some teachers are ever-entertaining and fun, but there is very little room for being silly and playful, for being imaginative and creative, and for being a decision maker able to make choices. The students are not encouraged to develop their own voices and become empowered. Students are not viewed as capable of self-discipline or as able to be constructive thinkers (Thayer-Bacon, 2000). They are told what to do, say, and think all day. Students at *Los Estados Unidos* are taught to be passive, docile, and not to question authority—not qualities one would consider necessary for a thriving democracy-always-in-the-making, but much more in line with patriarchy and the banking method of education that Paulo Freire (1970) vividly described not so long ago.

Ironically, though *La Escuela* is in a country that does not have a strong democratic tradition because of its patriarchal, collective, familial focus, the school greatly values a pluralistic, relational democratic structure and is doing what it can to help students practice the skills they will need to be active, participating democratic citizens. *Los Estados Unidos*, which is in a country that is considered a model for liberal democracy, routinely denies students chances to practice being contributing, responsible democratic citizens because of its focus on helping each individual reach his or her full potential through individual hard work. Because the classical liberal view of democracy treats individuals as if they are separate from others, and views others as impeding on and slowing down individual progress, learning how to help others and work together collaboratively to achieve more caring and just lives is not something actively taught at *Los Estados Unidos*. Tragically, what they teach at *Los Estados Unidos* is contrary to the cultural values that parents with Mexican cultural roots teach their children at home, for, at home, students are taught that the meaning of self is derived from family and community. Students at *Los Estados Unidos* must find a way to make sense of this contradiction, either by embracing the school's values and letting go of their familial values, or vice versa. It is not possible to embrace both individualism and a collective approach; the two are logically exclusive and contradictory.

Angela Valenzuela (1999) writes powerfully about the price Mexican students pay in acculturating to American schools in *Subtractive Schooling*. In her 3-year ethnographic study of a large, inner-city high school in Houston, Texas, she shows how schools in the United States are instrumental in maintaining colonial relationships. The schools' assimilationist policies and practices work to divest Mexican students of their culture and language, and, therefore, erode the students' social capital (p. 20). The effects of subtractive schooling are easy to see when we look at Mexican immigrants who are recent arrivals, Mexican-oriented (born in Mexico but came to United States as small children), and American-born Mexican Americans (for whom English is their first language). The longer the children are in the United States, the higher the drop-out rate and the increase in social problems. The first generation of Mexican students in American schools has a 17% drop-out rate, and the second generation has a 24% drop-out rate (Slavin & Calderòn, 2001). Valenzuela argues that the later-generation Mexican American students who drop out of school are opposing a process that disrespects them: They drop out of American schools in opposition to *schooling*, not *education*.

Valenzuela (1999) explains that the Mexican family's role of inculcating in children a sense of moral, social, and personal responsibility, what they refer to as *educacion*, is based on a view of relationships that she describes as *reciprocal*. Reciprocal relations focus on caring for people, unlike *aesthetic caring*, in which caring is directed toward things and ideas. *Educacion* refers not only to formal academic training, but it "additionally refers to competence in the social world, wherein one respects the dignity and individuality of others. . . . [A] person who is *mal educada/o* is deemed disrespectful and inadequately oriented toward others" (Valenzuela, 1999, p. 23). When teachers deny their students the opportunity to engage in reciprocal relationships, as I observed at *Los Estados Unidos*, they invalidate the definition of education that the children's families have taught them. "[S]ince that definition is thoroughly grounded in Mexican culture, its rejection constitutes a dismissal of their culture as well" (p. 23). Valenzuela describes teachers in Mexico as having an ethic of social responsibility, a strong commitment to their students, and less of a focus on rules. Her description supports my own observations of *La Escuela*, and her concerns were illustrated for me at *Los Estados Unidos*.

The founders and staff of *La Escuela* follow a path to democracy that does not emphasize individualism at the expense of community, or vice versa. They travel a relational path that recognizes the transactional qualities of individuals in relation to others. *La Escuela* serves as an excellent example of a form of democracy that is always-in-the-making, a form of democracy that moves beyond Locke's and Rousseau's liberal democracy.

CONCLUSION

La Escuela and *Los Estados Unidos* represent different models of democracy. While liberal democracy at *Los Estados Unidos* emphasizes individualism, it ironically uses a form of authoritarianism that is highly deterministic to teach students the value of individualism, thus undermining students' sense of empowerment. Because the children who attend *Los Estados Unidos* are also taught at home that elders have the highest authority in terms of knowing what is best for the family and community, the children enrolled in *Los Estados Unidos* submit to the school's authoritarian approach without much of a fight. At *La Escuela*, the focus is on transactional qualities of individuals in relation to others to teach students that a democracy-in-the-making depends on members who feel that they have shared responsibilities to make contributions and actively participate in their classrooms as well as their social and political institutions.

Both schools are meeting their missions successfully, but because they start with different assumptions about democracy, they end up with very different results. At *Los Estados Unidos*, the goals are to raise individual students' test scores and to place as many students as they can in higher tracks in the middle schools. These goals are established by state and national standards and are the terms on which the schools are evaluated. With a classical liberal definition of *democracy*, based on an assumption of individualism, the focus at *Los Estados Unidos* is on individual achievement and the hope that the method of teaching will result in more opportunities for individual students. At *La Escuela*, the goal is to encourage students to be politically active and to see themselves as people who can help make change and improve conditions for their local community. The definition of *democracy-always-in-the-making* at *La Escuela* is based on the assumption that individuals affect others and others affect individuals, that relationships with others are transactional. With this premise, the staff is able to help create for students a sense of cultural belonging and commitment toward their own communities. Their students are choosing to continue to live and thrive in their local communities in Mexico, rather than migrating to the United States to find jobs.

I am not arguing here for the loss of individual rights at the expense of communal rights, for a communitarian description of democracy over a liberal description. Like most Americans, I also fear that the social community can too easily become deterministic and deny individuality and difference. I also want individuals to have the chance to develop in creative and unique ways and become able to offer their critical perspectives to the group, thus helping to effect social changes. Rather, I posit that individualism and communitarianism are logically exclusive of each other and are based on contradictory values—individualism favoring the self at the expense of others, and communitarianism favoring others at the expense of the self. However, we do not have to choose one assumption over the other, for both have fatal flaws. We can move beyond this either/or logic to a both/and logic that allows us to see how we can embrace the assets of both individualism and communitarianism, without having to absorb their deficits. We do this by assuming a transactional view of individuals-in-relation-to-others.

It was a great joy to discover a school, *La Escuela*, that so flawlessly serves as an example of the both/and approach. I feel very fortunate to have observed a school that does such a fine job of modeling a democracy-in-the-making with a pluralistic and relational focus. I left that week of observation inspired and excited, as well as exhausted. I certainly intend to follow up on their development and to maintain and nurture the friendships I made there. As I have said more than once now, the staff at *La Escuela* has much to teach us. I will return to the lessons of their success in the final chapter.

It should be clear how much the staff at *La Escuela* is able to achieve because they share responsibility for running the school not only with parents but with the students as well. Students are treated with the same respect and dignity as their parents and are expected to learn self-discipline and self-monitoring, which they do because they are given the opportunity to do so. Students are placed in a variety of situations where they must develop those skills. Just like their parents, they are viewed as important and valued contributors to the school community, and their contributions are sought and greatly appreciated. As a result, the students feel a deep affection for their school and consider it *their* school. While I was there, a high school student living in the United States and attending school in New Mexico came to visit the school for the day. It was his summer vacation and his aunt worked at *La Escuela* and his cousins were students there. He had been enrolled in *La Escuela* for 1 year when he was younger, and still felt a strong attachment to the school and wanted to visit it. We chatted and compared notes, and found we agreed that this is a special school that one wants to return to again and again. No wonder many of its former students find their way to working at the school later on as adults.

La Escuela serves as a strong example of a democracy-always-in-the-making that moves beyond liberal democracy with the help of a transactional view of relations, personal, social, and environmental relations. But it is not the only example. There are many more schools I had the good fortune of discovering. The theory of democracy I am developing is not only transactionally relational, it is also pluralistic both in terms of embracing the value of cultural diversity, and in terms of believing that there are a variety of ways to explain our world and our experiences. There are many ways that democracies-always-in-the-making can be expressed; this is not an essentializing theory.

Let's move on and hear the voices of the many teachers and students I spent time with in schools in the United States where the majority of the students were African American and in the West African schools I visited in Ghana.[7]

Chapter 3

Shared Authority

African Americans are the largest collective cultural group in the United States today, although as we learned in Chapter 2, Latinos will surpass them in size by 2010. Again, I recognize that "African American" is a complex, diverse, and fluid cultural category. My understanding of African American cultures and my research of their roots in predominantly West Africa, where most of the slave trade originated (Wigwe, 1990), confirms for me that African American cultures represent another collective, communitarian culture, one that believes that "it takes a village to raise a child" (Asante, 1987).

I now live in the South, where there is a long history of African Americans and the racism they faced as slaves forced to immigrate to the United States. Racism against Blacks has certainly not been located only in the South, but has been pervasive throughout the United States. It is also not just an attitude confined to our past: African Americans share with Mexican and Native Americans a long history of colonization and discrimination by Whites that continues to this day. There exists in the South not only the humiliating story of slavery, but also the uplifting story of Blacks striving for more education by developing segregated public schools as well as historically Black colleges. The early development of these schools is a triumphant tale of Black communities pulling their resources together to build and staff schools, with very little support from the White communities. Some of these schools still exist and thrive today (J. Morris, 2004). Because of my interest in the coexistence of oppression and achievement, I spent the second year of the C.A.R.E. (Culturally Aware, Anti-racist, Relationally focused Education communities) research project immersed in the research on African American schools and their history of education in the United States, and continued my school visitations in schools where African American students were the majority population.

I turned to some key historians to help me understand the history of African American educational development (Anderson, 1988; Butcher, 1988; Woodson, 1990). I also found several scholars who are doing important

recovery work for the history of schools in their communities or in the segregated schools they attended prior to *Brown v. Board of Education* in 1954
and the Civil Rights Act in 1964, which forced schools to begin desegregation efforts (J. Morris, 1999; Morris & Morris, 2000; Noblit & Dempsey, 1996;
Walker, 1996, 2001). There are also important writers who are recovering
and recording African American teachers' stories (Baker, 1995; Delpit, 1995;
Foster, 1990, 1997; Fultz, 1995a, 1995b; Ladson-Billings, 1994, 2005; Walker,
2001). Despite efforts to improve education for African Americans, Black students still suffer from a high drop-out rate; in urban areas it is quoted as being
as high as 50% (Ayers & Klonsky, 1994; Lomotey, 1990), and students' un-
derachievement is persistent, pervasive, and disproportionate (Kozol, 2005;
Lomotey, 1990). Scholars tell us that 44% of African Americans and 54% Hispanic Americans are functionally illiterate (Peterson, 1996). My life partner
teaches English in a local high school that is 90% African American with 95%
of the students on free or reduced lunch, and his school faces many of the
educational issues these scholars describe. In no way do I want to diminish
the harmful effects of racism on African American students and their families
and the importance of continual work to rid our society of these effects. However, I also want to celebrate the vibrancy and resiliency of African American
abilities to survive and even thrive under very harsh conditions in the United
States, and I want to honor African Americans' valuing of education and its
importance for their freedom and opportunity to live a good life.

In this chapter, I present what I learned from my visits to African American
and West African schools under the general theme of *shared authority* using
several teachers' stories.[1] I will consider the key concept of *shared authority*
in a democracy-always-in-the-making in contrast to classical liberal, conservative, and radical views of individual authority. An excellent essay written
by Henry Giroux (1986/1997) on authority will help with this consideration,
as well as the important work of several Black scholars, especially bell hooks
(1994). I begin with teacher stories from my visits to Junior Secondary School
(JSS; similar to U.S. middle schools) and River High School (RHS). In the sections titled "Invest in Your Future" and "Take Care of Your Business," I present
stories from River High School and Mountain Middle School (MMS). These
teaching stories help us discover how the concept of *authority* translates for
different teachers in the schools I visited. At the end of each section, I discuss
the theoretical implications of the practices I observed as I consider how to
put theory and practice together and look at the possibilities for getting beyond liberal democracy. With the help of the teachers introduced throughout
this chapter, I show how the emphasis on individual development changes
to a transactional view of individuals-in-relation-to-others in a democracy-
always-in-the-making.

"YES, MADAM"

In Ghana, religious and moral education is a regular part of the curriculum in the public schools. A Presbyterian church started the public school I visited, and it is now run by the state. Even the recycled uniforms the children wear still display badges that say "Presbyterian Primary School" from the days when the church supplied the resources for the school. The school day starts with all the children lined up outside their classrooms, singing patriotic songs and saying the Lord's Prayer. Aside from a daily half-hour class on religious and moral education, the children also participate in worship for a half-hour on Wednesdays, where all the children in the Junior Secondary School come together to sing religious songs, hear Bible verses and a short sermon, and give monetary donations to help others. I observed the JSS religious and moral education teacher, Fortune, several times during my weeklong visit, and present below some of my field notes from those observations.[2]

Day 1, Tuesday

In Fortune's class of 33–57 students (the number varied depending on the day and the class), although the majority of the students are Christians, she teaches them about Christian, Muslim, and Traditional religious beliefs (indigenous beliefs). One day, her topic was the Islamic religion; another day it was on taboos for the three religious groups. The students do not leave the room for different classes; instead, the teachers come to them. When Fortune walks into the classroom she announces, "No talking." All the students in unison respond, "Yes, Madam." Again she says, "No talking," and again they respond, "Yes, Madam." Now she is ready to begin. She asks a couple of questions and the students answer for her. When the students answer correctly she says, "Clap for her" or "Clap for him." All the students clap a rhythm in unison, "clap, clap, clap-clap-clap, clap." If a student says a wrong answer, the whole class and the teacher moan, "Ehhh!" Next, Fortune goes over to the teacher's table and picks up a bamboo cane, while I wonder what it is for. She walks up and down the aisles, teaching the students about Islam. She goes over the five daily prayers of Islam and when they are observed. Each prayer has a name, and she has all the students repeat the names several times together. She writes the same information on the board and has the students record it in their copybooks. (This oral recitation–board-copying technique occurred in most of the classes I observed, as a means of compensating for the lack of books and supplies. Fortune has the only religion/moral education book for the class.) She reminds the students that they have an exam on Friday. The she writes the questions on the board and instructs the students to copy them and answer them. "Any questions?" she asks. "No, Madam." "Any questions?" "No, Madam." "Take your time and write for me. If you misspell I'll just count it wrong, because I can't read it." "Yes, Madam," they respond. At 4:30 P.M., Fortune walks out of the classroom while the students work until the dismissal bell rings.

Day 2, Wednesday

I finally had the opportunity to see what Fortune does with the cane besides just hold it in her hand or use it to point to the board. After worship, the afternoon classes begin with attendance, which takes some time as there are 57 students in the JSS afternoon classes, with two or three students sharing one desk. Fortune waves her cane and bangs it on the teacher's table to tell the students to get quiet. Students place their copybooks on the teacher's table for her to grade, and while another teacher teaches the students a vocational skills class in the room, Fortune sits at the teacher's table and grades the students' work. Periodically, as Fortune grades, she lectures to the students, but as she is speaking in Ghanian dialect, I do not understand what she is saying. Then she asks the class: "How do you spell 'prayer'? How do you spell 'observed'? The person spelled it 'prayr' and 'obserrvd.'" "Ehhhh!" moan the teacher and students. She is publicly correcting the students, but does not reveal the name of the student who misspelled the words. The vocational skills teacher finishes writing on the board what the students must copy and is done with her lesson. Then Fortune announces, "If you got below 40%, you are going to get lashes." She waves the cane. She sends a boy to bring her a second cane from another classroom. Then she passes the copybooks back to the students so they can see their grade. The two girls sitting by me both received grades below 40%. They start to whimper. I ask them softly, "Is she joking? Does she really mean to hit you with the cane?" They assure me she is not joking. Fortune starts with the row right next to where I sit, and asks the students to voluntarily come to the front of the room one by one if they have received below 40%. She canes the students, starting with the two girls sitting beside me. Each child comes to the front of the room and faces the blackboard as she gives them several light swats on the butt and then a hard one on their thighs. The number of lashes varies with each student, depending on how they respond to the caning. If they dodge the lashes they get more, and if they are too stoic, it seemed that they got more lashes, too. One, two, three times hard. Some boys get six to seven hard lashes and one on the back. Tears begin to stream down my face and I feel sick. All the kids who got below 40% on their test were caned. I saw eight kids caned before I left at 2:05 P.M.

I talked to the adults we were staying with that evening about caning. I discovered that they were all caned, as were my West African friends in the United States, which I learned upon returning home. In fact, now that I have been searching, I haven't found a West African who wasn't caned. I was told that caning is not allowed in the cities anymore—but out here in the little villages it is still done. My hosts and students from Ghana all talk about how caning is needed for discipline, motivating children to learn and work harder. They talk about the abolishment of caning in the cities, such as Accra, and how they are now having more discipline problems. My colleague in the United States, Handel Wright, laughed when I asked him if he had been caned and said, "I didn't know I was supposed to be traumatized by caning until I came to the West."

"ANYONE NOT A HAPPY CHILD?"

The high school I observed in the southern United States is a city school on the east side of town that is 90% African American, even though the city is only 6% Black. Ninety-five percent of the students are on reduced or free lunch programs. The school has a long history and is highly regarded by those who have graduated from River High and those who teach there, although it has the lowest test-score results in the city. The year I observed, River High was the state champ in football for its division, and it has an award-winning dance and music program. In an effort to increase the White population at River High, a magnet school for the performing arts and a science academy were developed and located in beautiful, new, state-of-the-art wings that wrap around the old building. I spent several days observing the band teacher, Ms. Lincoln. River High is on a block schedule, as are all high schools in this state, which means the students have four 90-minute class periods each day, instead of six or seven 50-minute periods. A one-semester course in a block schedule is the equivalent to a year-long course in traditional schools. Block scheduling works very well for classes like English, where students can have more time for reading, writing, and classroom discussions, but it does not work so well for band classes, as students don't have the sheer physicality to play an instrument for 90 minutes and need the consistency of a year-long course to maintain their technical skill. However, Ms. Lincoln has found a creative way to use the 90 minutes she has with her students. Lincoln went to River High as a child and she has lived in the area her whole life. She taught younger children for years but sought out the position of music teacher at her alma mater when it became available. She teaches Beginning Band during third period, from 11:45 A.M. to 1:52 P.M. Monday, Tuesday, and Thursday are for playing instruments, Wednesday is for working on sheet music, and "Friday is free for all." There are

15 or 16 students in this class, all African American and predominantly male. From my field notes:

Day 1, Wednesday

From 11:45 A.M. to noon, Ms. Lincoln allows the students to eat and chat and goof around because they have the last lunch period, which is not until 1:20 P.M. (school starts at 8 A.M.). In her office right off the band room, she has drinks and chips for the students; they know where the food is and are allowed to help themselves. She makes sure her students do not go hungry. She starts class at noon, and, from noon to 12:30 P.M., the students sit in their band chairs in a semicircle facing Ms. Lincoln and chat with her. She sits or stands at the front of the semicircle and her band assistant, an African American male named Nathan, stands or sits near her and joins the conversation. On this day, Nathan congratulates the basketball team on their win, and a student tells the class about the first African American, a woman, to win a gold medal in the Winter Olympics (which was being held at the time of my visit). The kids share and discuss news stories as they finish their chips and drinks. When they are all talking at once, Ms. Lincoln waves her hand and says, "I can't hear everyone at once," and they respond by talking in turns once again. At 12:10 P.M., Ms. Lincoln asks the students a trivia quiz question from Black History month about a woman who, like Rosa Parks, was the first woman to refuse to give up her seat on a railroad car for a White person. The answer is Ida B. Wells. "Who was the founder of NAACP?" Answer: W. E. B. DuBois. Ms. Lincoln then reminds the students: "I hope your teachers have signed you up because I know *all* of you will be at the game on Friday. You're playing at halftime. I want all of you freshmen to show the upper class how to behave at an assembly." There is lots of talking again. Ms. Lincoln asks: "Anyone else have something to say? Who's got something on their mind? Anyone not a happy child?" A student shares an inspirational story. There's a yellow tennis ball on the floor and Ms. Lincoln picks it up and bounces it a few times. (I wonder what role the tennis ball plays in her class.) Ms. Lincoln says, "Speak now or forever hold your peace." She asks them what they think about the Reading Across the Curriculum program the school is trying out. The students don't like it, it's boring; they need to get better stories. "Put some interesting books there," a boy says. When a student went to interrupt her, Ms. Lincoln held the tennis ball up in her hand and aimed it at him and said, "I will, don't interrupt me." Their suggestions for the Reading Across the Curriculum program include "The teacher needs to read with more enthusiasm." Ms. Lincoln then asks how many of them are up to par in their reading, and about half of them raise their hands. "Do you feel this program will help you?" "No." "Well, then what do we have to do now?" Ms. Lincoln says, "My *mother* was an English teacher." She's showing them that they need help with their broken English. There is a discussion about phonics. Ms. Lincoln says, "I don't know if they do that anymore. Last thing—then we have to move on—How many of you feel like you got a good educational foundation at home?" (Two students raise their hands.) "How many had a parent read to you?" (Three students raise their hands). She wants more feedback and suggestions from the students. "Now, you need to get a desk and come to the board." I look at my watch and realize she has invested 45 minutes in "building community" in her classroom and sharing her time with them. It is clear that she views her responsibilities in terms of teaching her students as being beyond the boundaries of music.

At 12:30 P.M., the students get desks and pull them to the side of the band room where there is a portable blackboard. Ms. Lincoln settles them in: "What time is it?" They say in unison, "Your time." Ms. Lincoln replies. "It is *my* time so stop playing." They all get quiet and listen to her. She gives them directions. "We will be *reading* today. Isn't that something we talked about, reading? Somebody read or I'll call on someone." She waits and repeats, "Somebody read." Someone reads the worksheet directions. She instructs them on how to highlight what she emphasizes in their notes, and helps them see what will be on the quiz on Friday. Lesson 2, "Somebody read." Treble cleft. Lines. "Every good boy does fine. FACE." (These are mnemonic devices for musicians.) She waits for them to draw a treble cleft, then do the next step. All the students work on their own. Ms. Lincoln tells the class, "You can go on if you are ready." A few minutes later, she says, "We can't go any further, this is taking you too long to do." Moaning, they get back to work. Ms. Lincoln announces, "Okay, put your pencils down. Now it is time to be on the board. Guess who's going to be on the board?" She brought up the girl who was not working hard when the students were working on their own. Ms. Lincoln had her name the lines and label them on the board. A boy got Ms. Lincoln's tennis ball and tossed it to her at her request. After a few minutes, she threw it at a boy who was not paying attention, hitting him on the chest. He stopped what he was doing. She shows the girl how to make sure she'll get it: "Say the mnemonic out loud." (Ms. Lincoln is referring to the mneumonic device "Every good boy does fine.") Ms. Lincoln asks, "Who else is having trouble? Don't be afraid that you don't know, just say you don't know." She teaches another kid at the board what to do. She then has the other kids call out a letter for the student at the board to write on the staff. She reviews the mnemonic again, writing the letters on the staff and then without the letters there to help them. A third student named Jamal goes to the board. Ms. Lincoln is excited: "You've got it!" Then she asks: "Everyone got it? Eliot?" She checks off their folders to indicate that they have completed this work and then dismisses them for lunch.

Day 2, Thursday

I arrive at 12:15 P.M. The students and teachers are talking, laughing, and sharing stories. They're talking about gambling, and what high-stakes gambling is, double or nothing. Ms. Lincoln asks a student, "What job have you got? If you could bet that much money on a card game!" They're talking about playing cards and gambling in the school cafeteria during lunchtime. She warns them that there are cameras in the cafeteria that would record them gambling and that if a parent complained they'd be in trouble. Ms. Lincoln says, "It shouldn't even be—better put up the cards." Then someone talks about how money is allocated at the school and how he heard the principal talking about the budget for the football team. Two guys must be on the football team because they both cheer "Yeah!" and high-five each other, with one saying, "New helmets!" Then there is a discussion of GPA and what is needed for eligibility to play sports overall, for a semester, and for 6 weeks. Then the same boy who brought up the football team's budget says, "We need a lottery for education." This triggers a discussion about Hope Scholarships, and what Georgia and Florida are doing for education with their lottery money. Then another boy asks, "What happens to your stuff in your locker when they cut off your lock?" He's advised that they save the library and school books but throw away everything else. Ms. Lincoln tells him, "The rest goes to BFI" (BFI is the trash company). Next, the same boy talking about the budget had brought in a book to share with the class, and he reads passages from it. It's about racially biased criminology. We learn that the local prosecutor says that 15% of the crimes committed in the city are committed by Blacks, but that 75% of the crimes reported on the news are about Blacks. After the student reads a passage, Ms. Lincoln asks, "What is the point he's trying to make?" They talk about how violence in the cities is taken as a given, but is shocking to Whites when it happens in the suburbs. Ms. Lincoln remarks, "Society makes us believe it is us. We don't do those crimes." Then the students and teachers give several examples of awful crimes White people have committed lately: shootings in schools, leaving a baby in a trash can, drowning five kids in a bathtub. They talk about Columbine High School. They label it "suburban neglect." Ms. Lincoln offers the students her opinion on gun violence, but tells them emphatically that this is just her opinion and they don't have to agree with her. She tells them that she grew up here in the 1960s and that she was born in 1957. She tells them how it was in the 1980s and 1990s when they started having drive-by shootings. "We were killing each other. Yet the media did not pick this up as important news, as a tragedy, until it hit the White communities. Now it has come around full [circle] and it's about violence, period, for everyone. I hated the tragedy of Columbine, but I also felt like, 'now you want to do something?'"

They talked about crack houses and brothels in their neighborhoods. One boy says, "We don't know what it means to say 'I'm Black and I'm proud.' We can see what you went through though." Ms. Lincoln responds, "The 1960s were hell on earth. We're saying to you, look at the opportunity *you* have. Especially in education. I remember segregation, riding in the back of the bus, taking food with us when we traveled because we couldn't get off the bus. We want you to be proud, and to take advantage of what you have."

She talks about how they have street skills—there's always a bootleg—a back door that depends on luck. She wants them to count on education to be their ticket to a better life, not luck. Ms. Lincoln asks: "Anyone else want to say something?" She thanks the student for the book he brought, talks to the class about Blount County having debate teams, and then tells them she'd like to see one at River High School. She tells the students that several of them would be good at it. She reminds them to go hear the brother sing at Bethel, 7 P.M., tonight. "Alright, anyone else?" "Who has their folders today? Bring [them] up." Now it is time for class work.

As I move to compare these two teachers' teaching styles, I do not pass judgment on the Ghanian teachers. I think their efforts to teach are heroic, for they teach in conditions *no* American teacher *ever* has to face today. There is no plumbing in the JSS, so there is no running water or bathrooms. Children buy water and food from the women vendors who come at recess time and set up under thatched roofs, or they bring it from home, or they go without. (It was over 90 degrees on the days I observed, which was during the cooler rainy season.) They use the cornfields for a bathroom. There are no copy machines or computers and printers at Fortune's school; there are only cracked and worn blackboards upon which to write lessons and tests. There are no shelves lined with books, not even pencil sharpeners. Children bring double-edged razors for sharpening their pencils. The teaching conditions are so different that they are beyond comparison. However, since the two teachers so clearly model different views of *authority* in their teaching styles, it presents an opportunity to consider various views at the theoretical level, which I do in the next section.

CONNECTING THEORY WITH PRACTICE, PART I

In terms of the classroom, classical liberal democratic theory relies on a concept of authority that is individualized and advocates a child-centered approach. Giroux (1997) describes liberalism's view of authority as one whose ideology is of "need fulfillment" that casts students in an "othered" role as deviant, underprivileged, or uncultured. It uses authority to promote self-control and self-regulation in order for the self to reach its full potential. It views the child as a unitary subject. In my field observations of teachers in the United States working with African American students, I have seen several teachers who reflect this liberal approach. Their pedagogy is one of cordial relations, seeking to keep the students "happy." It amounts to a kind of negotiated agreement between teacher and student that "I will not ask too much of you, student, if you do not cause too much trouble and grief for me." As Giroux (1997) rightly points out, the liberal view of authority is silent on the connection among authority, culture, and power. Classical liberals emphasize the positive aspects of authority and ignore "the 'messy webs' of social relations that embody forms of struggle and contestation" (p. 99).

From a classical liberal perspective, Ms. Lincoln's job is to make sure her students learn as much about music as they can during the time they have with her. Her focus should be on individual achievement, relying on the myth of merit to cajole her students into being highly motivated and hardworking so they will reach their full potential as musicians. Her students walk into her room with whatever natural talents they have inherited and her job is to make sure other students do not impede any individual's progress. What is going on in the students' lives is really not her business. When the students walk into the band room they should be able to block out all contextual distraction and focus on the task at hand. A classical liberal would judge Ms. Lincoln as not using her time efficiently, wasting half of her 90 minutes on food and conversation, with no musical education occurring. They would also worry about her efforts to teach students moral lessons, which is not within the boundaries of her subject area. During the time that she does teach music, they would approve of her efforts to attend to each student and make sure that all of her students are learning, although they may be concerned that the slow students are hold-ing the fast students back from learning. They also may be concerned that her style of discipline and attention-getting is potentially harmful, although they would admire its efficiency at getting the point across without taking any teaching time away from the other students' learning.

In Ghana, people have struggled with creating a democracy since the Brit-ish left in the late 1940s. They have had several coups resulting in dictators who have rewritten their constitution four times. Still, they are proud that their country is more stable than most in Africa and that they are held up as a model for others to follow. They state that they are finally getting an understanding of what a democracy is. However, in their classrooms and at home, I did not observe this. The families, schools, and churches are all structured in a strong authoritarian style, with the elders maintaining strict control. The students are not assumed to have civil rights; they must obey, which they do so overall without complaint. From a Ghanaian perspective, Americans overindulge and spoil their children with their child-centered approach. From an American classical liberal democratic perspective, Fortune is viewed in troubling ways. Her approach to teaching is seen as oppressive. She uses corporal punishment to frighten her students into working harder. She publicly humiliates her students as a way of improving their skills.

Fortune relies on a concept of authority that Giroux (1997) describes as neoconservative. In his essay "Authority, Intellectuals, and the Politics of Practical Learning," originally published in 1986, Giroux situates his discussion within the context of the Reagan era and the new conservatives' fears of "loss of authority." The new conservatives' discourse on authority gives authority a positive meaning, something to be celebrated as representative of the American dream, which is based on hard work, discipline, promptness, and cheerful obedience. These are the very values Fortune seeks to teach her students in Ghana. Giroux points out that, unfortunately, this type of authority also supports reactionary and undemocratic interests, and we can see this concern in how classical liberals might respond to Fortune's caning of her students as undemocratic. The neoconservative concept of authority focuses on control, management, and efficiency. With this view of authority, teachers function as clerks, which accurately describes the teachers I observed in Ghana. Like the classical liberal view of authority, the conservative view is also silent on the connection between culture and power. Both views are what Giroux calls "the dominant educational discourse."

Giroux (1997) points out that while neoconservatives view authority only positively, leftist educators tend to view authority as only negative—as a loss of freedom, connected to a logic of domination, as unprincipled authoritarianism. It is certainly the case that leftist educators would judge Fortune as being an authoritarian. Giroux moves beyond leftist educators' views of authority and develops an alternative, dialectical view of emancipatory authority as a central element in a critical theory of schooling. For him, such a concept of authority is necessary in order for us to be able to analyze the relationship between domination and power. A dialectical concept of authority as emancipatory is necessary in order for us to reinsert into the language of schooling the primacy of the political, a task Giroux has worked on his entire career. With Giroux, schools become an ideological and political terrain; they are not ideologically innocent. He underscores Dewey's (1916/1996; 1927/1954) vision that public schools can be places where the skills of democracy are practiced.

Giroux (1997) argues that an emancipatory concept of authority will empower students (and teachers and parents) to be critical and active citizens in a democracy-in-the-making. It is my contention that Ms. Lincoln serves as a strong example of a teacher who allows her students to practice the skills of democracy. Lincoln is teaching her students to be active citizens. She knows how to successfully create what Giroux calls "a democratic counterpublic sphere" in her classroom. An emancipatory concept of authority such as Giroux describes emphasizes that authority is "a terrain of struggle." It also emphasizes that teachers can function as "transformative intellectuals," who have the ability to think and act critically, and who can teach their students to do the same. Transformative intellectuals are the bearers of "dangerous memory," and Lincoln certainly serves in that kind of role as she shares with her students what it was like growing up in the 1960s.

While Giroux's (1997) essay on authority helps us make sense of the difference between Fortune's concept of authority as conservative and Ms. Lincoln's concept of authority as emancipatory, there are problems with Giroux's concept of emancipatory authority that hinder us from fully appreciating what goes on in Lincoln's classroom. Giroux's emancipatory authority clings to a view of human subjectivity based on individual autonomy and agency, which is a holdover from classical liberal democratic theories. His view of human subjectivity creates problems for him, as emancipatory authority still ends up placing the teacher in the position of higher authority and students in the "othered" category as lacking power and in need of assistance in gaining power. A teacher who is described as a "transformative intellectual" is still in the role of leading and guiding those who are not as informed and are in need of transformation. The teacher, because she is an intellectual and a bearer of dangerous memory, has more authority than her students and can use that authority in ways that help them, as well as ways that harm them. Emancipatory authority has to work at defending itself against the possibility that the teacher's authority will co-opt the students' authority, repressing their struggle to end oppression.

Feminist theory can help us get beyond the Enlightenment's assumption of individuality without jeopardizing the emancipatory political project of describing schools as political terrain that have the potential to be counterpublic democratic spaces. What is needed is a transactional view of individuals-in-relation-to-others. I argue that what I observed with Ms. Lincoln and her band class was a view of authority as *shared,* which develops from a relational ontology and pluralistic (e)pistemology.[3] A relational ontology describes human beings as always existing in relation to other human beings, at an intimately personal level (Flax, 1983, 1990; Noddings, 1984; Ruddick, 1989) as well as at a broader social level (Smith, 1987, 1990). It also describes human beings as always existing in relation to their natural surroundings and the greater world at large, so that it embraces an ecological (King, 1989; Merchant, 1980; Warren, 1990) and holistic (Allen, 1986; Khema, 1999) description of selves-in-relation-to-others (Thayer-Bacon, 2003). From a relational perspective, there is no such thing as individuality and human agency—key concepts of classical liberal democracy to which emancipatory authority still wants to cling. There

is only us-in-relation-to-others, and a recognition that we are continually affecting others just as they are continually affecting us. We exist in a dance
together that, from a larger perspective, is inseparable and indistinguishable.
From a pluralistic (e)pistemological perspective, there is no such thing as one
Answer, one Truth that we can hope to find. There are many truths and many
possible standards and criteria that we can rely on to make our case for what
we think is the right thing to do, knowing full well that our criteria and standards will need to be corrected and modified as our perspectives enlarge and
our knowledge expands, through the results of our transactions with others.
This is not a naively relativistic argument that "anything goes," and none of us
can claim any authority. Rather, this is a qualified relativistic argument that
says all we can ever claim is a limited, situated authority that develops and is
enhanced by our relationships with others (Thayer-Bacon, 2003). Whatever
authority we can hope to claim is a shared authority.

From a pluralistic, relational perspective, Ms. Lincoln's style of teaching
makes perfect sense. Ms. Lincoln knows how to create a safe environment in
her classroom where students' voices can be heard and can contribute to the
conversation. How does she do this? First, Lincoln recognizes that her students
are growing teenagers with insatiable appetites and that they do not necessarily start out the day with a solid breakfast because of their economic situation.
She knows that her students cannot concentrate in class if they are hungry, so
at the start of the class, she takes care of that problem by providing them with
food to get them through until lunchtime. Second, Lincoln knows that her
students must sit still in desks all day, and that there is very little opportunity
for them to talk to one another or get up and move around the room. She
figures she can take care of their need to move, talk, and eat all at the same
time during the first 15 minutes of class.

Third, Ms. Lincoln knows that her students cannot leave the context of
their lives behind when they walk through the door into her classroom. If
she talks to them, she will get to know them better and find more ways to
connect the curriculum to their interests and concerns. She also knows, as
a Black woman who grew up in the same neighborhood and who attended
the same school, that she needs to help them become aware of and be able to
critique the social forces they deal with on a daily basis. She wants to arm her
students with a critical understanding of racism and how it affects their lives,
and help them overcome feelings of inadequacy or stupidity. She wants them
to feel proud of who they are and capable, for only then will they be willing to
struggle with learning how to play a musical instrument and have confidence
that they can succeed. It goes without saying that her curriculum is culturally
relevant to her students' interests. But music is not the only area of her expertise. She engages her students' oral capabilities by using a pedagogical style

that emphasizes auditory learning. She uses repetition, knowing that it reinforces learning. In summation, Lincoln relies on her knowledge of the African American social context and adapts her curriculum, goals, and teaching style to that knowledge. From a relational, pluralistic perspective of democracy, she is an excellent teacher who is helping her students learn the skills they will need to participate in a democracy-always-in-the-making throughout their adult lives.

Ms. Lincoln models a belief that students have important things to say and can teach us all a thing or two. If we give them the opportunity to share their views and bring in news and readings to share in class, if we share our authority with them, not only will we get to know them better, but we will be encouraging their communication and relational skills as well as their confidence. We will help them develop their voices and find ways to contribute those voices to their larger society. By opening up her classroom to her students' contributions, even giving them time together without adult direction, and maintaining time to teach them directly, she creates a classroom space where the students share authority with her. Note that she does not give up her authority. When it is her turn to speak she insists on having the students' attention, even if it means using a tennis ball to get it. But she gives her students the same attention she insists upon for herself when it is their turn to speak, and she continually asks the class if anyone wants to speak, thus making sure that everyone who wishes to has had a chance to talk. Her classroom is a democracy-always-in-the-making, and if we attend to her example closely, there is much we can learn, not only about the practice of teaching African American high school students, but about a theory of democracy that is ontologically relational and (e)pistemologically pluralistic in its basic assumptions.

Ms. Lincoln's style of teaching is very different from Fortune's in some ways and is similar in other ways. Both teachers take advantage of their time with their students not only to teach them about their subject area but to teach them moral lessons as well. Both are encouraging their students in their unique way to work hard and strive to achieve a high-quality education so they will have more freedom and choices in their lives. Ms. Lincoln hopes that, with a good education, her students will be treated with greater dignity and respect as adults living in a racist society. Fortune doesn't have to worry so much about racism in Ghana where everyone is Black. Instead, she has to worry more about job opportunities for her students living in a Third World nation with meager economic resources. Still, I did not observe teachers in Ghana like Fortune sharing their authority with their students. The teachers have two or three students per desk in rooms that are full to overflowing and they demand silence and obedience, which is reinforced with a cane if needed. There is no question as to who is in charge. Their pedagogical style is directive and strict. I discovered in Ms. Lincoln an African American teacher who is teaching her students about democracies-in-the-making by sharing her teaching time with them and arranging her room in a way that encourages students to talk. Ms. Lincoln knows how to create a comfortable, safe place where her students can voice their ideas and contribute to the curriculum and instruction. She knows how to develop a classroom where authority is *shared*. She plays music *with* her students, allowing herself to become the student as they teach her, just as they let themselves be taught by her. They are in process, creating music together that is sometimes discordant, sometimes united, and sometimes in harmony, but always connected and affecting one another, always in a transactional relationship with one another.

A transactional view of democracy stresses the interaction that goes on continually between teachers and students and how much they affect one another. It proffers a democracy that is always in process, with the group continually adapting to the needs of the individual, and the individual continually adapting to the needs of the group. It is a view of democracy that is not based on underlying assumptions of individualism, rationalism, or universalism that classical liberal democratic theory relies upon and which, in the end, undermine the very possibility of democracy. A transactional theory of democracy-always-in-the-making is based on a relational ontology and pluralistic (e)pistemology that underscore how connected we are to one another, how multifaceted and diverse we are, and how any claims of authority we can hope to make are enhanced by our relationships with others.

"INVEST IN YOUR FUTURE!"

I had the great pleasure of spending several days at River High observing an outstanding African American, middle-aged, female math teacher, Ms. Jefferson. River High is on a block schedule, and just as block scheduling does not work very well for band class, neither does it work well for math class. Ninety minutes is too long for students to work on new concepts, and they need the consistency of a year-long course to fully absorb mathematical concepts. However, Ms. Jefferson uses the 90 minutes she has with her students to the fullest.[4] She was recommended to me to observe by the other teachers in the school, as she has a reputation for being an excellent teacher. After observing her class for 2 days, I could see why. Following are some of my notes from her first-period math class. Ms. Jefferson teaches first-period algebra to an almost all African American class (there was one White male). There are 18 students in this class, 9 males and 9 females. From my field notes:

Day 1

I get to Ms. Jefferson's room at 8:25 A.M. and take a seat tucked away on the side, behind the girls. Students are coming in; they have sodas and chips. They are talking to one another. Ms. Jefferson has the desks set up so they face in toward one another. She's working on the computer. At 8:30 A.M., Ms. Jefferson says, "Good morning, everyone. How's everyone today?" The students are still arriving. She's sitting at her desk and begins passing out notebooks, calling individual names softly. The students are still talking to one another. They come up to her desk and get their notebooks. When she is done passing them out, Ms. Jefferson goes to the front of the room and gives the students feedback on their notebooks. She tells them they need to get better organized and have more notes in them. They need to buy subject dividers, which she tells them cost $1.00. "You buy $100.00 shoes and $300.00 prom dresses, you can spend $1.00 and invest in subject dividers. Invest in your future!" She wants them to invest in their education. She's not going to review their notebooks next time if they don't have subject dividers (some had homemade dividers, which she did accept).

Ms. Jefferson is now ready to start teaching; we can all tell by her tone of voice. When she starts teaching her voice changes, it gets louder and clearer; I can understand her easily now. There's a seriousness of purpose to her voice when she teaches; otherwise it's more teasing, softer, more humorous. "Please turn to the problems on page 131." *All* of the students have their books open and they're *all* settled in and quiet now. She changes her mind and decides to go to page 147 and practice reading the equations. She randomly picks a couple of equations from the page and practices reading them out loud with the class. She shows them how to read equations using three examples. Then they read some equations together. There's a noise in the hall that distracts the students, and Ms. Jefferson notices right away. "What is that noise?" A student responds: "I think it is walkie talkies." Ms. Jefferson: "Close the door, Shannon. I'm hearing very few people, what's the problem? Derrick, you can join in. Am I going to be lonely?" Ms. Jefferson assigns the students problems to work on and then walks around looking at their work and helping some of them individually. At 9:09 A.M., she checks the answers to the equations with the whole class. She asks, "Who got them right?" and the girls all raise their hands. Not one of the boys raises his hand. Ms. Jefferson has gone back to talking softly to them, encouraging them to work by teasing them (she's doing this publicly, across the room). Then she laughs. She gives them time to do the problem. "Do I have an answer, anyone?" "Mr. Bishop, wake up, hon. I know you're not used to being here this early. But what did you get?" She went over the problem. Ms. Jefferson then turns to the boys' side of the room and says, "See how they work?" pointing to the girls' side of the room. "Their mouths don't move. Don't stare off into space, I don't want you to stare into space. I want you to work." They are *all* working, which is contrary to what I have observed in other classrooms.

Ms. Jefferson asks: "Questions, anyone?" One girl says, "Please don't give us any homework." Ms. Jefferson: "But I have to." Student: "Why?" Ms. Jefferson: "Because I love you!" Student: "You don't love us giving us homework." Ms. Jefferson: "Yes, I do!" She gives them homework. One girl tries to get her to give her less, arguing that it's a hardship for her with church, and Ms. Jefferson says she only has to do 15 problems. Others laugh and say that's what everyone has to do. They're chatting with one another as they write down the homework assignment. At 9:50 A.M., Ms. Jefferson announces, "Calculators back up, please." She rechecks attendance. She times her class to end just before the announcements start. She is a master teacher. The bell rings after announcements, but Ms. Jefferson does not let the class go yet. Her students have to be sitting at attention before she dismisses them by saying: "Have a beautiful day!" Then they leave, laughing and smiling. After class, she tells me, "They won't work unless you make them. Jason, a senior, was working today; he must have thought you were evaluating him." She laughs.

Day 2, the Next Week

Last night was parents' conferences, and Ms. Jefferson starts the day by commenting on this. "Good morning, everyone. I truly enjoyed those parents that came. Those who couldn't get here last night, Lord help you." Student: "Ms. Jefferson, my mom couldn't come last night, she's coming today." Ms. Jefferson responds: "Not during class she isn't—I won't see her. Tell her to come during my planning period. I'm busy teaching during the day and I'm here 15 minutes before and after school and that's it." Student: "When is your planning period?" Ms. Jefferson tells the student. As she's moving around the room getting the students and herself settled in, she says, "I didn't get out of here last night until almost quarter to eight." More moving around, then she says: "I'll have your grades averaged next week." Ms. Jefferson asks the students to get out their assignment and put it on their desk while she calls the roll. Now she's going around the room checking their work. She uses this as a chance to interact with each student individually. As she goes around the room, if she sees work that looks good, she holds it up and praises the student to the class, showing everyone what their work should look like. She teases one boy whose parents came last night, because he doesn't have his assignment. She announces to all that he thinks he doesn't have to work now—and that's not true. Ms. Jefferson: "You need to work even *harder* after your mama comes in, that's how that works." And she laughs.

Now Ms. Jefferson is in front. In her teacher voice she says, "Turn to page 622." All are quiet and turning to that page. She slides out of her teacher voice and says: "There's the answers to the problems I asked you to do. Tell me why you don't have your homework. Now tell me, what's the problem? That's what I call lazy people." She points out the checkpoint (examples of questions with answers) in the book, and discusses why to use it. "Have something to show! Never, never go home with homework and come back with nothing. Teachers don't like working with students who don't try," she scolds. She uses the example of being in choir and not singing to help make her point. "If you didn't sing in choir, what kind of grade would you get? You'd fail! And your choir teacher wouldn't like having students who don't sing." Ms. Jefferson then says: "Let's take a look at the checkpoint." Now she's back to her teacher voice. I write in my field notes that there is a good feeling of camaraderie here. Ms. Jefferson seems to have a pattern of starting class with a moral lesson, a lecture on her students' character, to get them working hard. At 8:50 A.M., now comes the math. I watch as she does not let anyone go by unnoticed who is not participating.

It is striking to me how much more Ms. Jefferson expects of her students in comparison to other teachers I observed, and how all the students try to meet her expectations. She has established a great rapport with the students and they all seem to be having a good time while they work hard. They also are well behaved and follow good classroom etiquette. She only has to use her voice to get students to quiet down; there are no confrontations, at least none that I observed. The students police a lot of their own behavior, and do things like moving away from someone to quiet themselves down. In other classes I observed, the teachers are easygoing and let the students just slide as long as they don't give them any grief. These less-demanding teachers are not allies of the students, and they are not challenging the students to grow and improve. The students in those easy classes are bored. I saw them writing rap lyrics and playing cards to entertain themselves, or sleeping.

"TAKE CARE OF YOUR BUSINESS"

Mountain Middle School has the same population as River High School, only younger. Its population is over 90% Black and most of its students qualify for free or reduced lunch. It is the feeder middle school to River High School, and it is also a magnet school for the performing arts. These programs are located in beautiful, new, state-of-the-art wings that wrap around the old building. Several students and faculty members recommended that I observe the West

African dance teacher at Mountain Middle School, Lidia. They told me I would not want to miss her! With that in mind, I set up my visitation schedule so it coincided with Lidia's West African dance class. This meant arriving at the school in the middle of the day, as Lidia starts her day at River High School for first block, then drives over to Mountain Middle School for second and third blocks, and then returns to River High for the last block of the day. She does this with a co-teacher, Eric, who teaches the West African drumming class at the same time as the dance class, and Eric hauls the drums back and forth everyday in his car. So that the dancers can be accompanied by live drumming, as are dancers in West Africa, both the drumming and dancing classes meet together. In Lidia and Eric, I found teachers who use the 90 minutes they have with their students to the fullest. Following are some of my notes on third-period West African dance and drumming class. The year I observed, there were nine drummers, eight males and one female, and 16 dancers, 12 females and 4 males (all African American students). On the occasion I watched them perform publicly, there were two White male drummers, with the rest being African American. From my field notes:

Day 1

I was told that class started at 11:15 A.M., which is when I arrived, but class actually starts at 11:10 A.M. When I arrived, the students were sitting on the gym floor and Lidia was giving them a lecture on being responsible and held accountable; she urged them to write down the information she gave them on a calendar. They have a performance on Saturday, and most of the students have not yet returned their permission slips. Lidia says: "Take care of your business. I got one permission slip in the next day, and I'll bet you can't guess who that was." They guess correctly. "Gloria!" they say. The students start dancing at around 11:25 A.M. They face the mirrors and one student (Gloria) and Lidia lead the group in warm-up exercises. While they are dancing, the drummers play. In West African dancing, the drummers lead the dancers. Gloria is tiny, and a *very good* dancer. The drums are very powerful. I am sitting against the far wall near the drums, and they make my insides vibrate! Lidia stops the students. Lidia: "You all aren't paying attention!" Lidia shows them what she did versus what they did. Lidia: "Pick it up! Lazy energy!" Now a second student comes forward to lead the warm-ups. In response to something one of the students said that I did not hear, Lidia says, "Excuse me, I'm the teacher in this class, I make the placements here. Pick up your feet! Your knees should be waist high! This is West African dance! High energy! Maybe I need to split up this class, because I need some West African dancers. This is not a modern dance class."

I observed Lidia use this technique of threatening to cut them out of the class off and on as a way to motivate them to try harder. The students seem to be used to it; it doesn't seem to upset them. Later, when I ask the two teachers about this on separate occasions, they both tell me that they start out the semester working the students very hard physically, having them run daily to build their strength, but also hoping to run the students who don't want to work hard out of class. However, their class is very popular and they find that most of the students who sign up want to stay and are willing to do the hard work.

Now the students are going to rehearse the dance they will be performing on Saturday. They know the dance *very* well. They're really good! They look like they are enjoying themselves, I see several smiling faces. High energy! When they finish, they lineup beside me as I sit on the floor taking notes. Lidia pulls one student out of the lineup and brings her front and center and gives her individual coaching. Then she gives correction in general to the group. This is a technique she uses regularly in class. Lidia says, "I'm going to start pulling out people. If you don't know the choreography by now, you aren't going to know it. I might as well start the weeding out process now." They go through the same dance routine again. While they perform, Lidia sits on the floor and watches. She's down in front of the mirrors, facing them, in the center. When they finish, they sit on the floor beside me. They are breathing hard and are tired. Lidia yells: "Get off of the floor! You do not sit in my class! Gloria, show them what I choreographed. I don't want to see anything else." Gloria comes out and does the dance solo for the class to see. Lidia approves. "Alright, from the top."

The class does the dance again and I time it. It takes 5 minutes total. In the first 2 minutes, only the girls are dancing; in the last 3 minutes, both the boys and the girls are dancing. This is a very physical, rigorous dance. After this run-through, Lidia compliments the drummers. "I like that. That's a good feel." Then she says, "Let's go! From the top you all! Let's go! From the top!" The students do the dance for the third time (from 11:57 A.M. to 12:02 P.M.). She didn't wait even a minute before she started again. Three students are now sitting by the mirrors, two girls and one boy. Now there are three girls. They are tired. After the last run-through, Lidia asks the students to come back out on the floor and she resets them, reorganizing them and moving them to different lines on the dance floor. Lidia: "Places. Who am I missing?" The students tell her who she's left out and where they were originally. Lidia: "It's up to you all to remember who's in your lines. All right, from the top! That's the new order." (They proceed to dance from 12:05 P.M. to 12:10 P.M.).

I watch the students do this very rigorous dancing for the fourth time. They work hard in this class! There is no talking or goofing off. Again, three girls and one boy sit. The boys get more rest than the girls during the dance, since they wait 2 minutes before they come in and the girls dance the whole time. After this run-through, Lidia says to the students, as they line up again over by where I sit: "Come out, everybody. Let's go!" She notices someone sitting down. Lidia: "Didn't I just say no sitting in my class?" One boy says, "My stomach's starting to hurt." Her response is: "And? Then you need to take a class that requires less strenuous work." She pulls the students together and lets them sit while she gives them feedback. One at a time, Lidia gives the dancers their corrections, in particular concerning their level of energy. To several of them, she says that they are barely hanging on by a thread. Lidia: "You have to rehearse 1,000 times for one performance. There's no excuse—oh, my stomach hurts—walk through it." She uses an example of drummers and their hands. "Even if your hands are busted up, you have to play through it. If you don't want to do this, I'll help you find another class. As long as you are here, I'm going to push you. I'm going to push you until you break. Right before you break, that's a peak performance. Now you can go."

As soon as Lidia dismisses them, the students start laughing and talking to one another. They go to the locker-rooms to change their clothes, and they put away the drums. They come out to the hall to wait for her. While they are changing their clothes, Lidia comes over and talks to me, and that's when I confirm that they have a performance on Saturday. She tells me she is not usually this hard on them, but she worked them hard today to make sure they are ready for the performance. She described herself to me as a "plum, sometimes sour and sometimes sweet." Then she laughs. At 12:22, she says, "Let's go!" and she walks the students to lunch.

CONNECTING THEORY WITH PRACTICE, PART II

Several African American scholars have written about their experience as students in all-Black schools prior to desegregation. In particular, bell hooks (1994) talks about her experiences before and after desegregation in *Teaching to Transgress*, and Lisa Delpit (1995) compares her segregated/desegregated experiences with her daughter's experiences in *Other People's Children*. Vanessa Siddle Walker (1996, 2001) describes her segregated school in North Carolina in *Their Highest Potential*. Vivian and Curtis Morris (2002) researched their segregated school in Alabama as well in *Creating Caring and Nurturing Educational Environments for African American Children*. Michele Foster (1997) and Gloria Ladson-Billings (1994) have contributed significantly to research concerning excellent African American teachers by interviewing elderly teachers and recording their stories, as well as interviewing and observing many teachers who currently are having success helping their students reach their highest potential. The African American teachers I write about here have the teaching qualities described by these various scholars.

bell hooks (1994) talks about how much she loved school when she attended a segregated school, for her teachers made school feel like it was the most important place she should be each day. For her, school was a place of ecstasy—pleasure and danger. Home was a place of forced conformity, but school was a place of freedom to reinvent herself. Her teachers at Booker T. Washington and Crispus Attucks schools insisted that she be an active, engaged learner, unlike the teachers she later had in desegregated schools, who demanded passivity, and consequently made school boring and learning dull for her. Lidia and Ms. Jefferson are teachers who make learning exciting and interesting, even algebra, by giving their students the message that this is a *very* important skill for them to learn, and only through hard work and diligence will they master this difficult skill. Lidia and Ms. Jefferson are not afraid to work their students hard. They are tough teachers, but tough in a good way (Dempsey & Noblit, 1993). They hold high expectations for their students, and they want them *all* to succeed. As long as the students are willing to work, they will work with them. But they will not tolerate any "lazy energy." They push *all* their students to work hard. Anyone who is not willing to work hard is welcome to enroll in another class. Lidia communicates to her students that it is a privilege to be in her class, and only hard workers are allowed to stay. No one gets to sit down and rest, she says (but notice how she pulled the group together for a demonstration or repositioning just when they indicated that they needed to rest). These teachers make it a source of pride to be one of their students; it is a privilege and an honor. If you are in their class, people know you are working hard! That they push their students hard and insist that they be actively engaged is taken by the students and their parents, as well as their colleagues, as a sign of how much they care.

Both Ms. Jefferson and Lidia publicly praise students when their work is good, by holding it up for the others to see or having them perform in front of the others. They name the students who are responsible and get their homework done and their permission slips turned in. The students who do not work to their fullest potential are cajoled to work harder publicly so the whole class can hear as well as privately at their desks or after class. Both teachers place the responsibility for learning clearly on the students' shoulders. Students are responsible not only for their own learning, but if you are an exceptional student, you are responsible for helping others by serving as a role model and peer tutoring. Both teachers also clearly see that an important part of their job is to teach moral lessons to their students. They regularly start their classes with lectures about the importance of being responsible, working hard, and investing in your education. They expect the students to monitor their own behavior and help monitor the behavior of their neighbors, so that none of their class time will be wasted on behavior management and all of it will be used to the maximum for learning.

As we saw with Ms. Jefferson, successful African American teachers are teachers who get to know their students and their families if at all possible. Walker (1996, 2001) and the Morrises (2000) describe how, historically, the teachers in segregated Black schools in the South were expected to live in the neighborhood of their school, visit their students' homes and meet their parents, shop in the same stores, and attend the various churches in the area. The parents viewed the teachers as role models for their children, and as pillars of strength for the community. In exchange, they were offered a great deal of respect and granted the authority to teach children. Walker, the Morrises, and Dempsey and Noblit (1993) have all documented the destruction that occurred to local Black communities when their schools were closed due to desegregation, for the schools served as community centers for African American families.

The schools I observed in the South still serve community-center functions. They are located on the side of town where most of the African American families live, shop, and attend church. Ms. Jefferson and Lidia both have children who attended or currently attend schools in this area; they know the community and the families in the area well. We saw how Ms. Jefferson expects her students' parents to be involved in their children's education, by showing up for parent conferences or coming to see her during the school day if they cannot make the evening meeting. But she does not let the parents interrupt her teaching for conferences; to her, that would mean that they disrespect the work she does. For Ms. Jefferson, her teaching is the most important thing she does during the day, and she wants to communicate to the parents and her students how important her teaching is. The time she spends with the students is precious, and she does not allow it to be interrupted. Lidia, too, used every minute of class time to practice for the upcoming dance recital so it would be a peak performance. Her students' parents chaperone for their performances and assist with costuming and performance preparations, but they do not interrupt her classes.

Given what I've related here about successful African American teachers, what does it teach us about the concept *authority*? We can look at Ms. Jefferson and Lidia from a classical liberal perspective, and point to their efforts to help each individual student reach his or her full potential as evidence that they maintain a classical liberal view of authority. We can praise them for their efforts to encourage individual achievement and cajole their students into being highly motivated and hardworking so they reach their full potentials as mathematicians and as dancers. We can admire these two teachers for their efficient use of time and their efforts to block out all contextual distractions and focus on the task at hand, the algebra problems and the rehearsal for Saturday's performance. But neither of these teachers fits the pedagogical style that Giroux (1997) describes as one of cordial relations, seeking to keep the students "happy." Both of them are aware of connections among authority, culture, and power, and neither ignores "the messy webs of social relations."

But we can also look at Ms. Jefferson and Lidia from a conservative perspective and see evidence of this approach to authority in their teaching styles. The conservative discourse on authority is a positive one, celebrating authority as representative of the American dream, a dream based on hard work, discipline, promptness, and cheerful obedience. These very values are taught by Ms. Jefferson and Lidia in their classrooms. Both teachers start out their classes with moral lessons on the importance of students "taking care of their business" and "investing in their education." The conservative concept of authority focuses on control, management, and efficiency, and both teachers certainly maintain control and manage their classrooms efficiently. However, Giroux (1997) describes the pedagogical style of conservative teachers as functioning like clerks, and also points out that the conservative view of authority is silent on the connection between culture and power. While I have observed African American teachers who do function like clerks, this is hardly true of Ms. Jefferson's and Lidia's pedagogical style. These teachers are not following someone else's authority; rather, they have claimed authority for themselves. And they are not using their authority to disarm their students, but rather to arm them so they will be better able to address the connections of knowledge to culture and power. This past year, Lidia's students learned a dance that enacts the history of slavery in West Africa and its movement to the United States, a powerful, moving dance that includes a whip being snapped and popped around the students as they enter the stage crying and screaming.

Following Giroux's (1997) categories for authority again, we find that leftist educators would judge Lidia as being an authoritarian and possibly Ms. Jefferson as well. After all, both teachers use public humiliation by announcing to their class the mistakes students make, and admonishing students to try harder and get their parents to attend parent conferences. Lidia in particular uses intimidation (threats to remove the students from the class) to frighten her students into working harder. From a leftist view, these teachers can be viewed as oppressive.

Remember, Giroux argues for an emancipatory concept of authority that emphasizes that authority is "a terrain of struggle" and that teachers can function as "transformative intellectuals" who have the ability to think and act critically and teach their students to do the same. They can create what Giroux calls "a democratic counterpublic sphere" in their classrooms. bell hooks

(1994) also uses the same kind of language as Giroux to describe the African American teachers she had as a child. Her teachers taught her that education was "the practice of freedom." They modeled for her the notion that teaching is "a revolutionary act of transgression," for it helps students learn the skills they need not only to survive in the world but to change the world. Her teachers served as "the bearers of dangerous memories." They were strong examples of teachers who allow their students to practice the skills of democracy. They knew how to successfully create what Giroux calls "a democratic counterpublic sphere" in their classrooms, which is exactly what hooks tries to create in her classroom today. The African American teachers whom scholars are interviewing and studying today are important voices to record, for they do indeed serve as the bearers of "dangerous memories."

But what about Ms. Jefferson and Lidia? Do they serve as strong examples of teachers relying on an emancipatory concept of authority? Are they transformative intellectuals? Or are they teaching their students to be more obedient and compliant? I think they do serve as examples of transformative teachers, but to fully understand how they serve in this role, we need to turn to bell hooks (1994). Giroux's concept of emancipatory authority hinders us from fully appreciating what goes on in Ms. Jefferson's and Lidia's classroom because he clings to a view of human subjectivity based on individual autonomy and agency, which is a holdover from modernist democratic theories.

bell hooks (1994) relates in *Teaching to Transgress* that her key experiences for learning that education can be the practice of freedom came from her early years in segregated schools. Once she entered desegregated schools, she lost the early role models she had until she entered college, where she found feminist classrooms where professors were striving to create participatory spaces for the sharing of knowledge. hooks also shares with us two key sources who underscore this approach to education: one being Paulo Freire, also a subscriber to Giroux's concept of emancipatory authority, and the other being Thich Nhat Hanh, the Vietnamese Buddhist monk. hooks learned from Thich Nhat Hanh how important it is to commit oneself as an educator to a process of self-actualization that promotes one's own well-being. hooks found with these teachers a concept of authority that is not based on individualism but rather on a transactional view of individuals-in-relation-to-others.

It takes a close look at Ms. Jefferson's and Lidia's teaching styles to realize that they do not approach teaching with an assumption of individualism in the way that classical liberals, conservatives, radicals, or even emanicaptory freedom fighters such as Giroux do. Like Ms. Lincoln and bell hooks, they create a community in their classrooms where everyone feels a responsibility to contribute. It is a shared commitment and a common good that binds the teacher and students together. In her classroom, Lidia creates a place where mind, body, and spirit come together. Ms. Jefferson does as well, as she builds a community that is based on a climate of openness and intellectual rigor. Their experiences as Black women raised in a racist and sexist capitalistic society inform their awareness of oppression and the relationship between domination and power. As Myles Horton learned at Highlander, individualism is a luxury that oppressed people do not have (Thayer-Bacon, 2002); they cannot ignore "the messy webs of social relations." Their very survival depends on the enactment of a concept of authority that is based on a transactional view of individuals-in-relation-to-others, a view that never deludes itself into thinking "I can make it on my own." hooks, Jefferson, and Lidia developed their pedagogy by relying on a concept of *shared authority* that recognizes schools as ideological and political terrains and classrooms as spaces where the skills of democracy can be practiced.

There are many examples of excellent African American teachers in American schools today. In this section, I presented only two stories—those of Ms. Jefferson and Lidia. They model working with students who come from various backgrounds and experiences in ways that are empowering and help them reach their full potential as individuals-in-relation-with-others. Ms. Jefferson and Lidia come to their classes prepared to work hard, for they know the work they do is of critical importance. Their classrooms are exciting places, where students know the importance of the work they do and that they can only succeed if they join together and help one another do their best. No one gets left behind, and no one is allowed to slack off. All of the students are expected to be engaged and active learners. Ms. Jefferson and Lidia know that in their classrooms students will learn important skills that will not only help them live in this world, but also change it. They know that, during the time they have these students, they have the chance to learn and grow with them as they share their authority, arming students for the difficult task of changing the political terrain in which they live.

CONCLUSION

African American sociologists writing about the arrangements extended families make for childcare describe the practice of "other mothering" in Black families in the United States (Collins, 1990). As I learned from staying with our host Ghanian family while visiting the local schools, the tradition of "other mothering" dates back centuries to the origins of West African cultures. So, too, does the authoritarian role that African American teachers and parents play in the United States, which I observed are not gender-specific. The authoritarian stance teachers and parents take in the children's lives in Ghana is taken as an expression of care. I met children who laugh and are joyful and are also helpful and courteous (children carry an adult's packages and give up their seat to an adult when one enters the room). In the United States as well, many of the teachers and classroom aides I observed in the predominantly African American schools exercised authoritarian roles that were understood to be expressions of care (Dempsey & Noblit, 1993).

I am not comfortable with this strong authoritarian role, and found it very difficult to observe it in Ghana and the United States while remaining a detached spectator. In the United States, I wanted to intervene on behalf of the children (I didn't), and in Ghana I wanted to remove myself from the classroom (which I eventually did when the canings continued). Like Giroux (1997), the experience of strong authority felt like violence to me, and it left me feeling very troubled. Just as my visits to the schools in Mexico and the Southwest United States and my physical experiences at those sites forced me to address the issue of welcoming others, so, too, my visits to River High and the Ghanian schools and my direct, physical experiences at those sites forced me to address the issue of authority and how it is expressed. I could only address these issues fairly by recognizing that I was raised with the liberal values Giroux describes so well, but with plenty of conservatism mixed in from my experiences being hit as a child (by a hand or a belt) and teaching in American schools at a time when children were still being paddled regularly for misbehaving. Liberal values support Maria Montessori's philosophy of education, and as a Montessori teacher-to-be, those values were expressed throughout my elementary teacher-training program. Liberal values teach that yelling at a child harms his or her psyche and hitting children with a cane harms their bodies. I realize that the meaning attached to these acts is culturally specific, and that I attached the meaning my culture gives to the behaviors I witnessed. The children being caned translate that act differently from the way I do. Still, it hurts them, just as it hurts any child as they cry from the pain. I do not support hitting a child with a paddle, hand, or cane.

While I view hitting a child as a violent act, this does not mean I view authority only negatively, as a loss of freedom connected to a logic of domination. I am a feminist, and as a feminist, I am very aware of how important authority is for one's presence to be noticed and one's voice to be heard. The history of women's experiences in most cultures throughout time is a history of men using their authority negatively to dominate women. However, there are vivid examples of cultures where this history of gendered oppression and domination is not the norm. Many Native American tribes stand out in stark contrast to this general history of gendered oppression, as do other indigenous tribes in various parts of the world, including Africa. Giroux (1997) presents an emancipatory authority that is "a terrain of struggle," but his concept of authority is dependent upon an individualistic view of human subjectivity, the very same view of human subjectivity upon which Locke and Rousseau depended. This will never get us to emancipatory freedom for all; it always leads back to freedom for some at the expense of others, for it is based on an either/ or logic that positions us against one another. Again, we find that we have not managed to get beyond classical liberalism.

I argue for a transactional view of human subjectivity that describes individuals-in-relation-to-others. The concept of transactional relationships begins with the recognition that we are always affecting others, just as we are always affected by others, and that the boundaries between "us" are very porous indeed. Any authority we can claim as relational human beings is a limited, situated authority that we share with those around us. Our relationships with those around us enhance as well as hinder our understanding of the social world, and move us beyond our own contextuality while keeping us trapped within our own limitations. Ms. Jefferson's teaching stories as well as those of Ms. Lincoln and Lidia expand our thinking and illustrate the concept of *shared authority*, in contrast to the conservative views of authority of Fortune and countless teachers in the United States. These teachers who share their authority with their students serve as wonderful models who portray what teaching looks like when it helps students learn what it means to be an active, participating citizen of democracies-always-in-the-making. Ms. Jefferson and Lidia are not the only examples of this pedagogical approach; thankfully, there are many more.

In the next chapter, I present Native American tribes that have a view of human subjectivity as transactionally related.

Chapter 4

Shared Identities

For a White researcher to observe a Native American school is a story in itself. Rightfully so, Native Americans are mistrustful of the people whose ancestors colonized them and attempted to destroy them. It has only been since the 1960s that the U.S. government has put enough money into providing adequate schools that are within driving distance of Native American communities, and allowed tribes to create Tribal Councils that have authority over the schools. Still, it is an illusionary authority, as the money for the schools comes from the U.S. government, which cannot be counted on to deliver the amount budgeted, for this depends on who's in office and the state of the U.S. economy (Senese, 1986). In addition, many Natives on the reservations do not believe the Tribal Councils represent their views, and also see the Councils as incompetent. Some tribes describe them as "apples," red on the outside but white on the inside, traitors to their culture (Deloria, Jr. & Lytle, 1984).

I was not able to obtain an invitation to do research from any of the schools I contacted directly.[1] For the schools I did visit, I was the first person to spend a week with them. Many educators visit for an hour or two, maybe an afternoon, but none stay for any length of time. When I learned this, I felt incredibly honored to be there and have this experience. I came with deep respect and appreciation for the people in these schools, listening attentively in conversation with the administrators, teachers, and students. Once they got to know me, they let me into their world, sharing with me more than I could ever have imagined.

In this chapter, I discuss what I learned from my visits to Native American schools in an effort to better understand the important role *shared identities* play in democracies-always-in-the-making. Following the pattern I established in previous chapters, I begin in the first section with stories from my visits to schools on the Navajo Reservation. I focus these stories on the role of the curriculum in relation to the teachers and students. Through these stories, we can see how shared identities are expressed by different teachers and curricula. In the following section on the intertwining of theory and practice and the possibilities for moving beyond liberal democracy today, I discuss the theoretical implications of the practices I observed. There are many powerful writings by Native Americans that describe the experience of forced assimilation and acculturation and the *soul wound* it has left them with (Lobo & Peters, 2001). In a moving article by Richard Morris (1997) titled "Educating Savages," he focuses specifically on the issue of shared identities, and his insights contribute significantly to the discussion in the first three sections about the Navajo Reservation: "The Rez," "A Street Is Something You Walk on," and "Where Are the Native Americans?".

In the second part of this chapter (the sections called "Creating a New Generation of Warriors" and "Education Is Like Medicine"), I describe my visits to Young Warriors High School, where the important role *shared identities* play in encouraging citizens to contribute to their school and community is on display. The stories illuminate the role Grandmother and Father play in the lives of the students. Shared identity is further examined in stories of the school director and founder of the school and one of its original teachers. In the section that considers putting together theory and practice, there is a discussion of the theoretical implications of the practices I observed. An excellent book by Eduardo and Bonnie Duran (1995), titled *Native American Postcolonial Psychology,* contributes greatly to the analysis in the sections concerning the urban school site.

This chapter reveals that when the emphasis on individuals changes to a transactional view of individuals-in-relation-to-others sharing identities in a democracy-always-in-the-making, an antidote is created that counteracts the poison that has done much to dismantle Native American societies—individualism, upon which liberal democracy depends.

THE REZ

Navajos got their first paved roads in 1961, transforming transportation from horses and carts to pickup trucks. When you enter the Rez, you are entering a Third World nation not unlike Ghana, where the side roads are packed dirt and people drive to the top of a hill to pick up a signal and use their cellphones. You enter a world where housing projects are home to people with a 70% unemployment rate, serious problems with drugs and alcohol, and high suicide rates—a byproduct of the devastating effects of colonization. You also enter a place of breathtaking beauty with splendid mesas, plateaus, and rock formations and stunning sunrises and sunsets that go on for miles and miles. The Navajo Reservation is located on land where the Diné (*Diné* is the term the Navajo people use to refer to themselves) have lived forever as "the chosen people."

The Mesa's schools are public and receive state funding from Arizona. The school buses have four-wheel drive and travel within a 50-mile radius, on dirt roads, to transport students to and from school. The Navajo Nation is organized into approximately 100 chapters. Eleven chapters go to Diné Primary School. It takes around 24 buses to get all the children to and from school. School starts at 8:00 A.M. and ends at 2:30 P.M. for the primary kids; the buses take them home and return in time to pick up the middle school and high school students. Some teachers arrive at 6:30 A.M. and leave at 2:30 P.M.; others arrive at 7:30 A.M. and stay until 3:30 P.M. Kids begin arriving around 7:30 A.M. and go into the cafeteria for breakfast or into the computer lab to play. The school building is laid out in three large hogans (a hogan is a traditional Navajo home in octagon shape), with each hogan having eight or nine classrooms that branch out like pieces of a pie. At the center of each hogan is an area with couches and chairs that serves as the central meeting and greeting area. The building structure was designed by the staff and built in 1993. I found it easy to get lost in the school because the octagon shape of the hogans offered no edges or corners to guide me. I arrived on the first Monday after Christmas break, just in time for the monthly fire drill.

For the first time, Diné Primary has a Navajo principal, a woman named Ruth. The White male principal prior to her assignment was there for 15 years and trained Ruth before he left to teach in a nearby university. She taught in the school for several years prior to becoming principal, and came to Diné Primary from another Navajo school where she had also taught for several years. The only White people in the building are the counselor who sponsored me, the art teacher, two teachers who have been teaching on the Rez since the days of the Bureau of Indian Affairs schools, and the female librarian, who is married to a Navajo teacher in the school. Everyone else is Native, mostly Navajo, but not exclusively. For example, the male librarian, John, is part Cherokee. As more and more Navajos earn college degrees and teaching credentials, they are replacing the White teachers and administrators at all levels of the schools on the Rez and reclaiming the education of their children. However, it is important to point out that they have had some strong White allies help them get to where they are today; the previous principal is one such ally, who was there for 15 years and oversaw the school's success in receiving the A+ rating it now enjoys.[2] Diné Primary is an award-winning school as a result of his leadership and collaboration with all the teachers working there. Parents who live off the Rez bring their children to stay with family members on the Rez just so they can attend schools like Diné Primary.

By the end of the week, I realized that Diné Primary School is indeed a very special school. Even with its large size (around 24 classrooms), the teachers know one another well. They have all worked there for a long time, as teachers do not usually give up their jobs until they retire. The only male teacher I observed is married to the librarian, and their daughter teaches in the school as well. The counselor is divorced from one teacher in the building and remarried to her sister. Mothers and daughters and cousins teach in the building. The schools are a major source of jobs for people in the area, and many who grew up on the Rez and want to stay there find work at the school. Teaching jobs are highly coveted and do not often open up. Consequently, the school feels like an extended family. The teachers are close to one another. Their children all attend the schools in the area and they live in the school compound or on their own land not far away. They all come to the Mesa for medical care and for a night on the town (e.g., a basketball game or dinner out). The teachers also know the students and their families well. Everyone is on a first-name basis, including the students with the teachers.

The three different "pod" areas of the building are labeled by the cardinal directions, east, west, and south. Each pod's common space is decorated differently by the teachers in the pod. In the common areas, there are bathrooms and drinking fountains for the students, and a conference room with adult bathrooms and a kitchen and workroom for the teachers. West pod has multi-age classrooms for children in grades K–2. East pod has looping classrooms, where classrooms of children of the same age stay with their teacher for grades K–2. South pod had a mixture of multiaged and looping classrooms. Teachers have a choice of which kind of room they want. The staff feel strongly that keeping students with the same teacher for the first 3 years of school provides a good foundation for their education.

The classrooms have tables shaped like circles or rectangles, with three or four seats per table, and a couch and rug area as well. Each classroom is *full* of materials. The school is *beautiful* and new and the center hub of the school is a huge library. There are books *everywhere* in this school. There's an ultramodern as well as traditional Navajo cultural feel about the school. It is painted in desert colors and proudly displays cultural artifacts such as weavings representing the Mesa's pattern. Of the various schools I saw on the Rez, this was the most beautiful and the one most full of Navajo culture.

The kids in Diné Primary School wear the same clothes kids wear everywhere (jeans, chinos, sweaters, t-shirts, sneakers, and hiking shoes. I've seen kids in Mexico, Ghana, Japan, and China all wearing the same Euro-Western clothes). Their clothes are clean and well kept. It's like any school population in the United States—but with the light brown skin and straight, dark-brown hair of Native Americans. The kids look healthy and happy. I see lots of smiling, friendly faces. They draw Spider-Man and talk about the Game Boy Advances, Game Boy Colors, and Playstations they got for Christmas. They snack on hot Cheetos. The kids know a little Spanish and Navajo, but English is their main language. They have totally assimilated with "American" culture. The young children choose to speak English over Navajo.

The staff at Diné Primary School worry about keeping the Navajo language and culture alive. They have a Navajo Enrichment Acceleration Program where the students learn traditional customs such as string art, traditional music, and the Navajo language. The school counselor, Tom, told me that in every classroom either the teacher or teacher's aide (TA) is fluent in Navajo. All the TAs in the intermediate school have some education background, but they are understaffed—a casualty of President Bush and Congress's No Child Left Behind program. TAs are required to have associate degrees now, but there are not enough TAs on the Rez with associate degrees. Tom told me that some of the kids are not fluent in either English *or* Navajo. The teachers work hard on developing fluency. The previous principal focused intently on improving the literacy rate of Navajo children. They now have a very successful program with the children leaving this primary school above grade level in reading. But by the time they get to middle school, they are behind in reading again. They lose ground in the intermediate school, where teachers spend less time on literacy and more time on math, science, and social studies. At the high school, the head of the math department said that the students are behind in math skills because they don't get enough of the basics in primary school, where so much emphasis is placed on literacy. A choice to focus on literacy skills comes at the expense of *not* focusing on another necessary skill, such as numeracy.

Following are two stories from my visit to Diné Primary School. The first is from a classroom observation, and the second is from a staff meeting.

"A STREET IS SOMETHING YOU WALK ON"

Leah has 17 students in her multiage classroom and they are all here on the first day back after Christmas break. Her room feels like a Montessori (1976, 1977) classroom.[3] Everyone is helping to take care of the room. The children have jobs that they rotate so everyone gets to help in a variety of ways. The kids have opportunities to work individually as well as together. Some of the kids are focused, hard workers, and some get easily distracted. When I visit, they are writing letters to their teacher to practice this skill. Some are almost done with the letters to the teacher and some aren't. There are a few signs on the walls: "Everyone help!" and "Be nice."

Leah laughs a lot and encourages the students often. There is a gentleness and mellowness about her that I find to be typical of people on the Navajo Reservation.[4] Everything is a potential lesson for Leah and a chance to build vocabulary and reading skills for her students. She is working with the three youngest children, who are still learning to read. Leah monitors everyone's work behavior while working with these three students. She gives them a new book to read and goes over the new words in the book, making sure the students can read and know what they mean. "Feet—meet—street." Leah asks, "What's a street?" A student answers, "You walk on it." Leah responds, "Yeah, you walk on it. They have streets in Gallup." One kid across the room is listening to the little ones as they read. He is prompting them. They read the story together, once and then again. Leah says, "This book you need to take home tonight. You can read it at the house and you better not lose it there." Then she laughs. Leah has the students tell her about the story and she writes their comments on the blackboard. She asks them to spell words as she writes and waits for them to figure out the letters before she continues. She gives them clues, such as, "Commas tell me to . . ." The kids say, "Slow down." Their sentence is: "I can run, stop, and walk with my feet." They read what she has written out loud twice, then they are to write it in their journals, draw a picture, and read the sentence to five people. That is their assignment. Leah has them remind her about capitals and periods. She is always teaching, not telling, getting them to tell her while she asks questions. Leah uses what I would describe as a whole language approach to reading (Ashton-Warner, 1975).

Every night ,most of the children in the school carry home a book to read. The school gives each child four brand-new, hard-bound books to keep each year. They expect to lose many books from their library each year, since books that are brought home often seem never to reappear. The teachers and administrators expect this and are not bothered by it. Many of the children do not have books in their homes or parents with strong literacy skills who can help them with their reading. So the children bring the books home and read to whomever is willing to listen.

When I heard Leah confirm a child's definition of a *street* as something you walk on, I was taken by surprise. I associate streets with something you drive on and sidewalks with something you walk on. Though I heard this interaction on the first morning I observed at Diné Primary School, I kept thinking about it, and eventually realized that there are no streets on the reservation. There are paved roads and dirt roads, but these are roads, not streets. For the Rez children, roads are where cars and trucks drive and also where people walk, since there is not very much traffic on them. The only way a child would have any experience of a street is if she or he is driven off the Rez to a nearby town such as Gallup. There are towns on the Rez large enough to warrant streets, but they are not incorporated and, therefore, do not have zoning or any of the infrastructure of a town. "Nearby" is a relative term, too, as the nearest towns are more than an hour from the Mesa.

Navajos have historically lived in clans around their homestead and moved from one hogan to another as they herd their sheep. They do not have a history of staying in one place and forming towns like the Hopis did. The Navajos spread out over their land and were nomadic to avoid overgrazing the land. Even today, in spite of the U.S. government's slaughter of their sheep and the consequent reduction in stock, as well as the forced boundary lines for land ownership on the Rez, the Navajos still live spread out across their reservation on small homesteads (*Between Sacred Mountains*, 1994). Very small towns have formed where the paved roads cross and the schools and trading posts are located. "Street" is not a common experience for a Navajo child.

I began to notice that much of what the children read about was not based on their own experiences and did not tap into their knowledge base. Over and over again, I heard teachers talking about how important it was to build up the children's vocabulary and expose them to the larger world, one they knew very little about. I started squirming at the perception I was hearing of the children as having deficits and the teachers' continual emphasis on what they lacked. The curriculum the children are exposed to continually reminds them of what they do *not* know, positioning them in a deficit status. The teachers work hard to fill the gaps between the children's reservation experience and the lives the books refer to. I started longing to see books based on the Navajos and their life on the Rez as well as in the towns in the surrounding states; the Navajos often maintain a place on the Rez as well as in a nearby city for greater employment opportunities. I became quite aware of the daunting task the Navajos face in running their own schools to creating an entirely new curriculum. The Navajo culture is absent from the books the children read; it is invisible and, thus, devalued, which means the life experiences of the children on the Rez are devalued as well in a world where literacy is so important.

"WHERE ARE THE NATIVE AMERICANS?"

When I attended a staff meeting on Wednesday, this issue of the students' books not reflecting their own experiences of life on the Rez came into sharp focus. The children are dismissed early on Wednesdays so the teachers can have time to meet at 2:00 P.M. This Wednesday, there are two sales representatives from a major publishing company selling a set of science books. The books are beautiful, hard-bound texts, and they come with many resources for teachers, such as activity ideas and test banks. The text I look at has a beautiful green cover with a green frog on it. I wonder, "When does a child on the Rez ever see a frog like that? They live in a desert!" Another book for a different grade level has a penguin on the cover. After politely listening to the sales pitch and looking over the books and support material, the teachers point out to the sales representatives that there are no pictures of Native Americans in the books and no discussions of Native American culture. This surprises the sales representatives, for their publishing firm is proud of its sensitivity to diversity, expressed in the pictures they choose. We look through the pictures again and, sure enough, we find images of African American, Latino, and Asian children but none of Native Americans. It is no surprise to the teachers that the books are biased. Even when they try to include diversity in their choice of pictures, the publishers and authors don't succeed from a Native American perspective. The students won't see themselves or their culture reflected in these books. The teachers will have to "bring in" Native American science themselves.

On my last day of visiting, I asked Ruth, the school principal, if the school planned to buy these science textbooks. She said the primary school is under pressure to be like the intermediate school and use textbooks and give grades. But the primary teachers resist. The teachers voted to do what they often end up doing: They will buy one set for the different ages they teach, which will be available as a resource for the teachers to use as a resource, but they will not buy books for the children. Ruth said they know they need to strengthen their science curriculum, but they want to do so in a way that strengthens the children's knowledge of their land and the life that grows around them. Again, I realized this means a lot of work for the teachers designing their own curriculum, as the Rough Rock teachers have done (*Between Sacred Mountains*, 1994). What choice do they have? Diné Primary School's mission is to help their children be bicultural and bilingual; they seek to maintain the Navajo way of life and strengthen it while also learning about the American way of life. It is a daunting task. Arizona has no bilingual programs anymore (as in California, they voted them out when money got tight). However, the Navajo Nation supports bicultural/bilingual programs. They've mandated it; they want it. Ruth says Diné Primary School is safe; New Mexico or Arizona isn't going to bother them on this issue. But I realized as I drove away that only the primary school is successful in fully integrating the Navajo culture into the curriculum. As the students get older, the curriculum becomes more like a standard curriculum found anywhere in the United States. The students are exposed to Navajo culture one day a week in the upper elementary and middle schools (both of these schools are run by White principals) and in a one-semester course on Navajo Studies in the high school. The children walk out of Diné Primary School strong and confident, but they struggle to maintain that confidence as they continue through their public schools on their Rez.

CONNECTING THEORY WITH PRACTICE, PART I

In "Educating Savages," Richard Morris (1997) writes as an Indian who went through a process so common to Native Americans who attend White people's schools. Morris tells us he lost connection to his family and his culture, and learned to hate his friends and family for being Indian. This loss of connection led to self-hatred. Morris's essay is about what he calls *transformational mimesis*, which he defines as "demonstration that the text has transformed the subordinate" (p. 154). The example he uses is acculturation or assimilation. He explains how acculturation/assimilation serves to put one's cultural identity under erasure involuntarily or without informed consent, by providing a ready-made "superior" alternative identity as the only means of escape for those "trapped" by their heritage. Transformational mimesis requires one to reject his or her culture's symbolic codes in order to become fully human.

A vivid example of transformational mimesis and how it occurs through assimilation can be found in the history of the Indian boarding school (Spring, 2004; Thompson, 1978).[5] The Indian boarding schools used methods such as isolation, denigration, and punishment to force acculturation. Indian children were to speak only English and were punished for speaking their own language. They couldn't dress in their own native clothes, nor were they allowed to practice rituals, beliefs, religions, ceremonies, and modes of living from their cultures. Most important to the forced assimilation plan, the children were not allowed contact with their families. If they did contact them, usually by running away, they were punished, often severely, when caught. The Indian boarding schools laid the groundwork for assimilation and fragmented the student from her cultural community. The result was a loss of living memory, the loss of heritage.

Morris (1997) explains that the lesson the students were taught was that you've got to be White if you are going to amount to anything. They were taught that the Indian way is the way of the past. These children, when they returned to their reservations, were poison to their own people, for they came back with White values that they used to disparage their own people. Morris relates this poisoning process very vividly through his own personal experience with his family. According to Morris, "Before Native Americans may participate in the democratic process fully, for example, they must cast off (among other things) the symbolicity of their cultures, take on the symbolicity of the dominant society, and mark themselves as counterfeit in the eyes of their people and of members of the dominant society. This process disallows their full participation either in the dominant society or among their own people" (p. 166).

However, the Native American story includes resistance stories, stories about survivors of forced assimilation and acculturation, and firm rejection of the effects of transformational mimesis. The Navajo primary school I observed is a vivid example of resistance to assimilation and acculturation to the dominant, colonizing culture, while at the same time accommodating the need for the children to be fluent in both languages and cultures. The children who attend Diné Primary School are growing up on the Rez, surrounded by their culture and their own people. They go home to their family everyday, and they come to school where their own people are their teachers. They are not isolated from their families and culture, and they are allowed to practice their cultural rituals and ceremonies, which they are even taught in their schools. They go to a school that displays cultural artifacts proudly throughout the building, and was built in the shape of their historic cultural dwelling, the hogans. Still, the families, teachers, and children feel the pressures to assimilate to the dominant culture. The families have televisions and radios in their homes that their children view and listen to, and they find that their children resist speaking the Navajo language and opt for English instead. What do their children want for Christmas? The year I was there, it was Game Boys and DVDs of *The Fellowship of the Ring*.

The children are being acculturated by the dominant culture, White people's culture, even on the Rez where they attend Navajo ceremonies. These children are not beaten in their schools; in fact, I never heard an adult raise his or her voice to a child and I never saw a child get into any trouble and receive some form of physical punishment. The atmosphere at Diné Primary School is wonderfully supportive and loving. But the pressure to assimilate is strong. The dominant culture, delivered in the benign form of attractive children's books, still reminds the children of their deficits and what they do not know—"a street is for walking on"—instead of what they do know. Their parents and teachers are resisting the assimilation and acculturation that they know is poison to their community and leads to self-hatred, and they work hard to help the children be bicultural and bilingual. The children leave the primary school strong and confident, and ahead in literacy. Most seem to love to read and to learn. But they lose ground as they proceed through a school system that teaches less about their own culture and more about the dominant culture. For me, observing this underscored the importance of shared identities for children to grow up with healthy self-esteem, able to contribute their voices and participate in a democracy of their own making. My observation also highlighted the poison of the dominant culture that Morris (1997) describes so vividly. The Mesa's high school has its mission painted on the high school interior wall: "To prepare our students to be successful learners and responsible citizens in a global community while retaining an identity with their traditional culture." My observations underscored how very difficult this mission is to accomplish, and the difficulties facing Native Americans trying to maintain and grow their traditional community while helping their children find ways to participate successfully as citizens in their larger world community.   •

"CREATING A NEW GENERATION OF WARRIORS"

What happens to Native American children by the time they reach high school? This question is addressed in the following three stories from Young Warriors High School, an urban high school in the Midwest. Young Warriors is a partnership school, supported in part by the public school system in the Midwest and in part by private funding. Even though it is directly across the street from the Indian Community School (ICS), which is funded by the Potawatomi tribe, it does not get funding from any particular tribe. The school director of Young Warriors is the founder of the school, Cheryl. She established the school in such a way that it is independent of control by any particular tribe or the public school system, yet it enjoys a degree of support from all of them. The students at the school receive free breakfasts and lunches from the Potawatomi tribe, and the school is assigned one public school teacher, Rita, whose salary is paid by the Midwest school district. Young Warrior High School has been in existence for 10 years. It has seven teachers and 100 students in grades 9–12. There is also a principal and counselor, and Cheryl, who now serves as the school director (she was originally also a teacher and the principal). Rita has taught in the school for 4 years and serves as the head teacher. She is White and Polish by background, which is a common ethnicity in Midwest. Three of the school's teachers are 100% Native American, two are of mixed heritage, and two are White Euro-Westerners, including Rita. Two are male and five are female. Both the principal and counselor are White males.

Young Warriors High School is on block scheduling, with four periods in the day: 8:10–9:30, 9:40–11, 11–12:30, then lunch and assembly, and the last block from 2:05–3:25 P.M. I arrived in the Midwest for what turned out to be a very eventful time in U.S. history, as it was the week that the United States went to war with Iraq. Cheryl tells the story of Young Warriors High School. From my field notes:

Cheryl is a Plains Indian. Her original focus for the school was on Native American traditional values ("traditional" means Native American culture as it was). She drove the teachers nuts the first year, insisting that Native American culture be represented in all curricula. The immediate problem they faced was—which Native American culture? There are 11 Native American tribes in their state in the Midwest alone. Furthermore, most urban Native American children are *mixed*. The staff realized that if a student was half white and half Native American, both cultures had to be celebrated if they were going to succeed in their main goal of uplifting the children. Cheryl is 62 years old and the mother of four children and described herself as a tired war pony. She started this school because she saw a need to reengage teens and create a new generation of warriors. She hoped the school would create a new generation of warriors, but the fact that this hasn't happened is a bitter disappointment for her. Maybe one student each year gains in social consciousness. The rest are dealing with survival of self.

The conditions are different for these kids compared with those when she was growing up. She grew up in extreme poverty on the reservation in the 1940s–1950s, but she knew she was loved and cared for by her mom. Her tribe is Ojibway/Cree, Turtle Clan. There was more overt racism and oppression when she was growing up than there is today. Cheryl's mom was an assimilationist, seeking to become part of the American culture, and her dad was a traditionalist, seeking to maintain his Native American culture. The issues for Native American children today are different from those she faced as a child growing up. Cheryl says that kids don't feel valued, loved, and wanted today. They have no mom or dad, and they have to worry about daily survival. Her unpublished philosophy is that you have to heal the spirit before you can engage the mind. Cheryl talked about Maslow's (1954) hierarchy and how food and shelter come first.

Young Warriors High School is for at-risk kids, but Cheryl says that all kids are at risk, just some more so than others. She knows that the school is on the right track, but she admits that it has problems with teachers, students, and supplies. She judged Young Warriors to have had 4 to 5 good years out of the 10 it has been in existence. Cheryl says one of their strengths is their willingness to adapt and change. Every year, they have a one-week retreat at the beginning and end of the year, and they "look at the good, the bad, and the ugly." She isn't married to anything but a curriculum that emphasizes *appreciation of difference*. They teach Indian culture and history, but even more important is Indian values. They teach the students that "You have a role to play in the circle of life, you are connected to and related to all spirits." They teach the students a belief in a higher power and to respect spiritual life. They teach the students to treat one another and the environment with *respect and love*. They teach the importance of community and interdependence. And they teach the students to be honest and keep their promises. Cheryl says she is criticized by Native American colleagues for her willingness to enroll diverse students. At first, she wanted only Native Americans; she was hoping to create a cocoon for them as teens. Then she realized that, while there are many differences, the root cultures of Native Americans and African Americans are similar. She opened the school to a diverse population, and she is happy to see that the Native Americans, African Americans, and Mexican Americans no longer see one another as "those people." Acceptance and empathy are emerging, for the students now understand that they are all in the same boat. The school has a corporate advisory board that meets once a year, and by school guidelines, 51% of the students must be Native American.

Cheryl told me she doesn't even like kids! She sees herself as the Creator's instrument. She talked about starting the school and that she used to be able to get substantial amounts of grant money. She stated that gambling is the "new buffalo," for it has become a major source of income for tribes. She notices the rise in racist criticism because the tribes are doing too well financially. People don't want the Native Americans to succeed, she says. Because Native American nations are sovereign, they were able to develop what they call *gaming*, not *gambling*, to a level unsurpassed in the United States. Cheryl ascribes the difficulty she has getting grant money to the financial success of the Potawatomi tribe's gaming venture. Though the school is not sponsored by the Potawatomis, the agencies nevertheless tell her to go to them for funding. The Indian Community School (ICS) has a distant, hands-off relationship with Young Warriors because they see the teens who attend Young Warriors as "troubled," and they do not want their students associating with them. When I observed at ICS, I was told how well their students do when they leave and enroll in public and private high schools in the city. However, Cheryl says the kids from ICS come to Young Warriors High School after failing in high schools in the area. She gets along with the Potawatomis and reaches out to others, and is good at networking.

Because of how difficult it is to teach at Young Warriors, the school has a 75–80% teacher turnover rate. When Cheryl interviews teachers, she is realistic in her assessment of the school, hoping to attract only those who will want the challenge and stay. Many of the students at Young Warriors have been abandoned by their parents, who have succumbed to the problems of poverty, such as drugs, alcohol, spousal abuse, and crime that lands them in jail. Cheryl wants the students to have adults who stay in their lives, adults they know they can count on to be there for them. That is the role she plays for them, as Grandmother. Even when she paints the bleakest picture of the school that she can, Cheryl says teaching at Young Warriors is still harder than the teachers had imagined. They don't believe her until they are there. She told me that Rita, their head teacher, didn't choose this job. As a new teacher, Midwest public schools sent her to teach at Young Warriors. On her first drive there, she had to ask for directions, for she had no idea where the school was. Rita is a former beautician and actress and, personality-wise, is not at all conducive to structure. At Young Warriors, she can be creative, inventive, and flexible, a fine fit for both the school and her. Rita's role in the school is that of Big Sister.

Cheryl's role in the school is that of matriarch—Grandmother. The students are afraid of her and do not want to disappoint her; they want to please her and earn her respect. Luke, who teaches Native American drumming, has the role of Dad, and his wife, Lynn, who teaches art, health, and parenting classes, has the role of Mom. They are a Native American couple who have been with the school from its beginning. The principal, Jeff, has the role of Uncle, and the counselor, Seth, is Big Brother. If the teachers can't get a role going with the students, they are seen as unnecessary and become excluded when they find they can't connect with the kids. Cheryl was not sure if three of the teachers I observed that week were returning. One of the teachers, the math teacher, was very unhappy. This was her first year teaching at Young Warriors, and she had come to realize that she needed more structure. In addition, the No Child Left Behind Act was making it impossible to keep Lynn and Luke, as they did not have teaching credentials, even though Luke has been teaching at the school since the year it opened and Lynn joined the staff the second year.[6]

Cheryl says Young Warriors' goal is to empower teens to make their own choices. She doesn't do marketing and doesn't seek recognition by the larger community, although the staff does enjoy an impeccable reputation and is known at a national level. The reward for them is the kids. When Cheryl started the school she was also a teacher, but now she attends only to administrative work. She sees her role as pushing and supporting the teachers and students in the school. The school size is actually larger than Cheryl and her staff want it to be. Ideally, they would have 70–75 students, which is what they started with. But with so small a number of students, they were unable to offer teachers competitive salaries and insurance benefits. So they agreed to take on 25 more students. Cheryl wants the school to be small enough that there is a sense of intimacy and the teachers and staff know all the students. My observations over the week showed me that the school did indeed have a sense of intimacy. The students and teachers all know one another on a first-name basis. The teachers know the issues the students deal with in their lives and address them directly, making it more possible for the students to succeed in the school and pass. And the students are succeeding. For students who have dropped out, failed, or been kicked out of other schools (the Native American drop-out rate is over 35%, Reyhner, 1992[7]), Young Warriors offers them a way to graduate and earn a high school diploma.

The teachers and staff at Young Warriors treat the students with respect, as young adults, and they have adapted the school structure to fit the needs of the students. They use a pass/fail system rather than grades, and base passing on meeting 25 competencies. Cheryl says, "If they have 24 competencies, they do not pass." The teachers give the students the message on a daily basis that they can pass, and make themselves available for tutoring before and after school. Many students have trouble with attendance because of other responsibilities. Inability to attend school regularly is a major reason many students drop out of regular high schools. Many of them have children and must stay home if their kids are sick; many have jobs supporting themselves and their families after school. They are teens dealing with serious adult issues, and sometimes those issues affect their ability to get to school or do their schoolwork.

The week I was there, the students talked continually about what was going on in U.S. politics and the threat of war with Iraq. When that threat became real on Wednesday, with the announcement that U.S. soldiers had invaded Iraq, the anxieties of the students became heightened. Many of them had family members in the military and were gravely concerned for their safety. The students had a schoolwide discussion about their plan to take a field trip to Chicago and voted to cancel it. Many decided it was not worth the risk of terrorist attacks, knowing that the Sears Tower in Chicago is on the terrorist "hit list." Others had children and they did not want to risk being injured. As an observer, I was struck by the mature conversations I heard that week by a group of high school students discussing political issues at a level of sophistication that I had not heard until the release of Michael Moore's documentary *Fahrenheit 9/11*. The students knew about the Bush family's connection to the Saudi Arabians and also about the oil issues in Iraq. For the entire week, they researched the issues on the Internet and discussed the topic with their teachers and one another.

Young Warriors High School is an amazing place to be. I came to the school bearing gifts for the students, teachers, and staff. At the end of my week observing, the students and staff thanked me for coming and gave me gifts in return. The greatest gift of all, though, is the one Cheryl talks about: the kids. I saw many young warriors developing at this alternative high school who will grow up and continue the work Cheryl began. They will continue the fight and give this old war pony some much-deserved rest.

"EDUCATION IS LIKE A MEDICINE"

I started the day at Young Warriors High School in Luke Lightfoot's class, as recommended by both teachers and students. For first period on Monday morning, Luke teaches Native American drumming. According to the schedule, class starts at 8:10 A.M., but it doesn't actually start then. The teachers wait, stall, and talk to students who are eating breakfast (breakfast is free for both teachers and students, and is provided by the Indian Community School across the street), while waiting for the students who have not yet arrived at school. Many students have situations at home that make it difficult for them to get to school on time; others get there early, for the warmth, food, and companionship.

Luke starts teaching around 8:30 A.M. Six students are here, two girls and four guys. He reminds the students about assignments that are due. Then he has them name the five tribes in the area and does a history timeline (12,000 years ago—oldest tribes here). He tells us that the Bear clan, his clan, serves as the police of the people. He talks about Native American culture and values. "Education is like a medicine," Luke says. He talks about his life in Chicago, and where he learned Native American history. Luke picks up a broom and sweeps the area where they will be playing the drum. As he sweeps, he tells us his mother was from the Snake clan, and that clan's job is to clean the environment, and so he sweeps in honor of his mother. "Keep the environment clean," he says to the students as he sweeps. Luke Lightfoot is a Native singer. In his room is a map of American Indians and Alaskan Natives in the United States. He tells the class he can stay for free in all the 480 tribal areas and that he is treated like a king—but he has to be a role model and do well, for people are watching him. Then he talks to the students about the medicine wheel being a circle, and that "A circle is *inclusive,* everything is in, contained within; it is *not* exclusive as some say." He draws a circle on the blackboard and gets the students to tell him the directions: north, south, east, west; the seasons: winter, summer, spring, fall; the colors: white, yellow, red, black (the order of the colors varies); and the ages of one's life: spring is 0–7, summer is 8–20, fall is 21–50, and winter is 51 and older. Luke talks about how the lower part of the brain is our collective memory of the past, and that all of us come from tribal people.

Four of the students look African American, one looks Native American, and one is sleeping, so I can't tell how he looks.[8] Luke mentions the year he graduated from high school and I learn that we are close in age. Luke continues on: He has three eagle feathers that were given to him in official ceremonies on three separate public occasions. An eagle feather is earned through bravery and service. A Native American girl with long black hair, Cheyenne, comes into the class at 8:45 A.M., sent by Rita; she sits at a side desk in a chair that looks like it is for a classroom aide (i.e., it is padded and not attached to a desk) and listens to Luke. He tells us he wasn't drafted for Vietnam because he was labeled "mentally unfit"—he couldn't take orders. He doesn't like being called names. It wasn't until he was 45 years old that he got over his inability to control his temper; rudeness still upsets him to this day. He's sharing stories, imparting moral lessons to the students. And he is letting them see that he is not perfect, that he has made mistakes, but that he has learned from his mistakes. As he tells the three feathers story, one student lays his head down (8:57 A.M.). Luke tells us he got three feathers without having to go to war. He says he is not feeling well, and he forgot something that he was supposed to bring in to class. He says his life is at a low right now. As he shares stories about his life and the problems he has, Luke tells the students his goal is to get them to think about such problems: "How do you handle them? With grace, with cheer? A smile on your face? School is so important—it is supposed to be about you, not about me. I'm trying to convince you that school is so important." Luke tells the students he has dreams: "To see a person of color or a woman as president. Equal representation—what does that mean?" Then he declares, "Education and Culture—you need both. People try to sever these two, and they sever us. Heart–Mind–Body–Spirit. They go together."

Luke has a medicine wheel/drum. He tells us heartbeat drumming comes from the womb—the mother's heart. He is debating about singing today because of the bad cold he has. But he decides to sing. So, for the last part of the class (9:12 A.M.), the students arrange their chairs in a circle around a big drum and hit the drum together with a long stick that is covered on the end that strikes the drum. Each student has a sheet of the words they are to sing (Luke gave me a copy to see, but took it back at the end of class). Cheyenne joins the students in their drumming and singing. She does solo parts and is very good. (She told me later that she had taken the class before and had learned the words then.) After one song, Luke points out that the drum is flat this week because of the moisture in the air. He also tells them he will soon be teaching at two other schools in addition to this one.

Luke only teaches Native American drumming for the first period in the day, but I saw him at Young Warriors off and on all day for the entire week I was there. He was always there for the smudging ceremony after lunch. The class takes a pre-test and post-test at the beginning and end of the 9-week course. They have to record themselves singing the two songs they have to master. The next song they sing is from the Stony Tribe in Alberta, Canada. They end their drumming and singing with 5 minutes to spare, which they spend talking about what they did this weekend; some students continue drumming on the tables with their fingers.

Luke has been teaching at the school since its beginning. He plays a role of Father in the school, and many of the students call him Dad. His wife, Lynn, teaches art, health, and parenting classes, and the students call her Mom. The next time I saw him was during assembly, which occurs every day after lunch, with all the students and teachers in attendance. They meet in a large room that is tiered; mounted swivel chairs with tabletops look down upon a stage area. At the first assembly on Monday, Luke talked to the students about Friday being a day to pray for world peace. "It's a day to think about world peace and not eat or drink all day." This is a problem for him because he is diabetic and has to get a shot of insulin in order to fast. He talks about Native American values, that we are borrowing this earth and that we need to think about the kids, the next seven generations. He told a story about the 1842 Irish potato famine and how the Choctaw sent the Irish money to help them out. In 1992, 150 years later, the Irish came to Oklahoma to thank them.

Next, a student comes to the front of the assembly room and lights an herb (sage) in a sea shell for the Blessing of the Ash. Using an eagle feather, she waves smoke from the burning ash on each person, and then each person waves the smoke over him- or herself from head to foot. It is a blessing and a cleansing activity that is very centering for the students. They used to do this ceremony at the beginning and end of the week, but now they enact it every day after lunch. It is completely quiet in the room while they do the ceremony. Some kids put their heads down if they don't want to participate in the smudging. They can also choose to sit in the middle of the assembly hall instead of near the outside aisles if they don't want to participate. It is mostly African Americans who have their heads down, but the number of those who participate varies all week. The teachers participate in the smudging ceremony as well. After the Blessing of the Ash, students quietly get up and go to their afternoon classes.

Rita leads the assembly at Tuesday's school meeting after lunch. She raises her hand and yells: "OK, quiet for 5 seconds." She waits 5 seconds then says: "Good afternoon, ladies and gentlemen." She reads the announcements and people start talking again. She stops and waits. It becomes quiet again. They plan the field trip to Chicago's Field Museum. Rita invites the other teachers to make their announcements from where they stand on the sides or at the back of the assembly room. Then Luke talks about Iraq, about praying for peace, about moral lessons, and thinking about fellow human beings. Then comes the smudging. It is a sacred ceremony similar to meditation. The hall is silent and they all wait.

At Wednesday's assembly, the principal, Jeff, speaks to the students about supporting the troops now that there's a war going on. He says, "They're in danger, whether you agree with U.S. policy or not." The students and Jeff discuss the possibility of canceling their field trip to Chicago's Field Museum next Friday. Jeff asks the teachers to poll the students during their mentoring time following the assembly as to whether or not they still want to go on the field trip to Chicago. After Jeff leaves, the teachers make their announcements. Luke sings a Native American song for Iraq and the soldiers. There is total silence in the assembly room, and then the smudging ceremony begins.

9:20 A.M., Friday

It is my last day observing at Young Warriors High School and I want to go back to Luke's class. There are five male students in attendance. They are having a discussion about Christopher Columbus and the naming of Native Americans as "Indians," purporting that what is taught in U.S. history books is a complete fabrication. Luke tells the students that 18 countries claim Christopher Columbus. He informs them that India was called Hindustan at the time of Columbus's voyage, not India. He explains that the name "Indian" is not a mistake made by Columbus trying to find a route to India: "Children of God is pronounced *Corpeus de Indios Dios* in Spanish. *Indios* means Children of God." He finishes class with: "The answers to these questions are in the archives. Your job is to try and find the answers." Luke's job is not only to teach the students moral lessons and serve as a role model, but to deconstruct the stories White people tell about current and past events. He is the Jacques Derrida of the Native American people. For today's drumming, Luke tells the students the drum can instruct us to turn away from the ways of war and toward the ways of friendship. Now they are drumming (9:24 A.M.). The kids listen to Luke's moral lessons. After one song, he talks about how "The drum can help you get to yourself and let go of the other masks, the 'tough guy' mask, that you put on [to] survive in that violent world." They play one more song, a short one. Then class is over. During the week, I heard a student say that she saw Cheryl standing outside the classroom while Luke and the students were drumming and singing. It brought tears to her eyes.

CONNECTING THEORY WITH PRACTICE, PART II

I came across a book by Eduardo and Bonnie Duran (1995), *Native American Postcolonial Psychology*, which discusses the issues Cheryl and her staff face at Young Warriors. The Durans are involved in therapy work with Native Americans that has been very successful. Part I of their book presents their theory and Part II investigates the Durans' clinical praxis for working with problems such as alcohol, family intervention, suicide, and community intervention. The Durans write about the pain Native Americans experience as a result of their colonization. They remind us of Black Elk's vision of restoring the hoop with seven generations, and suggest that now is the time for the restoration of the hoop.[9] They have developed a postcolonial paradigm to deal with the problems of living a healthy and balanced life in the Native American community. They argue that Western psychology is not able to help Native Americans, and to assume otherwise is psychological and philosophical imperialism.

The Durans (1995) present Native Americans as having a *soul wound*. They have experienced internalized oppression from years of colonization and genocide. Native American history with Westerners began with contact and environmental shock. The second stage was economic competition, when lands and wildlife (such as the buffalo), which were used for sustenance, were destroyed. The third stage was the invasion and war period, when the United States enacted a policy of extermination by military force (Brown, 1971). The fourth stage was the subjugation and reservation period, when Native Americans were forcefully removed from their lands and herded onto reservations. The fifth stage was the boarding school period, when children were forcefully taken from their families and placed in boarding schools, thus destroying the fabric of Native American life—the family unit. The sixth stage was the forced relocation and termination period, when people were moved off their reservations and into cities in the 1950s.

The Durans (1995) compare the Native American experience to the Holocaust, only it is not acknowledged. Native Americans have experienced forced acculturation, and the ongoing trauma that resulted from this (Morris, 1997). Their experience of oppression and being taught in boarding schools and missionary schools that their way of life must be abandoned in order for them to become American and succeed, has led to internalized oppression, which generates self-hatred. Self-hatred internalized results in suicide. Self-hatred externalized results in violent crimes, such as domestic violence. The Durans refer to the obliteration of the Native American male's role of warrior, which has led to repressed feelings of loss and rage resulting in alcoholism, suicide, and abuse. Shame leads to death. The Durans show that Native American women have been standing beside their men in support, as in the Sun Dance ceremony, for half a millennium (symbolically). They live with the constant reminder of defeat, because the colonizer is all around them.

The model that Eduardo Duran (1995) developed for his therapy practice describes the five stages of the soul wound Native Americans have experienced: (1) Impact or Shock, (2) Withdrawal and Repression (Warrior Regression), (3) Acceptance and Repression (Magical Thinking), (4) Compliance and Anger (Decompensation), and (5) Trauma Mastery (Healing). Duran advocates in his praxis that you have to name the trauma and encounter the perpetrator before healing can begin. The Durans encourage the validation of traditional values. They discuss the Plains Indians' use of dream interpretation, which they note is much older than Carl Jung's work. They compare the Western role of therapists with that of Native American shamans. Shamans use dancing, drumming, and chanting to achieve emotional arousal. The sweat lodge ceremony and the smudging ceremony such as the one used at Young Warriors also have therapeutic results. The Durans state that a therapist should be able to develop a "center" in the client from which she or he can gain strength. The patient needs to become aware of the cause of his or her suffering. For Native Americans, this means ridding themselves of guilt and exorcising the internalized oppressor. In the second half of their book, they discuss the problems named above through stories and describe how their approach works.

When I read the Durans' (1995) *Native American Postcolonial Psychology*, I had already spent a week at Young Warriors. I was struck by the extent to which the staff adhered to the Durans' principles and served as a vivid example of how to help young Native Americans and other involuntary minorities, such as African Americans and Mexican Americans, recover from their soul wounds (Ogbu, 1991). Certainly, the students' lives are powerful examples of the kinds of harm done to people when they are forced to acculturate to a colonizing culture that teaches them self-hatred. Cheryl and her staff help teens who live with the results of parents and communities that suffer from alcoholism, drug addiction, abuse, and suicide. It is a very difficult job to help these teens recover and heal. The children at Young Warriors are at different stages of the Durans' soul wound: shock, withdrawal, repression, compliance, and anger. Each day brings a new trauma for some students and relief for others.

Notice, though, that Cheryl takes on the role of the warrior to inspire her students. Notice that the school validates Native American values and develops in students a center from which they can derive strength. The smudging ceremony the school practices daily is a cleansing and centering activity that affirms Native American cultural values and ways of life. There are many more stories of teacher–student activities I observed than what I am able to include here, but just through Luke's drumming class one can see that the role he plays is that of a shaman, a therapist. He uses drumming and singing/chanting to engender emotional arousal and help with healing. He also uses the technique of critiquing American history from a Native American perspective to help his students become aware of the internalized oppression they experience, and to help them find a way to exorcise its effect: self-hatred.

Through my observations of Native American schools and reading about Native American cultures and how Native American students are faring in U.S. schools, I have come to realize that what they are going through represents a very important issue for any form of democratic theory—especially for a relationally focused, pluralistic democratic theory such as that which I develop here. They are struggling to maintain a sense of *shared identity* through their cultural roots and their traditions. It is only through the ability to maintain shared identities that they are able to develop healthy individual identities that enable them to participate as citizens in a democracy-of their-own-making.

A strong assumption of individualism, such as that in classical liberalism, takes for granted that the individual has a healthy self-esteem. It treats individuals atomistically, as if they sprout out of the ground like cabbages, whole and able to think for themselves. Democratic theory based on individualism assumes a position of power that ignores the role that childcare providers play in nurturing young children into adulthood, thus making their role invisible. It is a democratic theory that is from a majority perspective that can afford to ignore the important role that others' shared identities play in forming one's self-identity. Liberal democratic theories assume positions of power and authority—the colonizer's view; they are not theories that those with limited resources and power can afford to embrace. Collective communitarian cultures such as Native American culture are based on a very different view of the individual. In collective cultures, the community is the foundation for development of the individual. Rather than viewing others as impinging on individual freedom, collective cultures describe others as supplying the support and nurturing necessary for individuals to develop and grow. Freedom is something that comes with the help of others, not something that is thwarted by others. For children raised in collective cultures, to lose contact with their immediate family and larger clan or tribe is to lose the base of support that helps define who they are. To lose touch with their social group, to be asked or forced to abandon their cultural traditions, is to risk losing their self-identity. Self-identity is based on shared identity with others, and those others are significant others with whom one has deep emotional bonds.

CONCLUSION

We have learned from the teachers at Diné Primary School and Young Warriors High School and from the research of Native Americans presented here that the issue of acculturation by a majority culture that assumes a strong individualistic perspective must be addressed. When one comes from a collective cultural perspective, it is impossible to digest a heavy dose of classical liberal individualism without becoming sick. The sickness can come in forms that seem benign, but they have proven to be lethal to the psyche of Native Americans, individually and collectively. It is vital for indigenous parents, community members, and teachers to claim authority over how their cultural world views are represented to their children if they are to have a chance to grow up with healthy self-esteem. Self-identity is dependent on shared identities with others like us. This is the main lesson I learned from visiting Diné Primary School and Young Warriors High School.

The teachers and principals at Diné Primary School and Young Warriors High School know that individuals are not autonomous; they do not sprout from the ground fully grown and able to function and take care of themselves. They begin their lives as babies in need of someone else's loving care. That caretaker will not be able to raise his or her children and help them feel good about themselves if he or she drops out of school, suffers from unemployment, and turns to alcoholism and/or drug use as a form of self-medication to help him or her cope with the pain of living in a racist, capitalist, patriarchal society that does not recognize his or her way of life as viable. A transactional view of individuality recognizes that we become individuals through our relationships with others. We share our identities with others who help us become our own selves. And those others, our family members, are connected to others as well, their clan and larger tribe, within an even larger global community situated within a natural, living, breathing world.

My time spent with Native Americans and my research on Native American education have left me with vivid experiences I cannot forget and do not want to forget. The people I have gotten to know live within a country that presses upon them an either/or logic—either you embrace our way of living and the meaning we give to this world, or you die, a relic of the past. If you protest this arrangement too strongly, we will shoot you, for you have become a threat to our security. There is no middle ground for coexistence and cooperation from a Euro-Western perspective; the only option is to abandon your culture and assimilate to ours. Our way is the right way, the true way, and your way is primitive, savage, and backward, and full of myths and legends. I greatly admire these people who have become my friends for their courage and their fortitude, for their adaptability and their perseverance. They have found ways to survive and even keep their cultures alive for over 500 years of efforts to annihilate them. Since spending time with the Native American community, I find I am no longer able to complain about political conditions in the United States that I am unhappy about. What am I complaining about? My suffering is less than theirs. I am called to act, to become a warrior, too. I feel tremendous strength and courage, for I know it is possible to endure and survive, to live among the destructive forces of the last 500 years and move beyond them. We can get beyond Locke and Rousseau and change the path we are on. We have Native Americans to guide us, inspire us, and show us the way.

I know there is hope for us to move beyond the either/or logic upon which classical liberalism is built and recognize the need to embrace a both/and logic that emphasizes how connected and related we all are to one another, because I have met people like Cheryl and Luke Lightfoot. I came away from Young Warriors feeling a strong need to roll up my sleeves and get to work. And I came away with a great deal of realistic hope.

On the last day of observations at Young Warriors, after Rita called me up to the stage and gave me two gifts from the school, the teachers gave their announcements. Then the smudging ceremony began, the Blessing of the Ash. Everyone became quiet and Dan started the sage burning and began walking around, carrying the sage in a seashell, wafting smoke over people with the eagle feather. When he came to me he said very softly as he wafted the smoke on me, "Thank you for coming." My heart sang. I had worked so hard to get here and often wondered if I would make it, but I knew it was important to keep trying until I found a way. How can we begin to rethink democracies-always-in-the-making from a relational and pluralistic position, and not let Native American wisdom inform our thinking? For me, I carry that wisdom in my heart, with me still, and have planted sage in my garden, to smell it every time I walk by or need to remember.

I hear the voices of the teachers at Diné Primary School asking the text-book representatives politely and quietly, "Where are the Native Americans in these texts?" I tell my students, future teachers, to look for them in their texts. It is not possible to be included in history's textbook if one's voice is distorted or co-opted by the vast majority. The choices are too few—only assimilation or annihilation. It is important to listen with attention and receptivity, to listen with care so that we who are listening allow ourselves to be changed—forever. Then we will discover just how much we share in our common desire for plu-ralistic, relational democracies-always-in-the-making.

In the next chapter, I present another culture—Japanese and Japanese American—which I chose because, as a collective culture, they seem to be thriving within America's individualistic model of democracy. I was surprised to discover that, in some ways, they are not thriving. Children of Japanese descent, too, are struggling in U.S. schools.[10]

Chapter 5

Nurturing Communities

In East Tennessee we have a Japanese Saturday School that is located at a local college. On Saturdays, Japanese parents from all over the geographic area drive their Japanese American children (aged 6–18) to school so they can maintain as well as expand their knowledge of the Japanese language and culture. The school started 16 years ago with two families and five children, and now there are 150–160 students enrolled in Japanese Saturday School (JSS). The school is sponsored by the Japanese Ministry of Education and has a principal who was sent to them from Japan to help run the school, but like schools in Japan, the principal is there in an honorary role to represent the school to the parents and community at large (Ellington, 1992; Finkelstein, Imamura, & Tobin, 1991). The teachers and head teacher and administrative assistant run the school, making curriculum decisions and determining daily activities. The 14 teachers and head teacher are all Japanese, many of them college-age students with various majors, graduate students, or parents who live in the area. The teachers do not necessarily have teaching certificates or much experience in teaching, but they all have many years of experience as students in Japanese schools. They bring that experience to this school and have designed one that is very similar to what I experienced in Japan, with some adjustments to accommodate American culture. Students in my College of Education, Health, and Human Sciences who work at JSS invited me to visit the school. I spent the fall of 2003 attending Japanese Saturday School and have returned each fall for Sports Day.

Through my contacts at JSS, I was invited to visit an elementary school in Japan (School #3) in May of 2004, and had the wonderful opportunity of staying at the home of the mother of the school director for JSS. Asami Segi, a graduate student in the World Language/English as a Second Language program at the University of Tennessee, and a former teacher at JSS, accompanied me to Japan and served as my translator during the week we spent in School #3, which has 420 students enrolled in grades 1–6 (all of whom were Japanese except for one student who was Japanese and Filipino). We had great fun staying with Buba (Grandma) and we rode bicycles to school along with the children in the neighborhood. We even had the opportunity to go on the annual overnight field trip with the 5th graders (we went for the second day and returned on the train with the students). It was not until I visited School #3 that I realized how close JSS is to the Japanese school experience and that, through my visits to JSS in the United States, I was actually able to get a strong sense of what Japanese education is like at the elementary through high school level. JSS was the majority Japanese American school I visited in the United States and School #3 was the school in Japan.

In this chapter, I offer a broad comparison of Japanese education with American education. In the first part, I look at the role of the teacher in the classroom and some of the daily practices that make up the informal and hidden curriculum. I turn to Catherine Lewis (1995) and her wonderful *Educating Hearts and Minds: Reflections on Japanese Preschool and Elementary Education* to help me with my analysis. I spent one week in one elementary school in Japan whereas Lewis spent over 14 years visiting more than 50 Japanese preschool and elementary classrooms from 1 day to 4 months. Her richly developed descriptions helped confirm for me how the focus of preschool and early elementary curriculum can help children learn to work together cooperatively and that, contrary to our perspective of Japanese education, kindergartens in Japan center on free play, not academic instruction, and Japanese elementary schools strike a much better balance between work and play than elementary schools in the United States. Lewis's work informs the themes of *shared responsibility, shared authority,* and *shared identity* that I introduced in Chapters 2, 3, and 4 and develop further here. An excellent chapter in Chantal Mouffe's (2000) *The Democratic Paradox* contributes to my discussion about the value of conflict and how conflict leads to integration.

Americans have many stereotypes about Japanese education that are based on Euro-Western views of a society founded on Confucian thought and perceive Japanese culture as exotic and strange, or as a possible threat. More rare is a deep understanding of Japan as an insider to the culture or even as someone who can appreciate the culture. In the United States, Japanese students enjoy the stereotype of being perceived as high achieving and excellent, one of the "model minorities" believed to be successful (Nieto, 1992). Americans have a hard time seeing the racism Japanese families still live with, thinking that racism against the Japanese resides in our dark past in our placement of Japanese American citizens in internment camps during World War II (Spring, 2004). We see in this chapter that Japanese American students still have issues and concerns about their ethnicity and that they and their teachers and parents have much to teach us about moving in a more compassionate and equalitarian direction in our democracies-always-in-the-making.

EXPLORING THE TEACHER'S ROLE IN JAPAN

Teachers in Japan are highly respected (Ellington, 1992; Hood, 2001; Lewis, 1995). This deep respect can be attributed to Confucian philosophy, which was imported from China and has strongly influenced the Japanese culture (Ellington, 1992; Hood, 2001; Okano & Tsuchiya, 1999). Confucianism stresses moral perfection and the important role that education plays in achieving moral perfection. A teacher at the elementary level is just as respected as a professor in higher education, and is given the same honorary title of *sensei* (Stevenson & Stigler, 1992). The Japanese have developed rituals that show their respect for their *sensei:* When the teacher is about to begin teaching, the students rise and bow and greet the teacher, letting him or her know they are ready to learn; at the end of the class, the students rise and bow again to thank the teacher for the lesson (Finkelstein, Imamura, & Tobin, 1991). Being respected does not mean that the teachers in Japan are feared. They are honored for their knowledge and wisdom, not for the amount of control they impose on the students. In fact, it is not the teacher's role in Japan to be a disciplinarian, as it is in the United States. They do not have to worry about handling classroom management, for the students have this responsibility. Their job is to teach, and the students' job is to learn self-control and self-discipline with the help of their peers so they can learn from their teachers. I was struck by this difference in roles. The main concern of teachers in the United States is classroom management, and I was saddened to realize that American schools feel like prisons to Japanese American children and that American teachers scare them.

The following stories are from my observations at JSS in the United States and School #3 in Japan, and they illustrate the different roles teachers have in Japanese and American schools.

Opening of the School Day

I observed students arrive for classes in East Tennessee and in Japan. In Japan, the elementary children walk or ride their bikes to school, rain or shine. If it rains, they carry yellow umbrellas that make them easy to see. Parents do not escort their children to school; the children get themselves there. All elementary schools are located within walking distance of the children's homes (Ellington, 1992; Lewis, 1995). When they get to school, they change out of their outside shoes and put on slippers, and they then proceed to their classrooms, where they store their backpacks and visit with their friends. During this arrival time, there are no teachers in the classrooms or halls supervising the children's behavior. The teachers are in the teachers' office. In East Tennessee, the parents escort their children to school because it is too far away for the children to walk or ride their bikes. Parents may drop their children off in front of the school or park their cars and walk them to the school door, but they never enter unless they are volunteering in the school. Parents help in the school library and one parent sits at the end of each hallway as a hall monitor for recess, lunch, and breaks. The monitors are there at the request of the college on whose campus the school is located; it is not part of the custom in Japan. Even in East Tennessee at JSS, when the children arrive at school, their teachers are not in their classrooms or in the halls supervising their behavior. They are in the teachers' office having their morning meeting.

In a typical Japanese classroom, there is a desk or table in the room (it may be at the front, off to the side, or in the middle of the room) for the teacher to use, but it is kept empty until the teacher walks into the room with whatever he or she needs for that particular lesson. Japanese teachers do not store their supplies and lesson plans in this desk. Instead, teachers' desks are in a large, open room fitting 10 to 12 desks arranged a long column of face-to-face desks. Teachers who teach the same grade have desks beside one another, and at JSS, where there is only one teacher per grade, the elementary teachers are clustered together, the middle school teachers are beside one another, and the high school teachers share the same section of the room. There are no walls in this large room. If one stands up at his or her desk, it is possible to look across the room and see all the teachers. Teacher meetings begin with the principal thanking the teachers for work they did the day before or making an announcement (almost all principals are male; Okano & Tsuchiya, 1999). The principal might not even be there, in which case the head teacher starts the meeting. Then the teachers take turns running the meeting with a different teacher handling this responsibility each day. The leader stands at her or his desk and makes his or her announcements and then recognizes the other teachers, who rise to make their announcements. When all the announcements have been made, the leader adjourns the meeting.

Teachers in Japanese schools have a long day, arriving around 8 A.M. and staying until 5 P.M., averaging a 55-hour workweek (Okano & Tsuchiya, 1999). But they do not spend all of that time in a classroom, isolated from their colleagues and solely responsible for the well-being of their students. Between 8:30 and 8:45 A.M., homeroom teachers at the elementary level go to their classroom to run a classroom meeting, similar to the teachers' meeting, and then begin the first period of classes. At the high school level, students may meet in their homerooms at the end of the day. Teachers are engaged in teaching for a total of 20 hours per week, less than 50% of their time (Stevenson & Stigler, 1992; Okano & Tsuchiya, 1999). When they are not in their classrooms teaching, they are not expected to supervise students. They can usually be found in the teachers' room, working at their desks prepping for lessons or grading, on the computer doing research for lessons, or in a committee meeting (Stevenson & Stigler, 1992). In addition to the rows of teachers' desks, the teacher rooms have a work area where there are computers, copy machines, paper cutters, and so forth. There is also a lounge area with a refrigerator, sink, and microwave. Tea and often coffee are always available, as well as some kind of snack. Some of the schools have a couch and coffee table where the teachers can relax and eat their lunch.

Recess, Breaks (55 Minutes of the Day)

When teachers enter their classrooms to teach their lessons, it is not their role to take charge of the classroom and get the students quiet and seated in their desks. Student classroom monitors (*toban,* class leaders) have this job, and everyone takes turn having a day when they are a monitor. Since all the students know they will have to stand up at the front of the room and ask their classmates to get quiet and ready for the lesson, or lead them down the hall to physical education class, students listen when one of their classmates tells them to do something such as "Get ready for the lesson" (Lewis, 1995). The teacher goes to her or his desk and waits for the student monitors to get control of the class. Then the *toban* will announce to the teacher that the class is ready and the students will stand, bow to the teacher, and say they are ready for their lesson. The teacher bows to them as well, saying she or he is ready to teach them. When the lesson is over, the students stand again, thank the teacher for the lesson, and then bow, and the teacher bows in return. Then the teacher might leave the room or stay at the desk to organize his or her materials, but he or she is done overseeing the classroom. The students are now on break.

After each of the five periods of the day, students get a break. At School #3, the break is 5 minutes long between periods 1 and 2, and it is 20 minutes long between periods 2 and 3. Between periods 3 and 4, it is 5 minutes again. Lunchtime occurs between periods 4 and 5, and then the same pattern follows in the afternoon between periods 5 and 6 (5 minutes) and between period 6 and club activities (20 minutes). During breaks and recess, teachers are usually in the teachers' office having a cup of tea. Children can stay in the classroom and play with one another, get a drink of water or use the bathroom, run and play in the halls, or go outside and play. At School #3, all the kids in the elementary school take break and recess at the same time. Imagine 400 kids out on the playground unsupervised. You would never see this in America! Because of fear for children's safety and fear of lawsuits, children are *never* left unattended in the United States. Yet, in my 3 weeks of observation in Japanese schools, I never witnessed a child harmed nor did I see personal or school property damaged. I also didn't see children being wild and crazy. I saw laughing, running, noisy elementary children having fun with one another and I saw teenagers asleep during break or chatting with friends in their classrooms.

The situation was the same at JSS. All the elementary children take recess at the same time. No one lines up the children and marches them out to the playground. No one blows a whistle on the playground to line them up and bring them back in. They come and go on their own and don't seem to have any trouble finding their way back to class. The volunteer parents sit at the desks in the hallway reading a book or writing a letter and chatting with students; on parent went outside and leaned against the building smoking a cigarette. The parent supervision seems necessary to accommodate the rules of the college where JSS rents school space. When it is time for the next period at JSS, the parents ring a big, hand-held, old-fashioned school bell. At School #3, classical music comes on the intercom system as a signal that it's time for students to return to their classroom.

What happens on a day when the children cannot go out to play due to the weather? A typhoon went over Japan while Asami and I were there observing. On the day of heavy rain, the children were free to roam up and down the hall, in the multipurpose room, and in the gym. They were free to use the library, and many went in and checked out a book. Asami and I sat in the multipurpose room and chatted with students during their 20-minute break. During the 5-minute break, we followed the teachers down to the teachers' office for a cup of tea while the children played in their rooms and in the halls, unsupervised. The principal worried that children might get hurt, and apparently there were a few minor injuries due to roughhousing, but I never witnessed an injury even though I was alert to this possibility.

Lunchtime, Cleanup, and Rest Time (95 Minutes of the Day)

Lunchtime and the cleanup and rest times that follow lunchtime were different at School #3 from at JSS. But again, I think the difference was due to location. At JSS, the students spill out into the courtyard at noon and eat their lunches while they sit around and chat with one another. Only the first and second graders are allowed to eat in their rooms. Everyone brings their lunch from home. After they are done eating, they play ball games such as football and soccer on the large campus lawns. If they want to play in their classrooms they can do so as well. Lunchtime lasts for an hour, and then the afternoon often will become a time for more physical activity, such as tennis or another form of physical education. At the elementary school, children clean their classrooms at the end of the day, not because they have to, since the college has a janitorial staff, but because the staff and parents think it is an important part of the curriculum that teaches children the value of caring for their environment.

At School #3, lunchtime is from 12:25 to 1:15 P.M. for the entire school. The classrooms are turned into lunchrooms. Desks are pulled together into groups of four, and the red shelves in the front of the room are moved to function as the serving area. The children put on white chef hats and white aprons and then wash up. One student's job is to bring a bucket of water to wash the tables, and the children wash their desks and the serving shelves. Then the children put out their own placemat/scarf on their desks along with their chopsticks and holder. The teacher puts on an apron, too (each one is unique, reflecting the teacher's personality). The lunch preparation is completely done by the children, with the teacher in the role of assistant. The children go to the end of the hall and get the milk, bowls and plates (which are in dish racks), and silverware. This kitchenware is placed in the serving area, and then the children bring in the containers of food. A carton of milk and a straw are set on each student's desk. When the servers are ready, the students line up with trays and are served by their classmates. The kids are rowdy and excited while doing all of this. The teacher is still in the room, but does not direct and does not seem to be in charge. The teacher is not trying to control them, but watches and sometimes helps if there is a need.

On the first day of lunch I watched the kids serve fish ball and salad, and then rice, soup, and orange wedges (kids pull the oranges apart, they are pre-cut and in big plastic bags). Classical music plays throughout the school during lunch. The children wait until all are served before they eat. One student has the responsibility of making a tray for the teacher, and while I and my translator/graduate student were visiting, a tray of food was made for each of us as well. When all the children sit down, the two class leaders (*nichoku*, a boy and a girl who rotate daily so everyone has a turn) go to the front of the classroom and announce that it is time to eat. If there is food left over, this is announced and people who want seconds come forward and help themselves. When all are done eating, an announcement is made that it is time to line up for returning the trays. The children stack their dishes and trays back in the holders and the carriers take them away. They fold up their mats and aprons and caps, and put away their chopsticks. The food and clean dishes are trucked into the school and distributed to each floor by elevator. When lunch is finished, the children return the dirty dishes to the metal containers in the hall. The metal containers are then returned to the elevator, which goes to the basement where the trucks are waiting to cart them away. I was informed that the leftover food goes to the pig farmers.

The next activity on the school schedule at School #3 is cleaning the school, which occurs from 1:15 to 1:35 P.M. No bells ring for this; the classical music continues to play. Just as the whole school eats lunch at the same time in their classrooms, the whole school participates in cleaning. There are no janitors on staff at the school; the students and teachers clean the school.

There is a wheel chart at the front of the classrooms that shows eight groups of students (*han*, 4–6 children in a group) and eight jobs (Lewis, 1995). Each day the jobs change. Groups 1 and 2 clean the classroom, group 3 cleans the stairs, another group does the hallway, and another is responsible for the girls' or boys' bathroom (they sweep, mop, and scrub with the help of a teacher). In the back corner of the room, there is a closet that holds the brooms and other cleaning tools and supplies needed for the various jobs. When the two groups are cleaning the classroom, all the desks are pushed to the back with the chairs on top of the desks. Half of the floor is swept by one group and followed by another group that has the job of buffing the floor. Four children form a train with buffing cloths and go chugging across the room, one right after the other, to shine the floor. They have a great time cleaning! After they clean one side of the room, they push the desks over and clean the rest of the floor. The older students have more complex jobs such as cleaning the principal's office. The whole school is cleaning during this time, to classical music, with the teachers helping and participating, but again, not leading or controlling the activity.

After cleanup time, the whole school rests from 1:40 to 2:00 P.M. Teachers may direct students to copy lessons on the board and turn them in, and then have their free time. Some children rest their heads on their desks, some read, and some chat with their friends. During rest time, the classical music continues to play. When it ends, it is time for period 5, the last period of the school day.

CONNECTING THEORY WITH PRACTICE, PART I

Given that the structure of schools and the curriculum are determined at a national level by the Ministry of Education (*Monbusho*), it is safe to assume that what I saw in School #3 is common across the country (Hood, 2001; Okano & Tsuchiya, 1999; Stevenson & Stigler, 1992). The activities I have described happen every day in schools across Japan. They happen in similar form in Japanese Saturday Schools in the United States as well. These activities are an important part of the school curriculum, taking up 2½ hours each day in elementary school (which is 7½ hours long for the older children). For the people of Japan, these activities are part of their children's moral education curriculum, teaching students how to care for their environment and care for one another. They teach children how to work together on jobs in a way that is fun while still doing a good job and completing the task. These activities teach children that they are needed and have an important role to play in the daily care of their school. Their daily care of the school helps the children feel a sense of ownership and pride in their school. These activities also teach the children that time spent with one another in informal ways is valued, as more than a quarter of the day is devoted to these activities, more than is spent on any one academic subject. These daily, informal activities serve as a powerful method for teaching children about *shared responsibility*, as that is exactly what is modeled for them and what they participate in each day.

As we discussed in Chapter 2, *shared responsibility* is an important concept in the relational, pluralistic democratic theory I am developing. This relational democratic theory is based on an assumption that people are social beings who are in transactional relationships with one another as well as with the natural world. Starting with an assumption of transactional relations leads to very different ways of looking at democracy. With a transactional relational view of democracy, I no longer see others as getting in the way of my own freedom and development; I see others as important contributors to my development. I realize I cannot ignore the effects others have on me, and I understand that I am dependent on others to help me become "me." This does not mean I am socially determined by others, however, for I affect them as well. The relationship goes both ways, and we are all changed as a result of our transactions with one another. A transactional relational view of democracy positions the state in a role of nurturer, guide, and facilitator. As a teacher, my role is similar. I have resources and an enlarged perspective due to my greater wisdom (from my greater experience and education) that allow me to see ideas in greater depth; these are ideas I can share with students. It is my job to help students learn how to work together and help one another; it is not my job to do for them, for that will weaken rather then strengthen them. It is my job to encourage students and challenge them, and allow them to make mistakes and learn from those mistakes. If I try to control and contain them, students will fear me and not seek to learn from me. If I help students learn how to control and contain themselves, with one another's help for feedback and support, they will see me as a benefactor and guide rather than as an authoritarian. I will be someone they can trust and feel safe to open up to and with whom they can risk further growth.

Shared responsibility is not all that these daily routines teach the Japanese children, however. The teachers' role with the students positions them in such a way that they *share authority* with the children—another concept we discovered in Chapter 3 that is important to a transactional theory of democracy. The children in Japan do not find themselves under constant adult supervision. In fact, for more than a quarter of their day, they are very loosely supervised, if at all. The rest of the time—for example, when they are being taught mathematics, science, or Japanese language—an adult is in the classroom with them, but is not exercising authority over their behavior. The children learn each day that they have a share in the responsibility of making sure that they learn, by learning how to manage their behavior on the school grounds during recess and lunchtime, and while in the classroom having lessons. They are encouraged to learn how to get along with one another and to solve their disagreements with the help of their peers (Lewis, 1995). Teachers wait for the students to inform them when they are ready to learn. And teachers observe how the children work together and ask them how things went on the playground. At the end of the day, when they have a class meeting, the teachers sum up their observations of the day and encourage the children to improve their communication and relational skills or work harder. The students are encouraged to set goals to improve their behavior as they reflect on how the day went. However, during the day, the teachers will let the children struggle with their problems and try to solve them on their own (Lewis, 1995). Their relationship with the students within the classroom and during these informal times puts the teachers in a position where they share not only responsibility with their students, but also authority. The teachers are viewed as important sources of knowledge, as well-informed guides and authorities in their subject areas, and as resources, but *not* as authoritarians who are in charge of the children's behavior (Stevenson & Stigler, 1992). The children are responsible for their own behavior. And *all* of the people in the school *share responsibilities* in the children's well-being, thus placing them all in a position where they *share authority* as well. By delegating authority to groups of children or even individual children, the teachers are able to maintain a benevolent role with their students rather than an authoritarian role (Ellington, 1992; Lewis, 1995).

According to Catherine Lewis (1995), the Japanese preschool and early elementary curriculum focuses on helping children learn how to work together cooperatively. Kindergartens are centered on free play, not academic instruction. At the preschool level, the children spend quadruple the time in free play, 50% of their day, that kids in the United States spend. This free play is unregimented and often unsupervised (similar to what I observed at the elementary level). Lewis tells us that early childhood teachers spend most of their time responding to requests and integrating children who are isolated. The free play supplies situations from which they can learn. If free play alone does not supply enough situations, teachers will create situations where the children must learn how to work together to solve problems, such as bringing in large, heavy blocks the children can only lift and build with if they help one another or bringing in supplies that are small in number so the children have to learn how to take turns. During classroom meetings at the beginning and end of the day, teachers will share their observations of problems with the class and then let the children work on solving them. Much time is spent teaching the children how to function in the school setting so they can monitor themselves. Teachers respond to students' misbehavior with questions, explanations, or discussions, not with demands, punishments, or direct requests for compliance. There is much more use of persuasion and much less focus on external control in comparison with U.S. teachers' styles of teaching. Students assume much authority in Japan, even at the 1st-grade level. The students are taught from early on how to quiet their classmates, solve disputes, lead class meetings, and shape class rules and activities.

Shared authority is *not* what students commonly experience in American classrooms. In American schools, the day starts with principals and assistant principals standing in lunchrooms or in front of the school where buses drop off children, monitoring students' behavior. Teachers must take turns arriving early to school and being stationed in the cafeteria, auditorium, and designated classrooms to monitor students' behavior before school starts. Bells ring to announce when students may be out of their classrooms or in the halls between classes, and teachers must take turns standing in the halls monitoring students' behavior as they pass from one period to another. Many schools now have security personnel (police officers) in the halls between periods and before and after school. In most elementary and many middle schools, students are lined up and escorted to the restrooms, again, under the supervision of a teacher. Little time is allowed for students to pass from period to period, and little time is allowed for lunch, which is always supervised in school cafeterias and usually staggered so that not too many students are out of their classrooms at the same time. There is no such thing as recess for middle school and high school students in America, or extended break periods in the morning or afternoon, and recesses have almost become a thing of the past for elementary students (Kozol, 2005). Whenever elementary students are in trouble for not getting their assignments done on time or for misbehaving in class, the first form of punishment they usually face is loss of recess time. In contrast to Japanese schools, American schools feel oppressively controlling and strict. (And I haven't even begun to describe how teachers relate to children within the classroom to monitor and control their behavior!)

In teacher education programs in the United States, the first thing future teachers are taught is the importance of claiming authority over their classrooms. They are warned that if they try to be the children's friend, the children will not listen to them but instead will take advantage of a lenient teacher. Future teachers are taught the cliché: "Don't smile until Thanksgiving (or Christmas)." They are advised that it is best to start out tough and strict and ease up once the children learn the rules rather than start out lenient and get stricter when children don't obey the rules. Underlying the differences between the American approach to classroom management and the Japanese approach is not only a difference in the view of individuals-in-relation-to-others, with the Japanese having a more collective perspective and the Americans having a more individual perspective. Their differing styles of classroom management also reflect

differing views about children and their development. The Japanese believe
children are born innocent and do not intentionally do harm. They view early
childhood as a time for playing and exploring and see elementary school as the
time when children are socialized and learn to work with others. Few demands
or controls are imposed on young children (Stevenson & Stigler, 1992). Parents
do not begin to make demands for obedience, respect, and adherence to rules
until children reach age 6, which they view as the "age of reason." In America,
parents assume responsibility for educating and socializing their children from
birth until they enter school. We assume responsibility for correcting, controlling, and guiding our children, based on our cultural adherence to the Christian concept of "original sin," which assumes that children begin life as sinners
in need of discipline and control by adults to help them grow and develop into
good people. Americans, steeped in the Protestant roots of Calvin and Luther,
believe that children left to their own devices will go astray (Johnson & Reed,
2002). When our children enter school, we expect teachers to assume responsibility for the continuing effort to discipline and control our children and protect
them from harm.

Classical liberalism values such as individualism and Christian assumptions such as "original sin" permeate American culture, and social institutions,
including government and schools, are based on these values. It is hard to
recognize and critique these values from an insider's perspective, for they are
the norms and standards by which all of us growing up in America have been
acculturated. Stepping out of our schools and into very different cultures'
schools helps a researcher significantly to gain a better perspective on one's own
cultural values and norms. It is a powerful way to enlarge one's thinking, which
is why I sought to spend time in Japanese American schools in America, and,
even more importantly, in Japan. However, there's no guarantee of enlarged
thinking just by visiting Japanese and Japanese American schools. I have read
many books written about Japanese education from American perspectives
that reveal authors who are unable to appreciate Japanese cultural values (such
as Schoolland, 1990; Finkelstein, Imamura, & Tobin, 1991). In order to have
any chance of understanding another diverse, continually changing, complex
culture, researchers must use caring reasoning to help them. Caring reasoning
insists that the researcher attend to the other culture receptively and generously, with an effort to try to understand the other culture before one moves to
critique. This is the only way one can have a chance of gaining deeper knowledge of the other culture, as well as of one's own (Thayer-Bacon, 2000, 2003).
For an American studying Japanese education, using caring reasoning means
giving up one's assumptions of individualism and original sin in order to appreciate the Japanese approach to education in school and in the home. If the
researcher is able to give up these key assumptions, she or he will be surprised

to find that Japanese teachers model a relational democratic style of teaching as much or maybe even more than American teachers do.

The researcher will discover that Japanese elementary children have more freedom to move around in their schools and more choice of activities throughout the day. This freedom helps the children learn how to make wise choices and develop self-control and self-discipline. She or he will find that the children have many more opportunities for learning social skills, for they have much more time during the day when they are socially engaged with one another during recesses, breaks, lunchtime, cleaning, and rest times. All of this time for social engagement allows the children to practice their communication and relational skills with one another. These are important skills for citizens in a democracy-always-in-the-making to have. The Japanese children are learning on a daily basis that they share responsibility in how well their community functions, and that they have important contributions to make to their community's well-being. Along with this shared responsibility, the children of Japan learn daily that they share authority in managing their behavior and how well they work together. They are given opportunities regularly to practice their leadership skills so they can learn how to actively participate as citizens in their communities (*toban* and *nichoku*). It is not a far stretch for Japanese children to go from learning how to be democratic citizens within their school communities to using those skills to participate as active citizens within their larger communities and their nation.

Shared responsibility and shared authority are important themes that support a democracy-always-in-the-making. Collectivism, with its tendency to devalue and diminish diversity and lead to social determinism, and individualism, with its tendency to devalue and diminish social influences, ignore context, and lead to solipsism, are both flawed ideologies when adhered to exclusively. Both positions are logical complements of one another. There are certainly strong criticisms that can be made about Japan's culture in terms of its tendency to homogenize its people at the expense of devaluing diversity and excluding others. Still, there is much we can learn from Japanese educational practices.

In the following section, I focus on the concepts of conflict and harmony.

"THE HEAD THAT STICKS UP IS POUNDED DOWN"

There is a saying in Japan that has been quoted to me many times by my Japanese students: "The head that sticks up is pounded down." This saying, which is literally a reference to nails and the need to hammer them into place, is also a reference to people in society who make themselves stand out and the need to put them in their proper place so they will not be the source of social disharmony. In Japan, there is an emphasis on sameness as a way to ensure equality and fairness, which Americans translate as stifling creativity and individuality (Schoolland, 1990). There is also an emphasis on belonging and inclusion, and the importance of community membership as a way to develop shared identity as Japanese people, which Americans translate as elitist and exclusionary (Finkelstein, Imamura, & Tobin, 1991). The tensions in this adage represent those between individualist and collectivist views of democracy (such as Rawls, 1993, and Barber, 1984, respectively). Further discussion of these tensions will elucidate the strengths and weaknesses of these views and help us see how a transactional view of democracy-always-in-the-making can address their weaknesses while maintaining their strengths.

Much of the discussion of Japanese education by American researchers centers around secondary education. It is difficult to find scholarship that looks at early childhood education. Yet, without an understanding of early childhood educational philosophy in Japan, it is impossible to have a holistic picture of the country's educational goals and why things are the way they are in Japanese schools. The same can be said about any culture's educational practices. Understanding early childhood education involves a study of child-rearing practices in the home, for the boundaries between the home and school are very porous indeed.

In Japan, which is stereotyped as being a strict society where there is little freedom of creative expression, parents actually impose few rules and very little responsibility on children under the age of 6, for the years 0–6 are viewed as "the age of innocence" (Ellington, 1992; Lewis, 1995). Children at this age are not expected to be able to reason and are not held accountable for their actions. They have a great deal of freedom and are given much personal attention. It is perfectly acceptable to ignore children's bad behaviors and pick up after them, for example, which are actions that would be judged as "spoiling the child" by many Americans. It is unacceptable to punish children by yelling at them or physically harming them, actions that are seen quite commonly in the United States (Finkelstein, Imamura, & Tobin, 1991). In general, Japanese parents are kind, gentle, and patient with their young children, and American parents appear strict and harsh in comparison.

In Japan, compulsory education begins at age 6, but 90% of the children attend 2 years of preschool (Stevenson & Stigler, 1992; Lewis, 1995). Education of 5-year-olds is part of the preschool system (this is the same in China; see Chapter 6). Classroom size at the preschool level is large by U.S. standards, averaging 40 students per teacher. However, this is not viewed as a big problem in Japan, for the roles of teachers and students differ from those in the United States. Japanese teachers consider it the parents' job to make sure their children get personal attention and love, and they do not try to be the children's parents. It is also not the teacher's job to exercise direct control over the children and ensure their safety, for that is the responsibility of all the children in the classroom. Early childhood educators are not hired for their classroom management skills or for their ability to shower attention on children, but instead for their willingness to be playful and their joy in working with young children. Maintaining childlike qualities is considered an asset for early childhood educators (Lewis, 1995).

Catherine Lewis's (1995) basic claim is that Japanese education succeeds because, early on, it meets *children's* needs—for friendship, for belonging, and for opportunities to shape school life. Similar to what I found in my own observations, Lewis describes Japanese preschools as unregimented and often unsupervised, and found that 50% of the children's time is spent in free play; 14% in an art or craft activity; 8% in singing, dancing, or exercises to music; 7% in ceremonies or meetings; 7% in lunchtime and snack; 5% in listening to a story; 5% in cleanup; and 1% in academic activities (such as re-creating a pattern with blocks). In contrast, preschool children in the United States spend 30% of their day in direct academic instruction.

The Japanese word for *classmate* means "friend." The preschool teacher's focus is on building friendships, a shared sense of purpose, and on all children having fun together. Lewis tells us: "I think academic development occurs, at least in part, *because of* this emphasis on friendship, connection, and collaboration" (p. 35). Lewis found that, while American preschool and elementary teachers worry a lot about children who demonstrate aggressive behavior, Japanese teachers worry more about children who are isolated and not seeking inclusion. An aggressive child is at least interacting with others and can learn to curb his or her behavior, but an isolated child needs help integrating with others so he or she can interact and experience more learning.

Japan has a long history of relying on cooperative learning in the classroom, especially at the primary level. As Lewis (1995) describes so richly, the small group (*han*) is the home base for the children. *Han* have four to eight kids in them and are always mixed groups. Teachers carefully design the groups so that they include friends, kids who like one another and work well together, and kids with different strengths and weaknesses so they can teach one another. At the preschool level, the *han* may stay together for at least a year, whereas at the 1st-grade level, the average length is 2 months. The children eat, play, work, and plan in their *han*. At School #3, I saw the children doing their weekly jobs and eating together in small groups of four. At JSS I saw the entire grade (10th grade is the first year of high school) in homeroom together and eating lunch together in the cafeteria or on the lawn. Within their class of 30 or so students they have smaller *han* in which they meet for planning projects like cultural fairs they have with other schools in the area.

For Japanese teachers, working together in *han* fosters children's social and academic development. They help children work on communication and relational skills as well as reflection and enlarged thinking (Thayer-Bacon, 2000). The *han* give them all opportunities to be teachers and help one another. The children learn to see each other's attributes and how to work well together. The *han* strengthen a child's sense of attachment to the class by developing a feeling of belonging and of friendship. The goal of preschool and elementary teachers is to create a school that is like family, where children feel included. The children seem to really enjoy school and their teachers, and the feeling is mutual for the teachers. Japanese teachers create an environment where all the children can learn and they encourage all the children to work hard, but they recognize that learning requires effort on the student's part, not just on the teacher's part. They give the vast majority of their time to teaching the same lessons to all the students in the class, but supplement those lessons with one-on-one assistance while students work on their assignments (Stevenson & Stigler, 1992).

Japanese teachers at all levels help the children feel included in their classroom and school communities through daily, weekly, and annual rituals such as school festivals like sports day, recitals, carnivals, and collective birthday parties. In the classroom, art projects like murals are often done in groups. In contrast to U.S. schools at all levels, teachers in Japanese preschools do not start out the year with a discussion of rules (Lewis, 1995). They wait 2 to 3 months until all the children have bumped into one another and can understand the need for rules—"promises," as they are called. The teachers let the children have concrete experiences that allow them to learn through their own activities, and they refrain from enforcing a new policy. Teachers also do not intervene in small scuffles. Lewis tells stories of times she observed children doing "unsafe" activities, such as attempting to climb tall towers they had built from large, sturdy blocks, or "destructive" activities, such as the time some children bombed the fish tank with clay bombs and the teacher on duty did not intervene. Instead, she brought up the topic of the fish tank in the class meeting at the end of the day and shared her observation with the class, engaging the students in a discussion of their behavior and how it might affect the fish. Teachers do not want to be seen as leaders, but rather as resources. They limit their authority and respond to students' misbehavior with questions or discussions, not with demands, punishments, or insistence on compliance, which is how most teachers in the United States respond to students' misbehavior. Teachers in the United States rely a great deal on rewards and praise as well as surveillance, but Japanese teachers believe that managing a classroom that way will diminish children's subsequent interest in a task.

Japanese teachers would much rather help the children learn internal control than rely on external control to manage the children's behavior. They view the problems that arise in school as valuable teaching opportunities. The teachers in Japan spend lots of time teaching students *hansei*, reflection, and helping them develop the habit of self-criticism. They establish an enduring habit of self-evaluation with their students through their daily meetings in which they reflect on their day. Lewis (1995) considers the four cornerstones to discipline in Japanese schools to be the rotating leadership system (their *toban* system of having students take turns as class leaders who help with classroom management), children's involvement in shaping the rules and norms, teachers' low profile as authority figures, and children's reflection on their own behavior.

CONNECTING THEORY WITH PRACTICE, PART II

As a former elementary teacher, I noticed in my observations that Japanese elementary school children all wear the same clothes for physical education class and the same bathing suits for summer physical education. I saw that they carry the same yellow umbrellas when it rains so car drivers can see them as they walk to or from school. I noted that the children wear the same inside slippers, only boys' are white with blue trim and girls' are white with pink trim. I highlighted in my field notes that the children all wear the same adorable white apron and chef's hat at lunchtime when they serve their classmates. They do, however, have different place mats, and the teachers' aprons were unique, reflecting their different styles and tastes. I noticed that the children all have the same school supplies, only the girls' paint pallettes are reddish and the boys' are blue. My attention was drawn to the fact that all the elementary children stay together in each grade for all subjects and work on the curriculum at the same pace; there is no sorting by ability at the elementary level. I observed that there is little ethnic diversity among Japanese students; in fact, there was only one child of mixed heritage whom I would not have noticed if Asami, actively aware of her difference, had not pointed her out to me.

All of these observations emphasize that the Japanese focus on sameness and their desire for homogeneity, and underscore Japanese fears that differences will lead to inequality. In Japan, teachers rotate through different schools as well as grade levels within a school as a way to help them grow and become more well rounded as teachers, and also as a way of maintaining high-quality schools and classrooms that are equally good (Stevenson & Stigler, 1992). Principals rotate schools as well, though the principal in Japan is more of a figurehead than the type of active leader that we find in U.S. schools. Teachers lead together in the school, similar to how students lead in the classroom, as was described in part 1. The curriculum is controlled at the central government level through the

Ministry of Education (*Monbusho*) even though the United States shifted curriculum control to the local level after World War II (Haiducek, 1991). As soon
as the United States ended its occupation of Japan, the Japanese reverted back
to a central form of administration for fear that control at the local level would
lead to the loss of quality of education and loss of equal school conditions. The
elementary schools all have similar resources and follow the same curriculum.
Japanese parents can enjoy the security of knowing that no matter where they
live, their young children will receive a good education (Stevenson & Stigler,
1992).[2] That is a security American parents cannot enjoy. Many Americans
choose where they live based on the quality of the schools, as the quality varies significantly between school districts and between neighborhoods within
school districts, usually as a result of the funds available, although the varying
quality of staff and level of parental involvement are also contributing factors.

    American values of diversity, individuality, and freedom of choice cause us
to have savage inequalities in our public schools (Kozol, 1991). I was deeply
aware of this, having been an elementary teacher working with children from
varied social class levels in southern California and Pennsylvania. However, I
was surprised to find that under the veneer of sameness in Japanese schools,
there is a great tolerance for disharmony and disagreement among students.
This tolerance for disharmony and conflict with young children seems to create the opportunity for greater social harmony and integration as the children
get older and become more mature. Where American teachers may rush forward to quell a disagreement on the playground, Japanese teachers are much
more comfortable allowing students to learn how to solve their problems
without adult intervention. Where American teachers are advised to avoid
controversial topics in the classroom, thereby sanitizing their curriculum, and
are pressured to limit their time on topics and focus on the answers to the tests,
Japanese teachers are much more willing to let problems go unsolved and leave
questions unanswered in the classroom. In fact, if students move too quickly
to a solution, especially in literature, math, and science classes, teachers will
expand the topic to get them to ask more questions (Ellington, 1992; Lewis,
1995; Stevenson & Stigler, 1992).[3]

    We can learn a valuable lesson from Japanese early childhood educational
practice that applies directly to democratic theory. The lesson has to do with
the tension between harmony and disagreement, a tension between homogeneity and diversity. Through their organization of the students into small
groups, their emphasis on learning how to get along and be friends, and their
daily practices of shared governance, Japanese teachers help their students
develop a strong sense of *shared identity* with their fellow classmates, a theme
of great importance for democratic theory, as discussed in Chapter 4. At the
same time, through their willingness to tolerate young children's quirkiness

and creative exploration—in fact, their encouragement of it—they also teach the children the value of plurality and diversity. They teach the children that disagreement is expected and okay, not something to hide or pretend doesn't exist, but rather, something from which they can learn. These teachers show us that if we give children freedom to interact with one another, trust in their innate goodness and abilities, and encourage their efforts, they will learn how to get along and appreciate one another's contributions. Learning how to get along is something the students seem to do very well, for by the time most Japanese students are in secondary school, or even elementary school, they can function with ease in a harmonious school climate that is envied by American teachers. American researchers tend to see this social harmony as a result of pressure to conform by a collective culture, as a sign of social determinism, and a result of a lack of cultural diversity. However, if they look at the preschools and elementary schools in Japan, they will realize that the children have been given lots of opportunities to disagree and create social disharmony. Through those experiences, the children learn how to get along. Their freedom as young children, their liberty, results in their ability to embrace the value of diversity and learn from it.

Chantal Mouffe (2000) explores this tension between the value of harmony *and* disagreement in her book *The Democratic Paradox*. She approaches the problem by looking at liberalism's valuing of liberty (individual freedom) and democracy's valuing of equality. Mouffe highlights the paradoxical nature of modern liberal democracy not because she wants to get rid of this tension but because she thinks the tension is good. I agree with a central argument of Mouffe's, "that liberal democracy results from the articulation of two logics which are incompatible in the last instance and that there is no way in which they could be perfectly reconciled" (p. 5). This is why I argue that we need to move beyond liberal democracy with the help of a transactional view of individuals in relation to others. As I discussed in Chapter 1, liberalism is based on an assumption of individualism that undermines the possibility of a democracy, which is based on a valuing of diversity and pluralism as well as equality. I described individuals as existing in relation-with-others, relying on a relational ontology that recognizes we become individuals out of our social interactions with others, while at the same time acknowledging that we affect and change our social groups through our individual contributions and interactions with others. The relationship is transactional; it goes both ways and all are affected.

Mouffe (2000), however, is not making an argument for moving beyond liberal democracy; she underscores the value of living with this paradoxical tension between equality and liberty. She is worried that a consensual politics of the center (what she describes as the Bill Clinton years) jeopardizes the future of democracy. She is concerned that concepts such as globalization are being used to eliminate conflict. Mouffe argues that strife plays a primary role of integration in modern democracy—that the value of real debate is that it opens up possible alternatives. For Mouffe, conflict and confrontation are good, for then "power relations are always being put into question and no victory can be final" (p. 15). She emphasizes the need to acknowledge differences and the impossibility of complete reabsorbtion of alterity.

Diversity and plurality must be valued in order for democracy to have a chance to thrive, and democracy, as always-in-the-making, is an ideal to be sought but never reached. Mouffe (2000) recognizes that there is a dark side to a politics of hostility and antagonism, and that violence cannot be eradicated. Too much emphasis on harmony hides this dark side and the fact that chaos and instability are irreducible. For Mouffe, a perfect democracy would destroy itself; democracy should only be conceived as a good that cannot be reached. I agree with Mouffe and deconstructionists such as Derrida that chaos and instability are irreducible. But I do not think the solution to the very real fear of too much consensus, an "unanimity and homogeneity, which is always revealed as fictitious and based on acts of exclusion," is to maintain a paradoxical tension between two logics that are incompatible (Mouffe, 2000, p. 19). It does not have to be an either/or situation; it can be both/and. If we start with a transactional assumption of individuals-in-relation-to-others, we can find a way out of this paradox without having to sacrifice the value of diversity for the values of peace and harmony. Japanese preschool and elementary education make the case for the value of strife in integrating diverse others into a democratic community.

Putting 40 young children together in a preschool classroom where there is plenty of freedom to explore is bound to lead to strife. Add limited supplies and equipment, and the opportunities for strife increase significantly. Strife will occur for even three children under those conditions! In Japanese preschools, there is a high level of energy and tremendous amount of opportunity for creative imagination to go to work in all sorts of unpredictable ways. Yet I watched approximately 400 elementary children escort themselves to recess and play on a playground for 20 minutes with no mishaps occurring while the teachers were in the teachers' lounge having tea. I watched indoor recess on a day when a typhoon hit the island and children played in their classrooms, out in the halls, and in the gym without incident, while the teachers retreated to the lounge for tea. The students didn't need teachers to monitor their behavior, they had already learned how to do their own monitoring. Rather than trying to squelch strife or ignore differences, the focus in Japan seems to be on leveling the playing field so all have an equal footing and a good chance to do well in school, working to motivate children to put their best efforts forward, helping all children feel included and valued in the classroom and school community, and allowing children to find ways to creatively contribute to stimulating and meaningful problems through direct experience.

I agree with Mouffe (2000) that pluralism and diversity are essential for democracies to have a chance of thriving. The "fact" of pluralism makes the dream of consensus and harmony an impossibility. In fact, this dream begins to look like a nightmare that can only be supported through bullying and exclusion. It is interesting to note that bullying and exclusion are two key concerns for Japanese teachers and parents, and these issues are discussed frequently in the newspapers, on television, and in their scholarship (Okano & Tsuchiya, 1999). Yet Japanese schools enjoy much less violence and crime than American schools, as does the Japanese society at large (Stevenson & Stigler, 1992).

In the name of individual freedom and choice, American parents who do have choices are willing to send their children to more dangerous schools and have them walk to and from school through much more dangerous neighborhoods than Japanese parents are willing to tolerate. (Not all American parents have a choice about where they live or send their children to school.) And yet, when our children get to school, we think nothing of taking away their freedoms and controlling their every action, making our schools feel like prisons. Ironically, American scholars describe Japanese secondary schools as feeling like prisons (Schoolland, 1990). Scholars need to spend time with the younger children in Japanese preschool and elementary school to find out how free they are and how oppressive American schools feel in contrast. There is much we can learn from this example. The solution is not to find a way to live with the dangerous and destructive paradox of two contradictory logics, liberalism and democracy, and the conflict and violence that results, but to move beyond liberal democracy by embracing a relational ontology that describes individuals-in-relation-to-others. A relational, pluralistic democracy-always-in-the-making recognizes the value of disharmony and disagreement in reaching the goal of integration, just as the preschool teachers in Japan recognize that the same values help them reach the same goal in their classrooms.

CONCLUSION

In this chapter, we found that the role of the teacher in Japan is very different from the role of the teacher in U.S. schools. The difference between the two roles underscores the difference between America's individualistic culture and Japan's collective culture. I hope I have been able to capture how it felt to me when I spent time with them. There is a sweetness in Japanese teachers and the relationships they establish with their students, based on shared authority, shared responsibility, and shared identity that made me think that Japanese children must be frightened by American teachers when they transfer to our schools. Our teachers must seem very bossy and controlling. When I returned to the United States after observing in JSS and School #3, I talked to my students and friends who are parenting Japanese American children, to confirm my suspicion. "You are right," they gently confirmed for me. They are embarrassed to have to affirm my intuition, and they wish it was otherwise. I am appalled. As a parent I can imagine what the adjustment would be like for my own children to go from a Japanese school to an American one.

It is not that American teachers are mean, awful, terrible people, but our Christian cultural roots expect us to manage our students' behavior rather than allowing the students to manage their own. I can hear America's Puritan forefathers, Calvin and Luther, saying: A child left to his own devices will only get into trouble; "Idle hands are the devil's workshop." The responsibility, and, therefore, the blame, falls on the adults' shoulders to direct children's behavior, and this responsibility is not shared with the children. America's culture holds teachers responsible for students' safety and well-being and accountable for how much they learn (as can be seen in the current No Child Left Behind policy). We expect our teachers to get to know each child's interests and needs, strengths and weaknesses, and find methods of instructing each child that recognize his or her unique learning styles. It's a tremendous burden placed on the teachers' shoulders. In order to help our teachers manage this level of responsibility, we give them a lot of authority in the classroom, although we continually undermine that authority by reminding our teachers that their students' parents have more authority than they do, and that the country has more authority than they do, for they are teaching the nation's future citizens. Teachers in America find themselves having to defer their authority to administrators, legislatures, and parents, but never to their students. If they share their authority with their students, they are warned that they will "lose control of their classrooms."

I learned from the Japanese teachers I got to know that when a teacher no longer has to worry about being an authoritarian who manages the behavior and ensures the safety of all her students, this opens up all sorts of possibilities for her. Her role shifts to one of well-informed guide, facilitator, and resource. When she or he is not being asked to care for each individual child and establish a close, personal relationship with each of his or her students, assuming that this is the parent's role and not the teacher's, this frees the teacher and reinforces his or her role as well-informed guide, facilitator, and resource. At the same time, Japanese teachers enjoy a higher status than American teachers as professionals in their country. What Japanese teachers do to establish *shared responsibility*, *shared authority*, and *shared identity* with their students is supported by the formal curriculum as well as the informal, hidden curriculum defining the treatment of children and their responsibilities, and, most importantly, it is supported by the culture within which the schools are embedded. We can see this through the examples I presented, such as the very structure of the school day, where 2½ hours are devoted to nonacademic activities in which children are expected to get themselves to recess and back to class, serve lunch, and clean their classroom.

In the second section of this chapter, I discussed the theme of *conflict versus harmony*, for Americans perceive Japan as an oppressive society due to the level of homogeneity that exists there. Japan has sought to isolate itself from outside cultural influences at various times in its history. It has closed its borders to protect its own citizens, only to find that isolation left it more vulnerable to attack in the end. Today, Japan embraces the goal of "internationalization," but in a way that reaffirms Japanese culture and their own homogeneity and continues to maintain a divide between us/them (Haiducek, 1991). For example, Japan encourages cultural exchanges and having American colleges set up campuses in Japan, but *Mombusho* refuses to recognize American colleges and universities as equal to Japanese ones, thus maintaining a separation and supporting the Japanese hierarchical educational system. The Japanese can be open to other ideas and outside influence because they are 100% confident they are Japanese. Their conviction of racial unity and cultural homogeneity rests on an ultimate belief that the essence of Japanese culture is transmitted genetically (Finkelstein, Imamura, & Tobin, 1991). The goal of internationalization compels Japan to draw a sharper line than before to achieve unity of race, language, and culture. As a Caucasian, I am positioned as *gaikokujin* (an outsider), and was asked to visit Mr. Suzuki's *juku* to speak English with his students, as a native speaker, while Asami, an English as a Second Language teacher, seethed beside me, for Mr. Suzuki had never asked her to speak English with his students. For me, it was a reminder that my outside position made me "exotic" in Japan; for Asami, it was an example of reverse racism.

The children asked for my autograph in Japan. In many parts of Japan, there is little opportunity for them to meet foreigners, and they are excited when they do. Their excitement reminded me of how fortunate we are in the United States to have the diverse population we do; people from all over the world live in America and see one another on a daily basis. I have come to believe through this study that America's cultural diversity is its greatest asset, a topic I will examine further in the final chapter. Following is a discussion of Chinese culture, the last collective cultural group I studied for this project.

Chapter 6

Paradoxes Explored

The Chinese have the longest legacy of Asian cultures living in the United States; they have been here since 1785. Koreans mainly started arriving in the early 1900s and Japanese came to Hawaii to work as contract laborers on the sugar plantations in the late 1800s, but Chinese immigrants started arriving in the United States in the late 1700s and came in large numbers during the California gold rush years of the 1840s and in the 1860s for the building of the transcontinental railroad (Pang & Cheng, 1998). In 1880, the Chinese population in the United States reached 105,000, 0.002% of the U.S. population, but 10% of California's population (Choy, Dong, & Hom, 1994). The growth of the Chinese population in the United States ended in 1880 until recently, for with the 1880 Angell Treaty, China agreed to voluntarily restrict immigration to America. In 1882, the Chinese Exclusion Act was signed by President Arthur, barring Chinese laborers from entering the United States for 10 years. In 1892, the exclusion was extended for another 10 years through the Geary Act, and, in 1904, it was extended indefinitely. In 1924, the Immigration Act extended the exclusion to all Asians. The study of Chinese migration and the reception they received in the United States is a study in racism. It is a study of "yellow peril" propaganda, a belief in cultural inferiority, and anti-Chinese riots leading to exclusion politics (Choy, Dong, & Hom, 1994). In 1910, 79.1% of American Chinese were born in China. Most of the men kept their families in China, and only 6.5% (4,675) of the Chinese population in the United States were women (Chen, 2002). The Chinese population in the United States declined from its peak at 105,000 in 1880 to 62,000 in 1920 (Choy, Dong, & Hom, 1994).

Keeping in mind that cultures are complex, diverse, and fluid, of the five major collective communitarian cultures I studied, China was the most difficult to find information about.[1] Conditions are changing significantly in China today, but Americans are just beginning to learn about these changes. I have become highly suspicious of what I read about China after having traveled there. What the United States media have historically presented about China has been very biased, especially after China became a communist coun-

130

try under Chairman Mao's leadership in 1949. I have learned to read with a sharp, critical eye, for China is very different from what I expected prior to my arrival. The level of bias and the history of racism against Chinese people in America is very strong indeed, and is in great need of critical analysis.

It is only recently that Chinese students studying in the United States have been able to publish research about their culture and Chinese American students have been able to study the history of the Chinese in the United States. Shehong Chen (2002) studies Chinese immigration to the United States from 1820 to 1924, with a particular interest in the transformation of Chinese identity between 1911 and 1927, using as her main source three Chinese American newspapers published in the San Francisco area. Gloria Heyung Chun (2000) explores the history of the Chinese in California between the 1930s and the 1990s, using memoirs, autobiographies, and fictional writing by authors such as Maxine Hong Kingston, Frank Chin, Shawn Wong, and Gish Jen. Both of these scholars show that American-born Chinese have been active agents of history. They help us understand Chinese influence on American history and Chinese American influence on China. The treatment of the Chinese relegated them to the status of secondary citizens, despite their birth in United States. Historically, they have had two responses to the racism—separatism and accommodation. But Chun tells us that today many Chinese no longer see the need to negotiate their ethnic identity with mainstream America. They are the second largest immigrant group, with Mexicans being the largest (Chun, 2000); there are places in California, such as Monterey Park, that are 50% Chinese. Chinese Americans still struggle with underemployment and inferior wages, but the "post-ethnic perspective" both Chen and Chun take acknowledges that individuals occupy several positions and identities simultaneously. Chun (2000) explains that, historically, Chinese Americans,

> like the Monkey King, were superb tricksters. Through shifts and vicissitudes of public opinion, they changed their guise from era to era, and in the process learned that identity, far from being something that could be preserved and placed apart, was something that was made and unmade, depending on circumstance. (p. 59)

I began my observations of Chinese education by attending a Chinese Sunday school for a semester with one of my doctoral students, Yan Cao, who taught in the school. We live in a location that many Chinese scholars are drawn to because of the excellent opportunities to study in strong graduate programs in math and science and find work once they complete their studies. They live with their families and worry that their children are not learning about the history or current state of their Chinese culture. They worry about their children learning and maintaining the Chinese language and spending time with other Chinese children. There are around 200 families in the area, enough to support a Sunday school. A local community college offers them a place to meet. On Sunday morning, parents bring their children to this school and volunteer to help with the organizing and teaching of the classes. Both parents are usually Chinese born, and their children are Chinese Americans born in the United States. These families are part of the recent "open door" policy and the development of academic exchange programs that followed the normalization of relations between China and the United States in 1979 (Huang, 1997). In 1978, China sent its first 52 students to the United States since the formation of the People's Republic of China in 1949. In 1983, 1,000 students studied abroad; in 1986, 10,000; and in 1987, 100,000 (Ning, 2002). The numbers continue to grow.

My second location for observation was chosen because of the long history of Chinese immigration through the port of San Francisco. I knew from living in California that it has historically had a large Chinese population in comparison to the rest of the country and that the vast majority of the Chinese population in the United States still lives in northern California in the San Francisco Bay area. San Francisco's Chinatown is very famous and draws tourists every year. Chinese Americans are the majority population in the public schools in the city proper. Another of my doctoral students from China, Hongmei Peng, helped me find a school by searching on the Internet and conferring with people we knew in the San Francisco area. I call this school *Canton*, as that is the English term for the geographic area in China from which most people immigrated to the United States.[2]

Hongmei Peng chose my third location as well when we arranged to travel together and for her to serve as my guide and translator in the People's Republic of China. Hongmei is a certified teacher from China who taught Chinese in a middle school and high school (lower and upper secondary school, as the Chinese call it) in her home city of Guangzhou, which is the capital city of Canton. We decided to take advantage of her knowledge of the local schools and go to Guangzhou to observe in schools within walking distance of her home. The schools in her area are considered some of China's finest, and that added to the advantage of going there, as did the fact that the vast majority of Chinese students attend urban schools and immigrate to the United States from this province.

In this chapter, I examine through stories of my visits the tension between American and Chinese cultures and dispel some of the myths the Chinese have about American education and Americans have about Chinese education. I have come to appreciate the diversity in the United States as our greatest strength and as critical to the future of any democracy. I turn to Benjamin Barber (1984), Judith Green (1999), and Iris Marion Young (1990a, 1990b, 2000) to inform my analyses of *friendship* and *homogeneity*.

FRIENDSHIP

There are far more children in Chinese classrooms than in U.S. classrooms, yet this reality was softened for me by the fact that children in China start elementary school together in a class of 40 and stay together as a class for 6 years. This is something I had never heard or read about, but learned by observing in their schools. Often, the children have the same teacher for more than 1 year—usually their homeroom teacher, who also teaches them subjects such as Chinese and moral education. The children will have different teachers for subjects such as English, music, art, and physical education, but may have the same teacher for math and computers. When the children go to lower secondary schools (7th–9th grade), they continue to stay together in the same class, usually for 3 years, and have the same homeroom teacher. When they go to high school, they stay together as a class for 10th grade, but are divided according to their interest in liberal arts versus science and math, and stay together with their new class and homeroom teacher for the last 2 years of high school. Even at college, they stay together as a class for 4 years. The problem of large class sizes is certainly mitigated when students and teachers stay together and work and live with one another for a long time. A child in China may be in a class with 40 students, but those are the only 40 students she or he is with for 6 years, whereas a child in the United States may be in a classroom with 20 students for 1st through 3rd grade, but, each year, that child is with 20 different students. Then, for 4th through 5th grade, that child will be with 30 different students, and, in 6th grade, that child will have a different teacher as well as different students in each class. That means a child in the United States can be with 200–270 different children in the first 6 years of school, whereas a Chinese child is with only 40 students or 48 by the time he or she gets to upper elementary school. This is certainly a topic worthy of further exploration in relation to the development of democracies-always-in-the-making.

In my readings on Chinese education, I have not come across a discussion of the friendships that children develop in school. Neither did the topic arise until the last day of observation in an elementary school. What triggered the topic of friendship was my observation that the students knew the number of children in their class but the teacher did not. When I was trying to count how many girls and boys were in the 5th-grade math class, Hongmei Peng asked the students to check if I counted correctly, and they knew exactly how many girls and boys were in their class. Hongmei knew they would know this, and when I asked her how she knew, she explained to me that the students stay together in the same class throughout elementary school. We have discussed the ramifications of staying together in the same class and what it means for the culture and its values. For the students, this practice is so common and so much a part of their daily school life that it is taken for granted and not even discussed.

From a Chinese perspective, 40–48 children staying together in the same elementary classroom for 6 years means that the children have much opportunity to develop friendships with others in the class. They stay together while their teachers change, so the students develop closer relationships with their peers than they do with their teachers. Hongmei informed me that, given the large class size and the fact that children from 1st through 12th grade have 40-minute periods in their school day with different teachers for different subjects, some of which are taught only two or three times a week (e.g., music, politics, physical education), the smart students and the poor students tend to get most of the teacher's attention and the other students get little to no individual attention. The chance to develop a relationship with their teachers is almost impossible (except their homeroom teacher). Though the same group of 40–48 students experiences the same variety of teachers—all day long, every day, for 6 years—they nevertheless know who among their peers is a good artist, who can play a musical instrument or sing, who is a gifted athlete, and who is good at learning a second language (all children in China take English lessons starting in 1st grade). Even if a child does not sit near a friend in class, friends have many opportunities to play together: for 10 minutes between each of their six or seven periods, during lunchtime, and before and after rest time (lunchtime and rest time are discussed below). Many students who were in elementary school together remain close friends into adulthood. The friendships they begin when they are 6 or 7 years old do not get interrupted unless a student leaves the school for some reason. In the course of 6 years, those 40–48 students will get to know one another very well and will have the chance to develop deep friendships that last a lifetime.

A class of 40–48 students who stay together for 6 years is not something most American students experience in public schools. They may have small class sizes of 18–20 children for 1st through 3rd grade, but they do not usually stay together for those 3 years; each year, they have some of the same students in their class and some new students they do not know at all. Then, when they enter 4th grade, most public school classes increase to 30–35 students, and, for 4th and 5th grades, they are with different students each year. Each year the students in a class usually have one main teacher who teaches them reading, writing, spelling, math, history, and science, with other teachers for subjects such as art, music, and physical education. This pattern is standard across the United States, and the only time I saw another approach was as an elementary teacher in a private Montessori school.

Since it does not cost more or less to keep children together in the same class, it makes me wonder why the United States has developed such a different practice from China. I remember being in a class where I developed good friends, and then coming to school at the beginning of a new year only to find that my best friend was not in my class anymore. At the junior high and high school level, the first thing we would do when we got our class schedules was call each other to see if we had any classes, or at least lunch, together. In secondary schools in China, the students are guaranteed to have lunch with their friends, since they all have the same lunchtime. In China, as I watched junior and senior high school students, especially the girls, walk out of school hand-in-hand to get their lunches, I thought about how my best friend and I were only in class together in 6th grade, in Spanish class throughout high school, and sometimes in gym class. Once we left elementary school, I only remember having lunch together for 1 year in junior high school and in our junior year of high school.

China may have 1.3 billion people (with a strong commitment to zero population growth since 1979; Epstein, 1991), but the simple act of keeping children together in the same class for many years helps them develop a sense of community. It is a very simple structural design that supports at a deep psychological level a feeling of belonging and togetherness that children in America do not have. In the United States, we think smaller class size is important to make sure each child's individual needs are met by the teacher and that the child is not lost in a crowd of children. As a nation based on classical liberal values, we focus on individual rights and needs. We are not particularly worried about our young children developing deep friendships with other children, believing they are not capable of maintaining more than a few friends. When we enlarge class size at the upper elementary level, it is because of our belief that older children need to have plenty of choice in friends. We are much more concerned about the role the teacher plays in meeting our children's individual needs.

Interestingly enough, in China, by keeping a large class of 40–48 elementary children together for 6 years (and 50 or so together for 3 years in lower secondary school classrooms), the children have enough time together to develop close relationships with a few children and have a large pool of peers from which to select friends. They also develop the need to get along with one another, since they will be interacting together for 3–6 years. In my experience as a Montessori teacher, the need for the teacher and the students to get along with one another was also apparent, since we were going to be together for several years. Because my classroom size was never more than 20–25, the students and I became like an extended family. In China, the teachers (except the homeroom teacher) and students don't have the chance to develop a close relationship with one another, since the teachers don't stay with the class for several years as we did at the Montessori school. The children, however, are very close to their peers and develop a few great friendships they keep for life, no matter what the physical distance between the friends. Hongmei's best friend from elementary school came to the United States to study in graduate school at the same time she did. They planned this adventure together and helped one another have the courage to carry out their plans.

Before analyzing this issue of friendship and its relation to democratic theory, which will be undertaken with reference to the work of Benjamin Barber (1984) and Judith Green (1999), I want to describe how the issue of friendship was expressed in a public elementary school I visited in San Francisco whose majority population is Chinese American. I visited this school, Canton, prior to traveling to China, where I learned about their practice of keeping children together for many years. After my trip to China, I was able to better appreciate the motto of Canton—"Be a friend." It is clearly the case that the value of deep friendships has made its way across the Pacific Ocean from China to Chinatown, and can be found vividly expressed today in a Chinese American public elementary school.

"BE A FRIEND"

Canton Elementary School is located in the heart of San Francisco. It is a National Blue Ribbon School, and has been twice recognized as a California Distinguished School. I stayed with a family friend while observing in the school, and took the local bus to school along with people going to and from work and children going to and from school. The students on the bus reflected the population of the students in Canton, which is 61.7% Asian American (430, with at least 70% of them being Chinese American), 24.4% White (169 students, predominantly recent Russian immigrants), 1.4% African American (10 students), 0.3% Native American (2 students), 2.4% Mexican American (33 students), and 5% other (35 students). Canton has 679–694 students (the number varies depending on which report I read); 70 of them receive free lunch and 98 of them receive reduced lunch.

There are two streets to walk up to reach the school, one that takes you by the front of the school, and the other that goes by the playground in the back of the school. When I walked to the front of the school on Sunday, to make sure I knew where the school was located, I saw some interesting ceramic pottery totem poles in the front yard of the school. I later learned that these are friendship totem poles the children made with the help of their artist-in-residence, a potter. On Monday morning, I approached the school from the back, the way the students and their families approach it, and discovered a beautiful mural painted on the outside wall of the school. The mural is in blues and greens with abstract people of various colors holding hands in a big circle. At the top, painted in big red lettering, are the words, "Be a Friend." Every school day starts with the children assembling in lines with their class out back on the playground, which faces the mural, as the principal of the school greets them. Two children lead the school in the Pledge of Allegiance and the U.S. flag is raised on a flagpole that is centered in front of the "Be a Friend" wall. Then the principal announces who has birthdays that day. She tells them, "F is for feelings and taking care of them." She gives them a Big Canton Wave, and tells them to have a wonderful day, and then they go to class.

I followed the children into the school and up the stairs to the second floor. Here, I discovered there is a teachers' lounge at one end of the building near the 5th-grade classrooms. The teachers' lounge is an open room that looks out on a roof garden. I am drawn to go outside and look, for the walls surrounding the roof garden are painted with a beautiful mural of a landscape with flowers, plants, animals, and even mountain ranges, trees, and a desert scene. The floor of the roof is painted a deep green, like grass, and on the tallest wall there is a full-size picture of a girl and boy holding hands and holding up the earth with their free hand. Painted over them in white lettering are the words: "The Friendship Garden Mural, created by Class of 1996, funded by San Francisco Education Fund and X" (the name of a corporate sponsor). The roof garden has very large flower boxes, lattices, and a gazebo. I saw the Friendship Garden in January when the plants were dormant, but I can imagine how beautiful it must be when everything is blooming. I ask a 5th-grade teacher whose room is nearest to the roof garden for more information about it, and she says, "We had this roof space we decided we should do something with. So this is what we did." Later in the week, I meet a volunteer grandparent in her classroom who tells me she comes to school a few days a week to help out, and one of the things she does is tend the roof garden. I didn't realize then that when I went to Guangzhou, China, I would see beautiful gardens on the rooftops of every school I visited. Gardeners, teachers, and students tend them.

On day 2, I spend time in the 4th-grade classrooms, and in one class I listen to the children tell their classmates stories about what they did over the winter holidays. When one of them finishes their story, the students, not the teacher, call on someone else to tell their story. As I look around the room, I notice that the teacher has her classroom rules posted, as do all good teachers in the United States. They are:

1. Respect yourself and others around you—mutual respect!
2. Attentive listening.
3. Use your words to solve problems.
4. Say kind words—no gossip!
5. Be a friend!

"Be a friend" is not just a slogan but a philosophy that informs the curriculum. On days 3 and 4, I spend some time with the 1st graders and discover beautiful peace doves, each one uniquely decorated, hanging on a bulletin board outside their classroom door. On the door is a big sign that says "Making Friends," and all over the door are pictures of the students that they drew and colored. Each child has a bubble extending from his or her face that says something about the student. The children in this 1st-grade class are pen pals with another 1st-grade class in the school, and they come together for writing activities. In the section below on diversity, I'll describe their curriculum and classroom in more depth, but first I will continue with the theme of *friendship,* which pervades the practices of the teachers and the behavior of the children. On day 5, when I go to the teachers' lounge for a cup of tea, I discover that the 5th-grade class closest to the roof garden has a beautiful, big, lop-eared rabbit named Cottontail visiting them. Cottontail belongs to one of the girls in the classroom. During recess, the 5th-grade students go to a kindergarten class and bring the students up to meet Cottontail. Students in this 5th-grade class are reading buddies with the kindergarteners and get books from the library to read with them once a week, either on Wednesday or Friday. At Christmastime, the kindergarteners had a Christmas party with the 5th graders and made gifts for their buddies.

The children are not the only ones asked to befriend students in their classrooms; the adults model this as well. When 4th and 5th graders meet together for gym class, while they are running laps to prepare for a timed physical fitness test, the gym teacher chats with their teacher about her winter break. Teachers chat with one another and share lesson plans as they get their rooms ready in the morning. Some plan field trips that they will take with one another's classes (the 3rd-grade classes had plans to go on three field trips in the next three weeks: to the city library, to see the play *Rapunzel,* and to a symphony), and some come together for special presentations in their classrooms (I saw two 2nd-grade classes join to make quilts with the help of a local educator and her assistants from the Museum of Pop and Folk Art).

When the children have lunch, the 4th and 5th graders eat together, the 1st through 3rd graders eat together, and the teachers eat together. On Thursday and Friday, I find all the 1st- through 3rd-grade teachers in the teachers' lounge having lunch together. I listen to their conversation as I make myself a cup of tea. On Thursday, they talk about the state's budget woes and how they are affecting monies for public schools in the state, and, on Friday, they discuss the pros and cons of merit pay for teachers. Many of the teachers at Canton have worked there for a long time and are good friends (two teachers have been there for over 35 years). After spending 2 days observing the 1st through 3rd graders, I learned who the teachers are—some are young and new to the school, some are experienced teachers who have just recently transferred to the school, and some are substitutes who have been teaching there for a long time—I realize that *all* the 1st through 3rd grade teachers are having lunch together. No one is left out.

This theme of friendship extends to the parents as well. Canton has strong support from its parents. The teachers are able to have lunch together because the parents come in at lunchtime to be volunteer supervisors. The parents are predominantly Chinese American, and there are just as many men as women. The teachers escort their children to the lunchroom, where they meet the parent volunteers who have come to supervise the children during lunch and while they are on the playground. After the children have gotten their food and are seated at their tables, the teachers leave to have their lunch elsewhere. When the 4th and 5th graders are at lunch, the school principal walks around chatting with them. The assistant principal does the same with the 1st through 3rd graders. When the children are done eating, most leave on their own to go outside for noon recess, while some remain to wash the tables and benches.

At noon recess, four adults and the principal are on the playground chatting with one another as the children play. I talk to a man on the playground whom I'd seen before and thought was a teacher; his name is Peter, and he turns out to be a parent volunteer. Peter's daughter went to school here for 5 years but is now in 6th grade attending the neighborhood middle school. He still comes to Canton to volunteer. Friday is a rainy day and the children have recess indoors. I go to the portable classroom building to see what the children do for noontime recess when it is raining. There is no teacher in the 3rd-grade classroom (she's eating lunch with the other teachers, talking about merit pay), but there is a man, Lawrence, volunteering. He plays Scrabble with some kids while others play Life, Clue, and Owaree, a traditional African game. I talk to Lawrence and learn that his child had gone to school here. When I ask how old his son is, he sheepishly grins and says 21! How many schools have the pleasure of parents volunteering long after their children have graduated? This is the first school in America where I have seen that level of parental support. I am reminded of the school I observed in Mexico and the level of parental support it enjoys (see Chapter 2). Canton has obviously done a wonderful job making the parents feel welcome, valued, and appreciated for their contributions. The parents, both men and women, clearly develop a deep level of commitment to this school's well-being. Some parents watch their children's choir practice in the auditorium before school starts and volunteer in many of the classrooms, and they tell me they come in regularly, with several staying all day long. Canton lost its technical expert when it lost its funding, but the computer lab still remains open for student use during the midday when a parent volunteer helps—a Chinese American father trained in computers.

When school ends at 2:30 P.M., the children head for the playground where they pile their backpacks around the edge of the padded play area and play on the playground equipment. There is a group of parents and grandparents, men and women, standing around the grounds waiting for their kids. A few chat with one another. Some sit on the benches and watch the children play. They are in no hurry to leave. I observed this same pattern after school in Guangzhou, where the grandparents and parents planted themselves outside the school gate amiably.

Friendship at Canton is valued, encouraged, and modeled for the students by their teachers and family members. What Canton lacks in material resources, as a result of state cuts in educational funding, it makes up for in its wealth of human resources. This is not to say I am in favor of budget cuts or enlarging classroom sizes. The importance of *friendship* for democracies-always-in-the-making cannot be overestimated. I now turn to an analysis of this theme and the insights of Benjamin Barber and Judith Green.

CONNECTING THEORY WITH PRACTICE, PART I

In *Strong Democracy*, Barber (1984) argues for the need to revitalize citizenship, participation, and political activity in U.S. democratic politics, as these virtues are central to democracy. He advocates for direct political participation through a rotating lot system, neighborhood meetings, and televised town meetings. As noted in Chapter 1, Barber does a fine job of showing that liberal democracy is based on premises about human nature, knowledge, and politics that undermine democratic practices, primarily an assumption of the value of the individual and a view of social groups as hindering. He shows that the assumption of individuals as unitary wholes, roughly commensurable with one another and mutually exclusive, does not allow for an adequate account of human interdependence, mutualism, cooperation, fellowship, community, and citizenship. Liberal assumptions of humankind lead to a view of humans as solitary, hedonistic, and aggressive. For Barber, liberalism lacks a theory of citizenship.

In Chapter 1, we were introduced to Barber's (1984) concept of citizenship as something we become when we are able to choose freely and autonomously as political actors. We begin our lives as social beings, not individuals as Locke and Rousseau assume, but, for Barber, our social quality is within a private, dependent realm (our families), and this sociality renders us "slaves of dependency and insufficiency" who must acquire autonomy to break free. We are born capable of becoming citizens, but we are not citizens until we become autonomous and free, able to make choices of our own free will, deliberatively and responsibly. In Barber's efforts to link citizenship to the public world (as opposed to the private world of individuals) and to freely chosen action (to avoid the dangers of every community: anarchy and despotism), he turns to the concept of autonomy for protection. But Barber's reliance on the concept of autonomy for his definition of *citizenship* leads him back to liberalism's higher value of the individual and the view that the social group is a hindrance that we must break free of.

Understanding Chinese culture, with its collective view of groups as a source of strength and support for individuals, not as a hindrance to individual development, can help us achieve Barber's goal of developing an "adequate account of human interdependence, mutualism, cooperation, fellowship, community, and citizenship"—concepts upon which democracies depend. Chinese culture does not embrace a view of humankind that leads us down the path of liberalism. In the past, the people of China have been judged as having political views that will not lead to democracy because they do not embrace liberalism's assumptions. This Euro-Western judgment against the possibility of Chinese democracy illustrates classical liberalism's hegemonic power over the concept of "democracy." Since Locke and Rousseau, *democracy* has been defined from a classical liberal perspective with assumptions of individualism and rationalism embedded within the very concept and reinforced by the universal assumption that this is what *democracy* means for all of us.

Does the Chinese collective view of humankind—one that assumes the importance of the social group for the development of individuals—lead them away from the possibility of democracy? I don't think so, for the very reasons that Barber (1984) cites in his criticism of liberalism. Classical liberalism's basic assumptions of human nature undermine its chances of leading to democracy. We can understand the Chinese view of humankind if we think of the social group in terms of friendship. In so many ways, the children in China (and in San Francisco) are encouraged to see their classmates as friends who can help them rather than as hindrances to their personal growth and development. The children in China are given ample opportunities to spend time together and get to know one another. As we found in Japan in Chapter 5, teachers with collective cultural values worry most about children who seek isolation and do not have friends. They encourage students to make friends and learn how to cooperate with one another. They seat friends beside one another in the classroom and give them plenty of unsupervised free time to be together to solve their disagreements, thus teaching the children the value of fellowship and negotiated compromises. This is the opposite of what we tend to do in America, where we separate friends so they won't work together in the classroom (believing that such friendships will inhibit each child's individual development), and monitor and solve children's disagreements instead of letting them solve their conflicts themselves.

I did not notice any children in China who were isolated, for they were always surrounded by other children. But I know my observation of this behavior is not as refined and sharp as that of the teachers who work in the schools I visited. The students certainly have the time and supportive environment necessary to help them connect with others. Even a class of 40–48 students feels like a small community after so much time has been spent together. Children are encouraged to work together and help one another in numerous ways, and this emphasis on interdependence is linked to a concept of citizenship that is more social and community-minded than the individualism that prevails in the United States. There are many rituals performed in Chinese schools on a daily basis that encourage and reward students for learning to work together. These shared rituals bring the children together in a bond of common experience, not only with their classmates but with all the children in China as well, for these are national rituals. The children in China are taught how to be citizens through a model that values friendship and through rituals that bind them together "as neighbors bound together by common activities" (Barber, 1984, Chapter 9).

As a communitarian, Judith Green (1999) offers insights into the role of friendship in democracies-always-in-the-making. Friendships in China and in the predominantly Chinese American school, Canton, are based on face-to-face relationships amid diversity (there is more diversity in Canton than in the Chinese schools, as will be discussed below). Green bases her theory of *deep democracy* on the importance of valuing local, face-to-face relationships. This view is sympathetic with the valuing of friendship. Collective cultures are usually criticized by liberal individualists for valuing unity over diversity, but Green contends that the ideal of community values diversity within unity. In fact, she defines her *deep democracy* as focusing on the importance of developing "diversity-respecting unity in habits of the heart that are shaped by reflective inquiry" (p. ix). Through the friendships children in China develop, they learn habits of the heart that help them see one another as an extended family. Green's collective argument describes us as already members of a beloved community of shared hopes. This was apparent at Canton elementary school in the devotion of parents who volunteer and in the consistent modeling of the value of friendship throughout their curriculum (formal, informal, and hidden), making Canton feel like a beloved community of shared hopes. Those hopes are not only for one's own children when they are young and when they graduate from school, but also for all the children who attend the school. The children at Canton flourish in shared community life and help one another flourish through their collaborative efforts, with no detriment to themselves or others. Green argues that by helping the beloved community thrive, individuals will thrive as well. This view is certainly one that Chinese and Chinese Americans embrace. My observations in China and Chinatown serve as vivid examples of how this happens through deeply felt friendships established in school classrooms where children are taught habits of the heart and the importance of good citizenship over extended periods of time.

HOMOGENEITY

Homogeneity in collective cultures such as Chinese and Chinese American schools is a weakness that generates the worries that classical liberalists have about social determinism. The pervasive sameness of the schools I observed in China was striking, from an American perspective. We tend to think that our public schools are very similar, but in contrast to schools in China, American schools are diverse in many ways. In the following paragraphs, I discuss the differences between the two school systems and the paradoxes embedded within by contrasting the school in Guangzhou, China, with Canton in the United States, where the majority population is Chinese American. I then proceed to a discussion of the importance of diversity for a democracy-always-in-the-making, with help from Iris Marion Young (1990b, 2000).

Children in China wear school uniforms very similar to those worn by students in Japan. In Guangzhou, the high school students, both boys and girls, wear green shorts or pants that have white piping on the side, and white pullover shirts that have green, 3-button collars and a symbol of the school district on the front. On Mondays, the younger girls wear navy skirts and a button-down blouse; the boys wear navy shorts and a button-down collared shirt. They wear a more casual physical education uniform the rest of the week (blue shorts and a white pullover shirt with a blue collar). The children also wear a pin on their shirt or a red scarf around their necks that indicates membership in the Pioneers, the Communist Party's youth group. They are required to wear their scarves on Monday, for the morning meeting in which the Chinese flag is raised.

All the classrooms I observed in China from 1st grade through high school looked the same except for subtle differences. I was not given permission to take pictures of the classrooms, only the outside grounds, but I drew the classrooms in my notes and took pictures from outside. The exterior grounds of the schools are very attractive, with water fountains and ponds, sculptures, and many beautiful plants. In contrast, the classrooms are plain and functional and very much the same. This sameness exists in the number of ceiling fans, the number of fluorescent lights mounted on the ceiling, the clock to the right of the blackboard, and the large cupboard in the right or left corner that holds supplies and a trash can. The classroom buildings are at least two or three stories high; parts of the elementary schools and the lower and upper secondary schools are five stories high. The windows fill the upper half of the walls on each side of the classroom and have olive green or sage curtains that usually remain open unless the children close them when the sunlight causes a glare on the screen at the front of the class. The windows on the inside wall have full-length metal bars on them and the windows on the outside wall have bars that extend two thirds of the way up. The windows are open for maximum airflow (the temperature is very warm and humid in Guangzhou). Some rooms have air conditioning: the 9th- and 12th-grade classrooms, the computer labs, and the teachers' lounges and administrative offices. The walls are covered halfway up with white tiles, and the remainder is painted white (at the wealthier schools, the walls are covered entirely with white tiles). Desks are set up in four double rows with two desks side-by-side. All classrooms have the same standard desk with a shelf for books and a hook on the side for bags. The kids hook their lunch bags on the side of their desks and hang their backpacks on the back of their chairs.

The teachers have a large desk or built-in console at the front of the room, which is slightly raised above the rest of the classroom, creating a stage effect. Hongmei tells me that the university classrooms have the same arrangement. We talked about how this arrangement, positioning the teacher in front and above the students, reflects the importance of and respect for the teacher as a source of knowledge. There are no pictures or posters on the walls. A framed Chinese flag hangs above the front board and motivational banners abound with sayings such as: "Be serious," "Be creative," "Be diligent," "Aim high." At the front and back of the room are large slate blackboards; the one in the back usually is decorated by students in multicolored chalk, and the front board is used by the teacher to write lessons. Nowadays, the front board is often partially covered by a screen upon which the teacher can display PowerPoint slides. When I observed, all the teachers had laptop computers that plugged into the console and head mikes that amplified their voice when needed. Not all of the teachers used their laptops. Those who did use their laptops had prepared extensive PowerPoint slides to use in their lessons.

Like the Japanese (and Mexican) teachers, the Chinese teachers keep their supplies in their desks in the teachers' lounge, where they return when they are not teaching a class. The high school I observed has 4,000 students, 300 teachers, and 78 classes (the average class size is 51). All 300 teachers do not share one teachers' lounge. There are lounges throughout the school to which teachers are assigned according to grade level and subject area. The children stay in the same classroom all day—that is their space—and store supplies at their desks. All the desks in the classrooms are arranged in the same way. There are four columns of desks, with two desks side-by-side in each column; the only difference in this arrangement is how many rows of desks are in each column. In the upper secondary classrooms (10th–12th grades), 54–56 children sit in desks arranged in four columns that are two desks wide and 13 rows long. The lower secondary classrooms (7th–9th grades), with 48–51 children in them are arranged similarly, but the columns are 12 rows long. One or two children may have their desks up front near the teacher's desk, often by request to help them concentrate or see better. The elementary classrooms have 40–41 children in 1st grade and 48 by 5th grade. For the Monday morning meeting, the children line up in the courtyard and arrange themselves in the order that they sit in the classroom. They maintain the same order when spread out, arm's length apart, for activities such as morning exercises (see below).

Classes begin and end following the same pattern as in Japan. There are 10-minute breaks between classes in grades 1 through 12, during which time the students are free to move around the classroom, chatting and even wrestling with one another; roam the halls; use the restroom and drinking fountain; and generally just "horse around." It can be very loud during these breaks, as no adult supervises the students, but they always return to class on time. Rather than using the jarring bells and alarms that are commonplace in U.S. schools, classes in China begin and end with music that is piped through loudspeakers. Students are usually in their seats when the music begins at the start of class and stay in their seats until the teacher ends class, even if the music has already started.

ROUTINE RITUALS AND FREEDOM

There are four activities I saw the entire school engage in, which are apparently common throughout China and add to its homogeneity. They are Morning Exercise, Eye Exercise, a choric reading of Chinese and English, and lunch/naptime. The wealthier elementary school that I observed began the day with Morning Exercise, in which all the children lined up in rows on the basketball courts to do the exercises; the lower secondary school spaced the activities out after 2nd and 3rd periods in the morning. Here are my notes from my observation of two of these activities at the lower secondary school:

10:15 A.M.

Chimes are played: It is time for Morning Exercise. Half the students do the exercises after 2nd period and the other half does them after 3rd period. Loud marching music is piped into the classrooms at 10:20 A.M. and the line leaders pick up the students' exams. It's the 7th graders turn to do exercises.

The students pour out of their rooms, go down the stairs, and head out to the basketball courts and track. There are at least 550 students, possibly as many as 825 (there are 34 classes in the middle school). The students have designated areas on the courts to which they stroll and form six columns with four rows in a column, making 24 rows across. They spread out until the rows in the back are even. The crowd fills the entire basketball court, which is encircled by the track. Homeroom and gym teachers are scattered around the track. Five students lead Morning Exercise by positioning themselves in front of the crowd and facing them. They perform the exercises to the accompaniment of a tape that directs them. The teens are low-key and not very enthusiastic about doing the exercises. In typical teen style, they do the minimum they have to do to get by. As soon as the exercise tape ends, the students stroll back to their classrooms. By 10:35 A.M., they are back in their seats, ready for the next class.

Morning Exercise can be compared to recess in U.S. schools in that they are both routine practices that allow children to be physically active, but the Chinese elementary schools have recess *and* Morning Exercise. Their children are allowed to play freely at recess and between classes without supervision, similar to the Japanese elementary children's recess (see Chapter 5). The high school principals said that, from a Chinese perspective, U.S. schools have more freedom than Chinese schools. From my perspective as an American, the Chinese children have much more freedom during their free time when they play without supervision, and more time for physical exercise in general. In the United States, we do not do anything like Morning Exercise, and even recess is being cut back at the elementary level to make more time for practicing test-taking (Kozol, 2005). Children in middle and high school don't get a recess *or* Morning Exercise. Physical activity is limited to physical education class, which the Chinese students have as well.

A second daily practice in Chinese schools is lunchtime and naptime, which are practiced across the country at the same time every day by students as well as working people. The people have historically stopped at midday (noon) to eat lunch and rest, returning to work around 2 P.M. and finishing at 5:30 P.M. In China, the worker's day is from 8 A.M. to 5:30 P.M., with 2 hours off at midday for lunch and a nap. This schedule is followed by students as well, only their day ends at 4:30 P.M. for the older students and 3:30 P.M. for the younger students. Hongmei's family told me that the practice is changing as China moves to a market economy. While most people no longer go home for lunch and a nap, they do still stop to eat and rest where they are working. I observed construction and sidewalk-repair workers stop at noon to eat lunch and chat with one another before lying down to sleep right on the construction site or sidewalk where they were working. At the schools, the teachers eat and sleep in the lounges, at their desks, or on cots (they worried about finding us a place to sleep), and the janitors sleep on cots outside in a shaded area.

On the first day that I observed at the schools, I was surprised when noon-time came and class ended, the teacher left the room, and the students all got up to leave. For the schools I observed, high school classes end at 12:05 P.M., the lower secondary classes end at 12:10 P.M., and the elementary classes end at 11:40 A.M. High school and lower secondary students are considered old enough to leave the school on their own. They pour through the school gates, which are opened for lunchtime, and leave the school grounds to eat lunch at home or buy it from vendors in the city. The elementary children cannot go home on their own, so a parent or grandparent, family friend, older sibling, or babysitter picks them up and escorts them home. There are thriving businesses around the city schools, where vendors sell food, candy, and soda and other drinks to the students. Some students, particularly the younger children, stay at school and eat in the cafeteria or in their classrooms. They either bring their lunch from home or eat the food the school provides. The cafeteria serves food such as rice, noodles, meat, fish, stew, and broccoli and other vegetables. At one school I observed, there was a little snack store on the edge of the school grounds called the "Boys and Girls" store that sold soda, chips, candy, and ice cream. Many students use lunchtime to play basketball. Hongmei and I sit under a tree and eat the lunches we brought from home; we watch the students play basketball and chat with those who stroll by. This is also a time when I could ask Hongmei questions about what we saw that morning.

At 12:35 P.M., a bell rings at the gate and the security staff closes it and a teacher or two clear the basketball courts. A Brahms lullaby plays through the speakers signaling the start of naptime. The students who remain on campus for lunch go to their classrooms and lie down to rest. Many of the elementary children have their own pillows and blankets, and they lie on top of two side-by-side desks, the side counter space below the windows, or even the teacher's desk. Even some of the secondary level students sleep on top of their desks, though many of them just lay their heads down on their desks. The children who go home for lunch rest there. The lights in the classrooms are turned off and the curtains may be drawn as the students rest or sleep. Some might read or work quietly on their schoolwork. It is so hot in Guangzhou at midday that resting is about all you can do. Teachers in China also get a midday break during which they may run errands, grade students' work, or just sleep. A few walk the halls during the rest period. The principals enjoy this lunch/rest time as well, which I discovered when Hongmei and I took the principals and school district director out to lunch on our last day to thank them for their hospitality. We chatted and enjoyed a wonderful meal for 2 hours while their cell phones rang regularly.

At 2 P.M., the Brahms lullaby comes back on, gently waking everyone up; the security guards open the school gates again. From 2:00 to 2:30 P.M., the students who left the grounds for lunch and nap return to school. The basketball court fills up again with students playing. At 2:30 P.M., the chimes ring and it is time for classes to start again and for the security staff to close the school gates for the afternoon.

The elementary children have only one period in the afternoon, while the older students have two periods after lunch and rest time. This means that if the elementary children go home for lunch and nap, they are picked up at 11:40 A.M., brought back at 2 P.M., and picked up again at 3:30 P.M. Historically, in Chinese society, the 2-hour midday break was for family members to gather together, but this is changing as jobs change. More children are staying at school at midday because there is no one to pick them up, but most families are still able to make arrangements for the children to be escorted home. Children can stay for after-school care as they do in the United States, or someone can pick them up and take them home. The older children walk home by themselves, sometimes with their younger siblings in tow. Many grandparents are available to pick up the children, as women tend to retire at age 50 and men at age 60.

For 2 weeks, I experienced this lunch and nap schedule each day along with the students and teachers. I kept thinking about how much having this 2½-hour break changes the school day. Strangely, I have never found this practice mentioned in all my reading about Chinese education, yet it occurs on a daily basis all over the country. Nor have any of my Chinese students referred to this daily practice in our discussions about education. It is so common for them that they do not see it as a topic worth discussing. I have since talked to all the Chinese students I know at my home campus and found that they all grew up with this practice and that many of them still continue it in America by going to a quiet place like the library to rest at midday. The words of the high school principal returned to me ("Your schools have more freedom than ours do"), as I enjoyed lunch/rest time and thought about the fact that schools in the United States do not have midday breaks. I am guessing that American students, teachers, and principals would love this opportunity!

Not only do the students in China enjoy greater freedom of time than students in the United States, but they also enjoy greater freedom of movement, going off campus for lunch without signing out or needing a written permission slip or a call from a parent. Parents do inform the homeroom teacher if they want their kids to stay at school during the midday break, but even those kids can leave campus for lunch. They must return to class for naptime, however. After the music that signals the beginning and end of naptime is finished, the homeroom teacher or a designated student will make sure that everyone has returned. In the United States, it is usually only high school seniors who have the privilege of eating lunch off campus. Though rare, there are still schools that do not have a cafeteria and must let the students eat off campus. Most schools in the United States insist that students eat lunch at school, which they are given roughly 30 minutes to do, always under the watchful eyes of teachers, principals, parent volunteers, or lunchroom workers. How the United States handles the practice of lunchtime does not seem very free at all in comparison to the practice in China.

CONNECTING THEORY WITH PRACTICE, PART II

I greatly admire the Chinese practice of lunch/naptime, for letting children play freely at different times in the day contributes greatly to their physical health and well-being. However, I found the sameness of the classrooms and schools in China to be stultifying, and it caused me to reflect on the fears classical liberalists continually express about collective cultures. The fear is that if we start with an assumption of the importance of social groups over individuals, the result will be social determinism. The group will hold too much influence and power over the individual and will limit the possibilities for diversity and individual differences in the name of equality (which is equated with sameness) and harmony (also associated with sameness, with differences being associated with conflict).

Other American educators who have observed Chinese schools have said that they find activities like Morning Exercise scary; seeing the rows and rows of children lined up reminds them of soldiers in formation. I think, however, that this perception is created by media bias in the portrayal of China's collective culture, which was born in the 1900s when China chose socialism rather than a classical liberal philosophy to guide the development of its governing institutions and economic structure. When my colleagues are repelled by the structure of Chinese schools, they are not considering the logistics of getting 500 students out of school and onto the grounds for daily exercises. Perhaps what scares them is the sheer number of students doing the exercises. But in the United States we have had very large high schools since the early 1900s, when high schools were consolidated. These large high schools are predominantly located in our cities, as are those in China. What *I* find disturbing is American teachers marching their children to lunch and to recess in straight lines with their hands behind their backs (see Chapter 3). I never saw children in China escorted this way and never heard an adult yell at a child, which is routinely done in U.S. schools (see Chapter 3).

However, I do think the homogeneity in Chinese schools is an important issue for democratic theory concerning commonality and difference. While communitarians emphasize the importance of developing common experiences with others to help communities thrive, classical liberals emphasize the importance of valuing individual differences. When the principal of the high school in China told me they do not have the same level of freedom in his school that we have in America, he was referring to the amount of diversity we have in our curriculum. On that account, he is right. American teachers have much more freedom in their curricula to express their unique personalities and interests, and to encourage their students to do the same.

The lack of freedom in the Chinese curriculum was apparent to me in several ways. Hongmei and I visited room after room that looked exactly alike and watched teacher after teacher use the same teaching methods in presenting their lessons. We listened to many mind-numbing lectures where teachers did all the talking and students did all the listening, occasionally answering a question from the teacher and often repeating the teacher's words in choric fashion. However, we did observe some lessons where students were offered the chance to be creative and choose a topic of interest to them. This kind of creativity occurred mainly in art and music classes, which are important to the Chinese and are included regularly in the curriculum. But these subjects are less valued than mathematics, science, history, Chinese, and English because unified exams are not given in art and music, and, therefore, these subjects have little effect on the main goal of getting into a high school and college. The exception is when a student is found to be extraordinarily talented.

The contrast between schools in China and Canton Elementary School in San Francisco is quite illuminating. Canton is not a wealthy or "key" school like some I saw in China. Even though it has won a distinguished school award, it is just one of many public elementary schools in the city. Yet *every* room is unique. Classrooms have snowflakes hanging from the ceiling or students' pictures and writings dangling from clothespins on a line. The double desks are arranged in every way possible, and every bit of wall space is covered by bulletin boards, maps, teaching tools, and children's work. Extraordinary things are happening in this school where buckets are positioned to catch rain from leaky roofs, kids play germ ball in the halls when it rains (there's no place else to go, as the gym also serves as the music room and cafeteria), and there is no updated technology for the teachers and students to work with (the children score too high on standardized tests for the school to qualify for financial aid).

Children come to school early in the morning to sing in the choir, where they are learning the music to *Man of La Mancha*; play in the band, where they are learning to play wind instruments; and play in the orchestra, where they are learning to play the violin. In 3rd grade, they are learning how to make quilts with African American patterns; in 5th grade, an actress who is an artist-in-residence is teaching them *Macbeth* and the various ways it has been performed. In another 3rd-grade class, they are glazing their ceramic sculptures to be fired in the kiln, and, in 4th grade, they are learning how sentences build a paragraph with the aid of a huge colored-paper hamburger (the parts of the hamburger illustrate the parts of a paragraph—the top bun is the topic sentence; the bottom bun is the concluding sentence; and the lettuce, tomatoes, and onions are the supporting sentences). The student council is planning a pajama day, when all the children will come to school in their pajamas and bring a sleeping bag to crawl into when they read during the day. Canton is full of talented, diverse teachers and students who are co-constructing a very exciting, creative curriculum. My notes from Canton are rich with examples; almost every classroom I observed yielded a great deal of diversity.

Iris Marion Young (1990b, 2000) contributes greatly to current democratic theory through valuing pluralism, including plural definitions on the good, as well as the critical role of conflict in democracies. Young's focus is on oppression and domination, not distributive equality or standardization (see Chapter 1). It is not that she is unconcerned about the "huge issues of distributive justice facing education in most societies today" (2006, p. 93), but rather that she examines a form of justice that is not reducible to distribution. Young wants to transform the public to include group differences, arguing that a politics of difference will lessen oppression for disadvantaged groups and allow them to find ways to participate politically without foregoing their particularities. She seeks "public fairness in a context of heterogeneity and partial discourse" (1990, p. 12). Young criticizes an ideal of justice that seeks to transcend differences, and demonstrates that such an ideal leads to assimilation and perpetuates cultural imperialism. The "melting pot" metaphor used in U.S education in the 1960s and the encouragement teachers received to be "colorblind," are examples of assimilation that perpetuates cultural imperialism, with Euro-Western, middle-class, White, heterosexual, able-bodied male values serving as the norm embraced under the banner of universality and neutrality. For Young, equality does not equal sameness in a diverse society such as America. She shows that treating all people the same in a world where people are diverse leads to inequality, rather than equality. It leads to oppression in the forms of marginalization, exploitation, powerlessness, cultural imperialism, and violence, for in the name of sameness and impartiality, all particularities except the dominant group's are erased. In China, the valuing of pluralism is not such an important issue because the culture is much less diverse than in the United States (although there are more than 50 ethnic groups in China and distinctions between the populations in northern and southern China as well as between rural and urban China). But in a country such as the United States, valuing pluralism is essential to the achievement of a just society.

"Equality does not equal sameness" is a truth that teachers who work with diverse populations understand. Children do not come to school having had the same past experiences, and, while they are in school, their lives outside continue on their diverse paths. The students will teach their teachers about their cultures if their teachers are welcoming and good listeners. No teacher in the United States can be an expert on all the diversity represented in the classroom, but she or he can certainly model a valuing of plurality and design a classroom and curriculum that embraces the value of cultural diversity. If she or he is willing to view the students and their parents as teachers as well, they will all learn a lot from one another. Young's work supports what I have learned from this study, that social difference is a tremendous political resource in which Americans have grown very rich from their historical condition as a country of immigrants (where Native Americans have become invisible; see Chapter 4). Today we find educators using metaphors such as a salad bowl or a Chinese hot pot to empha-size how a classroom can be a place where children can maintain their cultural distinctions and contribute their own "flavors" to enhance the overall learning (eating) experience for all partaking of this delicious meal.

CONCLUSION

In this chapter, I described my visits to a predominantly Chinese American public elementary school in the United States and several public schools in the People's Republic of China. I explored more deeply the strengths and weaknesses of collective and individualistic cultures through the themes of friendship and homogeneity. Chinese teachers do a tremendous job of making students feel included and connected to one another under conditions that most American teachers would find daunting because of the sheer number of students in the classrooms and schools. As a teacher and parent, I have always advocated for smaller classes and schools as models that help children feel included and connected to one another as well as to their teachers, but I have learned from Chinese teachers and students that even in very large schools students can develop deep, long-lasting friendships if they are given enough time to do so. Extending the time students in a class stay together to 4–6 years ensures that students feel connected to one another. Changing teachers while the class stays together actually strengthens the bond among students. Chi-nese teachers, as well as Japanese teachers (see Chapter 5), are not expected to forge the same kind of bond with their students that parents and grandparents form with their children. Society neither expects nor desires it. A teacher who achieves that degree of closeness would be viewed as having overstepped his or her boundaries.

Aided by the considerable insights of Barber and Green (1999), I have examined what Chinese and American children learn about becoming good citizens and have explored the ways that we can help children develop the habits of heart that encourage them to see their community as beloved instead of viewing others as infringing upon their lives. Our children in America are taught to value their privacy and independence, need space away from others, spend time alone and work by themselves, and take care of themselves without depending on others.

In addition to examining citizenship from a collective, Chinese perspective, and how it is developed at school and at home, I have also addressed, through the theme of homogeneity and a discussion of freedom and diversity, the concerns that classical liberals have about collective cultures and their fear of social determinism. In exploring the sameness of Chinese schools and the diversity and plurality of American schools, I developed an argument, with the help of Young (1990b, 2000), for the importance of diversity and plurality for democracies-always-in-the-making.

Chinese teachers and principals are aware that teachers in America have more freedom in what they teach and how they teach, but I am not so sure that American teachers and principals are aware of how much freedom Chinese students and teachers have as a result of the students being allowed to monitor their own behavior in the absence of adult authority and control. It is easier for Chinese teachers to expand their pedagogical style and curriculum than it is for American teachers to loosen their control over students' behavior. Americans live in a society that expects adults to protect children and control their behavior, and holds them accountable if a child comes to any harm. In the name of protection, based on a logic of fear, adults are willing to infringe upon children's behavior since society insists that they do so. Consequently, American schools feel much more controlling and lacking in freedom than schools in China.

The freedom in curriculum and instruction that American teachers have enjoyed historically is being eroded by the recent push to raise standards and insist on teacher accountability by making all students take standardized national examinations to evaluate the success of teachers. Standardized examinations are standardizing America's school curriculum.

American teachers have enjoyed a freedom that allows them to use their strengths and interests and rely on local experiences to engage students' interest. They have been encouraged to be creative and inventive with their lessons and even in the decoration of their classrooms. They have enjoyed a freedom that allows them to use what they learn about their students' interests and experiences to help students connect new ideas and concepts to what they already know. The ability to adjust their curriculum and methods of instruction to fit the needs of their students is a tremendous asset in teaching the diverse students American teachers have enjoyed. However, we squander that freedom when we do not hold high expectations for all our students and assume that some children are more teachable than others. Increasingly, parents fear the educational inequality that results from factors such as varied teacher expectations and unevenly distributed school resources. In America today, we have the most highly educated teachers that we have ever had, with most teachers having master's degrees, but are experiencing the continual erosion of public trust in our teachers' abilities to do their jobs well. To rectify this situation, in the name of equality, our legislatures are imposing standardized test requirements on local school districts, teachers are losing their freedom to adjust their curricula to meet students' needs, and students are losing their choice in curricula (due to No Child Left Behind). Rather than doing the hard work of addressing the social factors in children's lives that might affect their learning, such as poverty and all its consequences (e.g., lack of healthcare, good nutrition, and a stable childcare support system), teachers have become the easy target to blame for uneven educational results.

Given the level of diversity we experience in American schools, it is vital that we find ways to value that diversity and recognize it for the tremendous treasure it is. This does not mean all diversity is good and should be maintained; for example, inequality in the distribution of educational resources is certainly a diversity that should not be honored. This is the point of a differentiated politics of difference, which is examined in the final chapter. My point here, however, is that if we do not find ways to learn from one another, we will squander our greatest resource—our diverse population. Our teachers need to maintain the freedom to adjust their curriculum and methods of instruction to fit the needs of their students or we will be guilty of colonizing young minds and insisting that they all be the same—the very fear we have about a communist society such as China. A high-quality, equal education for all children as future citizens in a democracy-one-day cannot be the same education for all children. In the following chapter, I will review the theory I have developed herein as well as discuss the educational implications of a relational, pluralistic theory of democracies-always-in-the-making by bringing the diverse voices from the C.A.R.E. (Culturally aware, Anti-racist, Relationally focused, Education communities) study together for a summary conversation on educational practice.

Chapter 7
_____

Conclusion—Project C.A.R.E.

I have followed Myles Horton's (1990) advice in Chapters 2 through 6, beginning each chapter with practice and stories from the field and then moving to theory, where I analyze the themes and issues the stories illustrate for a relational, pluralistic democracy-always-in-the-making. In this final chapter, I follow Horton's advice again and bring the theory and practice together. I begin with a summation of the theory I have developed throughout this text and follow with a discussion of the implications this theory has for schools in America and beyond. My voice becomes stronger in this chapter, but the teachers, parents, administrators, and students in the schools I visited for the C.A.R.E. (Culturally aware, Anti-racist, Relationally focused, Education communities) project are included in this discussion, and I invite you, reader, to join in the conversation, too.

THEORETICAL SUMMATION

I began this text by tracing the roots of liberal democracy back to Locke and Rousseau's classical liberalism and their assumptions concerning human nature and our capacity to reason. Both Locke and Rousseau begin their theories with an assumption that we start out our lives as free individuals and choose to join with others to form a society (I → others). "Others," however, are viewed as hindrances that infringe upon our individual freedoms—we lose some of our freedom when we choose to join with others to form a society. Others are something we must tolerate for our own protection and to help us meet our individual needs. The classical liberal role of government is what we associate with libertarian views today—that the best kind of government is a small one with limited powers, one that protects us from harm and keeps others from infringing upon our individual rights, but otherwise stays out of our lives. We need to be protected from a government that grows too large and seeks to have too much influence over our individual lives. This skeptical, distrustful view

of government makes a great deal of sense when we look at examples throughout time of governments that have gained too much power and did intrude
on their citizens' rights to free speech, to assemble, and to vote leaders in or
out of office. However, I argued in Chapter 1 that classical liberalism is based
on false assumptions about individualism, rationalism, and universalism that
cannot hold up to the criticism it receives from pragmatists, feminists, and
postmodernists.

I offered instead a *transactional view* of individuals-in-relation-to-others—
a view that questions the myth of autonomy (Locke and Rousseau's atomistic
individualism). A transactional description of selves-in-relation-with-others
(I ↔ others) describes us as becoming individuals out of our social settings—
our families in particular and our care providers, but also the larger neighborhoods and communities in which our families are embedded and the still
larger macro context of nations in which our communities are embedded. At
the same time that we are becoming individuals within a social setting, we are
continually affecting that social setting as well. Individuals are not aggregates
with separate boundaries that have no relation to one another. In fact, the
"self" is fictive and contingent. Our "selves" are multifarious and fractured,
a result of repressive forces imposed upon us by others as well as supportive
forces offered to us by others. Others bind us and help us become free, at the
same time. They bind us in that we are embedded within social contexts and
situated within particular times and locations, and all of that context affects
who we become. Yet, at the same time, others help us become free, for their
differences make us aware of our own situatedness, thus helping us enlarge
our thinking, critique our own embeddedness, and decide to make changes.
We do not decide our own identities under conditions of our own choosing.
Individual identity development always involves a dimension of coercion, but
it is also always developed in relation to others and always brings to the social
group a dimension of contingency and undecidability. We actively appropriate our own multiple positionalities, but we don't have complete control over
this.

I have discussed the classical liberal assumptions of rationality and universality less than the assumption of atomistic individuality because I have discussed
them both in greater depth in other research projects (2000, 2003). Please do not
misunderstand and think that I do not value the use of reason to help us think
constructively. I have certainly relied on reason throughout this book to make
my arguments and analyses. But the myth of rationality suggests that reason
alone will solve all of our problems and lead us to Truth. Like any tool we use
to build, garden, or cook, how we use the tool of reason depends on us: Will we
use it for constructive or destructive purposes? Reason does not have a life of its
own, and it certainly can be flawed. Reason cannot guarantee us certainty.

I also have not talked at length about classical liberalism's assumption of universality, again because I have done so elsewhere (2003). This should not be interpreted as an argument against universality and for extreme pluralism, which implies heterogeneity and incommensurability—that we are so culturally diverse that we cannot communicate with one another or establish common ground. My experiences in the schools I spent time in across three continents and five very different cultures have taught me how much we do share in common in pedagogy, curriculum, daily school rituals, what our children wear to school, the games they play at recess, the ways they tease one another, and the tunes they hum between assignments. Yet these visits have also reminded me to value the particularity of unique local school environments and to appreciate the tremendous diversity that exists in our world (which seems smaller and smaller as technology brings us closer and closer together). I am arguing for contingency, for locality in the everyday world of diverse people and their values and beliefs, as well as for commonality, not universality.

In making the case for multiple truths, I am also not arguing for naive relativism—that anything goes and that everything we do in our schools is equally good and right. I offer instead a differentiated politics of difference that recognizes that some differences should be tolerated, even valued and protected from intrusion or harm, while others should be eradicated. I witnessed examples of the latter in Ghana watching children being caned and in the United States listening to teachers yell at children (Chapter 3). In the southwest United States, I saw children march down the halls in alphabetical order with their hands behind their backs, practicing walking silently on a painted line as they went to lunch to sit at their assigned tables in their assigned seats, and out to the playground to play in their assigned area until the whistle blows, calling them to line up at their numbered spot and march back to class (Chapter 2). There are things we do in our schools that do violence to children, are harmful to their well-being, and make schools very unhappy places to be. These acts of violence and injury should not be tolerated. But I also know there is no one right way to teach children, but multiple, diverse ways that work quite well and help us achieve multiple valued ends. I am making the case for humility, flexibility, and openness to various possibilities, for tolerance and acceptance, even celebration, while at the same time insisting that acts that significantly harm our children be treated with unequivocal rejection. While there is much room for disagreement about what counts as "significant harm," there is room for agreement as well. Parents all over the world love their children and teachers all over the world feel the joy that comes from helping their students understand a difficult concept or develop an important skill. No one thinks it is okay to sexually molest or starve these beautiful children. All children represent the hope and future of their communities.

I agree with Dewey that a democracy is a mode of associated living, not just a political democracy, and that it must be struggled for in all our social institutions—political, economic, educational, scientific, artistic, religious, and familial. This comprehensive view of democracy is consistent with the transactional relational assumption described above, for it recognizes that social institutions are no more autonomous and separate from one another than individuals are separate from one another. Classical liberalism worked hard to separate some social institutions so that governments would not be able to claim authority over people's religious expressions (what church, if any, they were allowed to attend) or dictate to parents how to raise their children or even if parents should be the ones who raise their children (in slave cultures, children are taken away from their parents, as happened in the America's dark past with African, Native, and Mexican parents and their children). Liberal democracy fought to keep governments from overtaxing their citizens, so that people could reap the rewards of their own hard work and pass those rewards on to their children, rather than to the state.

Liberal democracy offered a way to critique social institutions by making the case that social institutions are not divine but humanly constructed, and, therefore, open to critique and reconstruction. However, no matter how hard liberal democracy works to separate social institutions from one another and draw secure boundaries around them, it never seems to work. There is a reason for this—the boundaries are socially constructed, artificial, and impossible to maintain. They are leaky and porous, flowing into each other continuously so that all we are able to maintain is the illusion of separation. Our views concerning the role of the government inform our views concerning the roles of parents, our spiritual leaders, and our teachers. In a society such as the United States, where governments are feared for their power, and a system of checks and balances is set up to limit their power, it is not surprising to find that parents also fear teachers having too much power and influence over their children and that a system of checks and balances is put in place in schools as well. Principals with strong authority direct the daily activity of the schools and observe and evaluate their teachers, superintendents evaluate the principals, and school boards evaluate the superintendents, while the states (and now the nation) design benchmark examinations for students in order to make sure that everyone is doing their job and is held accountable.

The effort to separate social institutions and protect them from the power of the government (or the church) is based on a view of government as one that intrudes upon us. Again, it is a view of associations with others as hindrances that we need protection from as individuals. Classical liberalism evolved during the 1800s to the point where the state began to be recognized as being important for more than just protection and safeguarding; it began to be viewed as necessary to secure and extend individual liberties by aiding those who are economically disadvantaged (Dewey, 1935; see Chapter 1). Democratic governments began to be viewed not only as necessary hindrances that must be kept in check because they continually threaten to become too powerful and infringe upon individual freedoms, but also as having an important role in assisting citizens to reach their full potential as individuals. Instead of relying solely on a myth of merit—that if I just work hard enough, I will be able to succeed and have the opportunity to reap the benefits of my hard work—people began to acknowledge that not everyone starts life under the same fair conditions. Some people get assistance to help them begin to establish the fruits of their labor, and some people do not. Some families have material wealth and can hire private tutors for their children or pay for the best medical services, while others cannot.

The role of government in a democracy shifted in the 19th century from one that supplies protection from harm to one that is also a provider. The role of protector relies on a logic of fear and distrust of others. The role of provider relies on a logic of paternity, viewing the government as responsible for the care of citizens who are not able to care for themselves. This view of the government's role is paternalistic in that it assumes a benefactor role from a position of strength, assurance, and wealth. It is a position of power that allows the government to judge what is lacking or deficient in people's lives and determine how to rectify that deficit. It positions the citizens it assists as lacking, deficient, and needy. A paternalistic government does not treat its citizens with dignity and respect or as equals. Rather, it treats them from a position of moral strength and judges them to be inferior and in need of help. A government in the role of provider is a government in a position of arrogance, which is certainly how mothers on welfare view the social workers who check on them to determine if they qualify for federal assistance, and is certainly how many nations that receive assistance from America view the United States.

If we look to social democratic countries such as Sweden, Finland, Norway, and Canada as examples, we find countries that, without assuming the paternalistic role of provider, have been able to create governments that ensure the equitable distribution of wealth to those who are lacking in material goods, thus breaking down extreme differences between the wealthy and the poor. Time and again, Americans opt for what they think benefits themselves and offers them the most individual freedom and choices, at the expense of others whom they believe deserve less because they must be lazy, incompetent, uninformed, lacking in ability, less deserving, or just plain unlucky. The values of individual freedom, choice, and competition trump the values of fraternity, equality, cooperation, and shared resources in American political decisions. To much of the rest of the world, while we may be envied for our perceived wealth and opportunities (which many immigrants find are not available to all, but to just a select few), we are distrusted and even despised for what they perceive as our selfish greed as we use up more than our fair share of natural resources and refuse to share with others or clean up after ourselves, and for our unfathomable arrogance in believing we deserve what we have (the myth of merit), even though our wealth has come from the exploitation of others less powerful (the Native Americans, Mexicans, and Africans we enslaved, immigrants from other countries such as Ireland and China, and now the exportation of our companies to countries where they can hire cheaper labor, such as Mexico, India, Pakistan, and Sri Lanka).

An outcome of the C.A.R.E. study was the position that governments in democracies-always-in-the-making should serve roles very similar to those that teachers serve in classrooms: roles as facilitator and resource, guide and mentor, advocate and supporter, translator and referee. These are roles teachers modeled for us in Chapters 2 through 6, and I will discuss them further below, from a teacher's perspective. Our government, church, and business leaders; and teachers, community members, and parents all share a responsibility to help our children develop into adults who will be able to participate in a democratic-society-always-in-the-making. We need the adults in our children's lives to create and nurture fertile ground for them to grow by making sure their basic needs are taken care of (such as a place to sleep, food to eat, clothing and shelter, protection from harm, loving arms to hold them). This means we need our governments to address universal issues such as healthcare, job opportunities, retirement benefits, and access to quality schooling to make sure the resources we have are shared so that no child goes without his or her basic needs being met. Laws such as No Child Left Behind that do not address social issues that affect children's basic needs are empty promises. It is easier for legislatures to blame teachers for lowered expectations and order children to take more tests than it is to address difficult social issues such as lack of healthcare, unemployment rates, and the rising cost of living that put so much stress on families that they reach their breaking point.

We need our governments to help us find ways to work together and solve our problems, not to solve them for us but to serve as facilitators, giving us forums for airing and discussing our issues and concerns and avenues for sharing our views with others beyond the reach of any particular forum. We need our governments to serve as a resource and help us find the information we need to solve our problems, including making available experts in human resources who are trained to deal with particular issues and concerns. We need our governments to serve as mentor and guide to help people develop their knowledge so they can become experts in problems that need solutions. We need our governments to advocate for us when our rights are violated and support us in our efforts to grow and develop. We need our governments to serve as translators to help us understand one another and find ways to work together, to help us overcome our flaws and limitations, appreciate and value our differences, and recover from our mistakes and misunderstandings. All of these tasks for the government of a democracy-always-in-the-making are similar to the roles Highlander played and continues to play for people who come there to learn how to organize and solve their problems.

We need our governments to help us gather our resources and serve as the place of deposit and distribution. We need them to keep an inventory of our resources and inform us when there is a need to replenish them. We need our governments to make sure we all have equal access to resources and that we don't use more than our fair share. As a referee, we need our governments to make sure we play fairly and follow the rules we agree upon and blow the whistle on us when we don't. If we find we do not like the rules we have created to live by, we need our governments to offer us a forum for discussing and deciding how we want to change the rules.

I agree with Barber (1984) that we need a theory of democratic citizenship if we hope to live in a democracy-someday, but Barber's free-choosing, reasonable, deliberative citizen relies on a strong concept of autonomy that leads us back to classical liberalism's assumptions of individualism and rationalism. I agree with Young (1990b, 2000) that we need to make sure we teach our children to appreciate their differences in our effort to affirm diversity and plurality. They need to know that they do not have to like one another or agree with one another, that it is okay to disagree. In fact, it is important for them to understand and expect that they will not find anyone who agrees with them all the time. However, in attempting to find ways to work together and share our limited resources, we must teach our children to continually pay attention to others' needs and how their choices and actions might be affecting others. Our children need to know that while they share much in common with others, they also have much that is different, and that this is not only okay but a great good, for it is through those differences that we are able to become more aware of our own limitations and open up possibilities for more solutions to our problems. I agree with Laclau and Mouffe (1985) that it is vital for our children to grow up aware of and able to recognize oppression and exploitation, to understand that domination and inequality are harmful to all of us as we seek to live together in democracies-always-in-the-making, and that they need to learn ways to resist these harms to themselves as well as to others. A transactional view of individuals-in-relation-to-others is what will help us maintain a pluralistic view of democracies and protect us from fears of social determinism, not Mouffe's (1993) individual freedom and personal autonomy or Young's (2000) self-development and self-determination.

What kind of democratic citizens can we hope for when we start with an assumption of transactional relationships, emphasizing how much we are connected to and affect one another as well as how much we are disconnected from one another? When we acknowledge how much we have in common with one another, as well as how different and strange we are from one another, then how much we can effect change in the world, and how much the world affects who we are and what we do. We have to hope for citizens who:

- are able to make decisions and not act solely on the basis of their own needs but take the needs of others into account as well;
- value others and treat them with respect and dignity;
- are caring toward others and able to attend to them with generosity and feel empathy for others who are different and strange from themselves;
- are patient and generous, able to share with others, wait their turn, and are willing to offer a helping hand;
- are self-reflective and seek to learn from their mistakes;
- seek to continually improve their ability to communicate and relate to others different from themselves;
- are able to take responsibility for their own limitations and fragilities and apologize and try to correct their mistakes and fix the harm they do;
- are intellectually curious and continually develop their inquiry skills and improve their ability to research, problem solve, and think constructively;
- are willing to work hard, expect much from themselves, and encourage others to work hard, too;
- are persevering and resilient, able to keep trying and not give up easily when they run into problems; and
- are brave and courageous, and are able to take action against wrongs and help to right them.

Within this general description of democratic citizenship, there is tremendous room for diverse expressions of these values. As I consider these qualities from the diverse cultural perspectives of Maria, Fortune, Lidia, Ruth, Luke, Asami, and Hongmei, I am confident they would all embrace the importance of these qualities, and would probably have more qualities they would want to add to the list. I am also sure they would find a variety of ways to express these qualities and would agree that there are more ways of expressing democracies-always-in-the-making than all of us included in this project can imagine.

EDUCATIONAL IMPLICATIONS

When we look around us, beyond our own cultural borders, we find in the rich display of humanity wonderful examples of alternative ways to think about schools. My study of five collective cultures made me conscious of deeply held assumptions I have about schools, assumptions based on my acculturation within American schools. This is exactly what I hoped for when I set out 6 years ago to visit schools in Mexico, knowing that I needed to enlarge my thinking and critique my own embeddedness.

I used to think it was very important for children to be in small classes in small schools to increase the chances they had to know and relate to one another and not get lost and disappear in the crowd. I wanted children to know their classmates and their teachers and get the attention and nurturing they need to grow and learn as inquirers. While there are great advantages to small schools and classes, I now recognize that this and other goals were based on the classical liberal values that the needs of my individual children be met and that every child have the chance to reach his or her full potential, and that underlying these values was the assumption that others are a hindrance to the individual child's development.

I learned from this study that large schools and classes can compensate for their size in a very simple way by keeping children together in the same class for several years. This was the lesson of classrooms in Ghana, Japan, and China, all of which have larger classes and schools than many, if not most, schools in the United States. In a world of unlimited resources, I would still want small schools and classes (no more than 500 students in a school and 20–30 children in a classroom, which is what I found in Mexico). However, we do not live in a world of unlimited resources, and I now know that we can overcome the problems of crowded classrooms by simply keeping children together in the same class over extended periods of time (at least 2 years, if not more).

It seems counterintuitive to keep the same children together for longer periods of time when one's goal is to expose children to diversity and enlarge their thinking. It would seem that the greater the variety of children our students are exposed to, the greater their understanding of one another would be. However, constantly moving children to different rooms with different students does not help them get to know one another or improve their understanding of those who are different and strange to them. Staying together with a diverse group of children helps them get to know one another at a deeper level, one that overcomes stereotypes and first impressions and encourages children to accommodate one another, improve their relational and communication skills, and develop long-lasting friendships. This was the lesson of the schools I visited in Mexico, Ghana, Japan, and China, as well as the primary school on the Navajo reservation.

If we want our future citizens to take others' needs into consideration, value others and treat them with respect and dignity, attend to and care for one another, be patient with one another and help one another, improve their communication and relational skills, and apologize and correct their mistakes, we need to give them plenty of time together. It would not take an infusion of new resources to meet this recommendation, for it's a scheduling issue, not a matter of physical location. Since we already have the space for students to be in a classroom for one period of a day, it wouldn't cost more for them to stay in that room all day. The advantage of moving children from one room to another for various subjects is that they don't sit in the same room all day and have more variety in their location. This is already done when students go to different rooms for music, art, and physical education classes. It is possible for students to move from one classroom to another while keeping the class together so they are able to maintain their classroom community. If the resources are lacking for children to move to different classrooms, they can stay in the same room while the teachers move from one classroom to another, as they do in Mexico, Ghana, Japan, and China.

When there are a large number of children in a classroom and few adults, the adults learn that they must turn to the children for help with maintenance and monitoring activities. They also cannot devote enough time to the individual guidance and coaching all their students need. By reducing the number of adults in a classroom and increasing the responsibilities of the students, the students learn that they are important and valued contributors in their school community, neighborhood community, and nation, as future citizens (see Chapter 2). The importance of student responsibility was clearly valued in the school I visited in Mexico. *La Escuela* is a school where the students are treated as trustworthy, able to be counted on to do tasks assigned to them, and able to generate their own ideas for tasks they want to contribute to the school. The school is also excellent at including the parents actively in running the school, emphasizing that it is *their* school and that its success depends on all of them working together.

Children in schools should not be forced to contribute their manual labor to keep schools running, as Native American students were forced to do when they were mandated to attend boarding schools against their own and their family's will (Spring, 2004). The children in the boarding homes were treated as slave labor. If we want our children to grow up feeling needed and necessary, willing to contribute and work hard, and willing to act courageously and take action against wrongs, adults (parents and teachers) need to share responsibilities with them from an early age. As they grow and get physically stronger and gain in their knowledge and skills, they will be able to contribute more and more. Through their valued contribution, they will gain in their feelings of respect and dignity, and through the trust we offer them, they will gain in their feelings of pride and in what they can accomplish and be counted on to do. Sharing responsibilities with students empowers them in vital ways for democracies, for they learn through those experiences how important their contributions are, not only to their school but to other social institutions, such as family, community, and nation as well.

There are numerous ideas for how students can share responsibilities in school and in the classroom. In fact, after watching children in Mexico and Japan in particular, I am convinced that they can basically run the daily maintenance and upkeep of their schools with a minimal amount of adult guidance. In both schools I observed (see Chapters 2 and 5), the students are responsible for the daily care of their school compound (outside the classrooms), sweeping, raking, mopping, even cleaning the swimming pool, as I observed the 6th graders doing in Japan. Inside the school they clean the halls, stairwells, and even the teachers' lounge and principal's office. They clean their own classrooms and even their bathrooms. Adults help them and work with them as team members and guides if they need help, but the children do the bulk of the work. And, at the elementary level, they do this work gleefully, having great fun splashing water around the inside of an empty pool and scrubbing it with big brooms. They even make a game of buffing the floors, which they do in a group, forming a train and chugging along. There is joy in doing practical life work.

I don't want to overly romanticize the physical labor of caring for an environment. By the time children are teenagers, the joy of cleaning does not seem so great. They have mastered those skills and are ready to learn new ones. Teenagers should have greater responsibilities, which they do in Mexico, where they were responsible for overseeing younger siblings and getting them to school and looking out for the younger children on the playground. They were also responsible for making marketing materials for the school and curriculum materials in their print shop. On Fridays, they were responsible for teaching a community activism curriculum that they designed and implemented. On Saturdays, they taught adult literacy classes. At some schools, the teenagers may be involved in cooking noontime meals for the students and teachers. In China, Japan, and Ghana, the students do much of the toting and lifting, carrying water to the school (this was done by 7-year-olds in Ghana), carrying containers of food to the classrooms for lunch (even 6-year-olds in Japan do this), and carrying students' copybooks to and from the teachers' desks (in their classrooms as well as their offices) for teachers to grade. Again, it is empowering for children to learn that they can do this work, that they can help care for their environments. Letting them work and help out also teaches them the value of effort, and that hard work can be rewarding. No democracy has a chance of forming and enduring if its citizens are not willing to work hard and put effort and energy into the well-being of their environments, great and small. We share this Earth together and need to teach our children how to care for it, not only for their own comforts and needs but for those of their children and grandchildren. If we follow the advice of the Native Americans, we need to teach our children to worry about the impact of their actions for the next seven generations.

We must not only share responsibility with students but authority as well. Sharing authority means that students take an active role in decision making and are viewed by adults as having important contributions to make to their communities: classroom, school, family and neighbors, clan, and larger spheres as well. Their experiences need to be considered valuable and their voices considered important and listened to with respect and care. They need, along with teachers and administrators, to be seen as sources of knowledge. A democracy-always-in-the-making is a form of human association where the participants (the citizens) decide what courses of action they want their collective community (classroom, family, town, country) to take. Maybe they vote, with each citizen having one vote, and accept the majority's decisions; maybe they require that two thirds of the population support a proposal for it to be passed; or maybe they discuss and debate the issues until they reach a consensus, as many smaller indigenous nations do. How a decision is made and who gets to make the decision are things citizens in a democracy must determine.

While it is very important that students share in the responsibilities of caring for their school environment, including the curriculum, it is equally important that they are not made to labor in ways that are harmful, abusive, or oppressive. When adults control how a task must be done, insisting that they know all the answers and the best way to do things and that students do things exactly as they direct or risk punishment, there is no room left for children to make a contribution of their own. In this case, the work and effort we ask of them is for us, not them, and our tool for enforcing their compliance is fear. When we insist that we are the only authority and refuse to share authority with our students, then we create a situation where our use of power is harmful to ourselves as well as those over whom we claim authority. It is a dominating form of power that positions the adult/teacher as the oppressor and the children/students as the oppressed.

Schools and their classrooms are ideological and political terrains (see Chapter 3). They are places where we teach our students about relationships between domination and power (just as parents teach their children at home). When teachers share authority with our students, we create a situation where power becomes generative rather than harmful and oppressive. We create a place where the skills of democratic citizenship can be practiced. Democracies-always-in-the-making need citizens who are willing to contribute to their community, and take pride in their contributions. We teach them to be proud of what they give to their communities by recognizing their contributions and honoring them for their significance. We teach them that we appreciate their efforts by thanking them gratefully. A transactional view of democracies emphasizes how much we are connected to one another and need one another to succeed. It does not view others as hindrances to our personal development but instead views others, our classmates and our fellow citizens, as absolutely necessary to help us do our best. We are connected to one another and affect one another's well-being so significantly that we are only deluding ourselves if we think we can make it on our own. Classical liberalism's assumption of autonomous individuals is a dangerous delusion, a fictional dream that ignores the loving arms that cradled us, the natural sounds that soothed us, and the food that nourished us, all of which made it possible for us to stand on our own one day and declare our independence, all the while continuing to need one another and our wider living environment in order to survive.

How does the value of shared authority affect the role of teacher in the school classroom? I recommend for schools that aim to teach students how to be citizens in democracies-always-in-the-making that teaching roles be very similar to the ones I described above for governments in democracies-always-in-the-making. We need our teachers to be facilitators and resources, guides and mentors, advocates and supporters, translators, and referees when needed. The many wonderfully diverse teachers in Chapters 2 through 6 modeled these roles for us in a variety of ways. The diverse examples offered above remind us that there is room for multiple expressions of teaching that can reach students in important ways. It's important for teachers to understand their students' cultural roots in deep ways to help them communicate and relate to their students in ways that will not harm them. Parents (or whoever serves as childcare provider[s]) are teachers' best resources for helping them understand their students, for parents live with the children and know them best; parents serve as children's first teachers. Parents continue in the role of teacher long after a child has a particular classroom teacher, and wise schoolteachers recognize that their students' family members are tremendous resources for them.

We need our teachers to help us as students find answers to our questions and ask us questions about things we don't even realize we don't know. We need them to teach us research skills and problem-solving skills so we can think constructively, inquire about things we don't understand, satisfy our curiosity, and solve our problems. We need our teachers to guide us in understanding all the knowledge our culture wants to pass on to us, to share with us the stories and lessons of our elders, and teach us the language that holds our culture together. We need our teachers to mentor us, coaching us on skills we need to learn and pushing us to try harder and put more effort into our struggles. We need our teachers to encourage us to keep trying and not give up, to cheer us on and teach us to not settle for less than our best efforts. We need our teachers to critique our mistakes and help us see when we are losing our way. We need them to encourage us to reflect on our actions and the errors we have made so we can learn from our mistakes. As advocates, we need our teachers to fight for us against injustices and make sure our voices are heard. We need our teachers to encourage us to believe in ourselves and teach us how to fight to defend ourselves, and let us try. By believing in us and letting us try, teachers help us learn to be courageous and defend ourselves. By modeling an advocacy role for our classmates, they help us learn the value of defending others as well. As referees, we need our teachers to make sure others are following the agreed-upon rules and are treating us fairly, and make sure we are following the rules, too, and treating others fairly. We need them to step in to protect us when others seek to harm us until we are able to protect ourselves, and we need them to stop us from harming others. We need our teachers to facilitate discussions for us when we need to negotiate with others over disagreements until we are able to communicate and relate to others well enough to negotiate on our own. We need our teachers to serve as translators and help us understand one another across our differences.

Teachers need to claim authority for their knowledge, and society needs to recognize their authority, or they cannot serve in these roles for us. However, we cannot become knowers, too, unless teachers are willing to share their authority with us as students. Democracies are dependent on citizens who are able to make informed decisions because they are educated and view themselves as knowers. Teachers who are able to share their authority with their students and view their students as teachers as well, will find that they empower their students, help them develop courage, teach them to be persistent and resilient, encourage their desire to learn, feed their curiosity, and keep their love of learning alive. Sharing their authority also encourages their students to learn from their mistakes, develop the ability to be self-reflective, and recognize their own limitations.

When sharing authority with students, teachers must be able to trust their students. In Mexico, this means helping students become experts at something of interest, such as recycling or how to do desktop publishing, and then having them teach what they know to others. It means teachers leave the classroom at the end of their lessons and students stay behind and are free to play, roam the halls, get a drink, go to the restroom, and get back into their seats in time for the next lesson. In Ghana, it means asking the senior students in the class to write the test questions on the board for all to copy down in their copybooks and answer. At Young Warriors High School, it means trusting that the students want to come to school and learn and earn their high school diplomas, and that if they are not there, it is for a very good reason and excuse their absence, letting them make up the work another day.

Sharing authority also means that communities, even nations, need to trust their teachers and recognize them as authorities, giving them the respect societies give to those who are viewed as knowledgeable and have valued skills to share with others. In Japan, teachers enjoy a great deal of respect and are recognized as authorities in their subject areas and valued for their skills in working with students. The Japanese society trusts its teachers to do a good job and expects children to work hard for their teachers. Teachers are awarded a level of authority that American public school teachers can only dream of, and see modeled in university settings with professors or in private school settings. Japanese society values the work teachers do and recognizes it as an important contribution to the society's well-being. Native American nations value their teachers as well and award them a great deal of respect, as I saw modeled at Young Warriors High School and Diné Primary School.

In the United States, we say we value our public school teachers but do many things that undermine their authority and show a lack of trust and a lack of respect for them as scholars and for their skills in working with their students. The most obvious examples of this are the ways administrators in our public schools treat teachers: making teachers clock in and out of their work days, interrupting their teaching time with announcements and unscheduled tasks (such as monitoring the halls, proctoring exams, or escorting their class to an assembly meeting) holding teacher meetings where administrators do all the talking and don't ask teachers for input or allow them to discuss their concerns. Continually in the United States, teachers are given the message that they are not trusted as authorities in their subjects, are not skilled in working with their students, and do not understand the needs that must be considered in running a school. They are told what to teach, when to teach it, how to teach, and how to assess their students' knowledge to be sure they learned what was taught. They are treated as part-time employees (9-month contracts) who work less than a 40-hour week and are given salaries that reflect this belief. These salaries do not recognize all the preparation teachers do for their classes, all the grading, and all the continual learning they do to stay current in their fields of study.

Contrary to Japan, where teachers of elementary children are offered the same level of respect as university professors, our primary and secondary teachers can only dream of receiving the respect and authority that American professors enjoy. The only time I find my authority as a professor questioned is in regard to the courses I teach for the teacher education program. Here I am called upon to defend the value of what I teach and my ability to do so with my students in my classroom, my own colleagues in teacher education programs, the associate deans responsible for getting the teacher education program through

NCATE reviews, and state legislatures that make demands of teacher education programs without consulting the scholars in this field. In any other course I teach for the doctoral program, my authority to teach is never questioned. What this says to me is that we are all guilty—legislatures, community members, parents, students, and fellow teachers—of undermining teachers' authority in America. In order for teachers to share authority in their classrooms with their students, they first have to have authority to share. We need to offer them the respect they deserve for the important work they do, the degree of difficulty involved, and the significant level of knowledge needed to teach successfully.

A transactional democratic theory depends on a concept of shared authority that encourages the use of power in generative ways as well as to protect us from the abuse of power. A recommendation of shared authority in schools assumes that the teachers have authority to share with their students. Their authority comes from their claim of knowledge, that they know much that the student wants and needs to know. Students gain in their authority as they become knowers, too, and are able to share what they know with others who want or need to learn from them. Classical liberalism is based on a distrust of others, a feeling that others cannot be counted on, that they might harm us, and that they will not do their jobs unless we monitor or even threaten them to make them work. Distrust of others is not a good foundation upon which to grow a democracy-someday. We must begin by valuing others and treating them with respect and dignity. Fortunately, there are many examples of societies that do trust their teachers to pass on what the society has determined is vital information for their young to have, and do offer their teachers a great deal of respect for their abilities to teach the future members of their society. In societies where teachers enjoy authority as knowers, they share their authority with their students who, as a result, become inspired and empowered to become active participants in their society and help it thrive.

Of course, all teachers have limitations in what they know and in their skills in working with others. One way to compensate for a teacher's limitations is to expose students to different teachers. The Japanese and Chinese method of assigning students to a homeroom teacher who stays with them for many years, while exposing the students to a variety of teachers in specific subject areas, is a wonderful compromise. This method offers the students a chance to get to know one adult teacher at a deeper level and become known by that teacher as well. The extended time (several years) homeroom teachers have with their students helps the teachers in their roles as mentor, guide, and advocate for the child. At the same time, having different teachers for several subjects also helps students get to know diverse teachers and be exposed to differing styles of relating and communicating, and differing values and beliefs. This exposure to diverse teachers helps students adapt and adjust to any one teacher's limitations.

Another way to compensate for individual teachers' limitations is to give teachers many opportunities to work with one another to improve their skills and continue their learning process. Experienced teachers can mentor new teachers on what they know about the school population and culture, and younger teachers can share with more seasoned teachers the latest research on education. Another important idea that Japan, China, and Mexico have is that of teachers' lounges—a central room where teachers can get to know and learn from one another; have their own desks to store materials, prepare for lessons, and grade students' work; a work area for making materials and a reference area for getting information for lessons; a place to eat and drink; and a place where they can relax and enjoy human companionship. Teachers in the United States are stuck in their individual classrooms, isolated from one another, and rarely have the opportunity to talk to one another about students they may be having problems with or to share information and resources they have developed to teach a difficult concept or lesson. Their only time to talk to one another is before or after school, if they have the same prep period, in the hall between classes (usually 5 minutes), or during lunch period (which can be as short as 20 minutes).

What makes this version of a teachers' lounge so easy to institute in some countries is that their societies do not expect their teachers to continually monitor every child's behavior and continually worry that others might harm individuals. Instead, these societies expect the children to monitor their own behavior and help and look out for one another. These values are taught in homes, in houses of worship, and in neighborhoods. Parents, neighbors, spiritual leaders, and law enforcement officers all teach us what behaviors are expected of us, what behaviors our cultural group considers to be normal and what behaviors are considered to be abnormal and unacceptable. They also teach us what the consequences are if we break the social norms and do not follow the rules.

In order for teachers in the United States to have the sort of teachers' lounges that teachers in Japan, China, and Mexico enjoy, our societal norms need to be adjusted so that our children grow up learning that they are expected to monitor their own behavior. This is not an impossibility, for we already have cultural groups within our geographic borders that embrace these values and teach them to their children (e.g., Mexican Americans, Native Americans, Japanese Americans, and Chinese Americans). However, conversations on this topic need to happen at a national level, so Americans can embrace the idea that we need our democratic citizens to be responsible for monitoring their own behavior and helping one another if the need arises. Our children, as future citizens in a democracy-someday, need to learn how to do this self-monitoring while they are children and can practice the skills for relating to one another safely. They will not learn how to do this unless we let them try.

From an American perspective, it takes a big leap of faith in children's abilities to ask them to monitor themselves. The good news is that there are examples all over the world where children have already proved they are capable of self-control and caring for one another's well-being, even in high schools in China with 4,000 students enrolled. What a difference this would make for American teachers if the burden of monitoring their students' behavior at all times was lifted from their shoulders! Maybe our schools would begin to feel like happy, joyful places instead of the jails they are becoming with police officers roaming the halls, as I witnessed in all three African American schools I observed in the southeast as well as in *Los Estados Unidos* in the southwest.

The third and final theme I developed in this book that is vital for the possibility of democracies-someday—relational, pluralistic democracies-always-in-the making—is that of *shared identities*. Native American teachers, students, parents, and administrators helped us greatly understand its significance (see Chapter 4). I have learned from all five of the cultural groups I studied that children need to grow up with a sense of shared identity with others like them in order for them to feel good about themselves. They need to feel included in a cultural group, to feel like they belong. This feeling of membership helps children feel safe and comfortable, assured that others understand them at a deep level because of what they share in common (language, rituals, historical experiences, geographic location, the milieu of their daily lives). They also need to feel good about the cultural group to which they belong in order to feel good about themselves. They need to hear their cultural members described in terms of making significant contributions to their society, and to see them serving as role models of highly valued quality traits (such as bravery and generosity). Majority children, who are surrounded by their culture and can take it for granted, grow up not even noticing how much loving support they receive from their family, friends, and society at large for their own development of a healthy identity. However, how do children from diverse minority cultures find ways to feel that they fit in to their schools and forget, at least for a little while, that they are a minority? How do they thrive and feel good about themselves when they do not find their cultures reflected in the stories the teachers tell and in the "facts" their books present as being important to know, or even worse, when the teachers and books tell lies, as they do with Native Americans? (Brayboy [2003] writes about his recent experience of finding on the classroom bulletin board in a public high school sociology course a portrayal of Geronimo as a serial killer.)

Societies that embrace the value of democracies-always-in-the-making must embrace the value of cultural diversity at a deep level. They must understand that diverse cultures need to be afforded space to gather and socialize with one another as they seek to practice and maintain their cultures. They must be allowed, even encouraged, to maintain their cultural distinctness in-

stead of insisting on cultural assimilation, which amounts to cultural imperialism. Our children need to be taught to value and appreciate one another for
our differences as well as for what we have in common. The best way to ensure
that cultures are represented fairly and favorably is to allow them to represent
themselves. They need to tell their own stories of their past and explain their
own interpretations of the present to their children as well as to others. The
best way to ensure that cultural diversity thrives within a country as diverse
as the United States is to allow local control of the curriculum, with parents
and teachers working together in consultation with scholars to decide what
needs to be taught to their children/students and how it is to be taught, and to
allow students to contribute as they grow and gain skills. Let the teachers, as
authorities in their subject areas, develop the curriculum to meet the needs of
the students in their classrooms with the local community's support.

In order for us to have the hope of achieving democracies-someday, we need
our teachers to be culturally relevant (Ladson-Billings, 1994), appreciate the importance of cultural diversity in their classrooms, bring culturally diverse perspectives into all aspects of their curriculum, and make sure the cultures of the
children in their classrooms are represented favorably in their curriculum. It is a
tall order, expecting our teachers to continually learn more about their students
and their cultural influences, but we cannot accept anything less without risking
squandering our greatest resource, our cultural diversity. Achieving this high
level of value for cultural diversity cannot be the sole responsibility of teachers. All of our social institutions must value diversity: our religious institutions,
homes, communities, places of employment, media, and so forth.

America is very fortunate to have the level of cultural diversity it has within
its borders. From a political philosophical perspective that embraces a relational, pluralistic democratic theory, I believe cultural diversity is our country's greatest asset. From an educational perspective, I believe it is our public
school system's greatest asset and will help us become a democracy-someday.
The United States is a place where our children can be exposed to tremendous
levels of cultural diversity just by attending school. Of course, the extent of
cultural diversity varies depending on where we live. However, I live in a state
that is not a port of entry to this country and not particularly known to be culturally diverse, and have observed schools with significant African American,
Japanese American, Chinese American, and Mexican American populations,
with more moving to the state every year. We have a significant number of
Korean Americans living in the area (enough to have a Saturday school), the
Cherokee reservation nearby, and one of the largest populations of Iraqis in
the country (Nashville was one of the voting locations for national elections in
Iraq). In port-of-entry states such as California, Florida, and New York, there
is even more cultural diversity than in my state of residence.

Because of the degree of cultural diversity in the United States, we do not have to work as hard as other countries do to expose our children to diverse cultures. Students in Ghana, China, Mexico, and Japan learn about other cultures by reading about them in their textbooks and on the Internet, viewing films, listening to music, and dining at franchises like Kentucky Fried Chicken or McDonald's. Some have the opportunity to travel to other countries but many do not, and depending on where they live, they may not get much exposure to international travelers in their home country. In every school I visited for this study, the students are being exposed to diverse cultures through their curriculum: in economics, government, religious studies, literature, music, and art classes. They are studying other languages as well, predominantly English, and striving to be bilingual, if not trilingual. In America, instead of embracing the importance of cultural diversity and seeking to ensure that all our children are at least bicultural and bilingual, we are reducing funds for ESL programs, seeking to pass a law making English our national language, building triple fences on our southern border with Mexico, and tightening immigration laws so fewer people can move here temporarily or permanently. After 9/11 and the terrorist attacks on our shores, Americans seem to have a greater fear of others who are culturally different, rather than seeing them as allies and friends who can help enlarge our views and enhance our lives.

In the United States, we are afraid to let curricula be controlled at the local level for fear they will become too parochial, while at the same time, we fear that a national curriculum will be too powerful and erase many cultural perspectives. We do not trust our public school teachers to be in charge of the school curriculum (although we do trust teachers in our private schools). We do not trust our local communities either, citing examples of curricula that teach very limited, biased representations of the world as justification for controlling our curricula at the state or national level. However, we also do not trust our states and nation to control the curriculum, for we know that this leaves our children vulnerable to indoctrination. We are certainly a country whose people are suspicious of one another, and for good reason.

We need to work at breaking down those suspicions and building trust, and that begins by recognizing how important shared identities are for each of us at a personal, local, and national level and even on a larger scale, for we are all inhabitants of this one precious Earth. If we embrace the value of learning from others who are different from us and strive to be rooted in our own cultures while being bicultural and bilingual, we can achieve a both/and approach to this problem instead of framing it as either/or logic. All over the world, children are learning about Euro-Western cultures—I heard Brahms lullabies played in Chinese schools to wake up students from their naptime and Mozart playing in Japanese schools while the children cleaned their classrooms, and I heard geography, economic, government, and religious lessons about Europe and the Americas taught to children in Mexico, Ghana, Japan, and China. Children all over the world are exposed to American popular culture: In Mexico, the students and teachers wore t-shirts with the names of American baseball and football teams on them; in China, in a lower secondary talent show, a student lip-synched to Michael Jackson's "Thriller"; also in China, we took our son to see *Star Wars III* in English the very week it opened in the United States (the film was available in several languages); and in the village where we stayed in Ghana, we watched the World Cup games along with everyone else around the world. It is a small world we live in, after all!

I am not worried that if curricula are developed at the local level by diverse cultures, it will result in a loss of commonality. Quite the contrary. There is already so much pressure, through global marketing and technology advances (such as televisions, computers, and planes), to become more alike and have more in common. Our world is shrinking, and I am more worried about losing our rich diversity. We can see this happening with young children on the Rez who insist on speaking only English and have little interest in learning the Navajo language well enough to maintain it. In China, this is a big concern right now as the country opens its ports to the Euro-Western world and expands trade tremendously. How will they maintain their Chinese values and beliefs? How will they make sure they do not lose their Chinese culture, not to mention their most talented students, to the lure of the Euro-West? Cultures do not stand still, frozen in time; they continue to adapt, change, and adjust to the forces around them, as well as contribute to those forces and change them (this is a transactional relationship). All over the world, people fear the loss of their cultures; we are more alike than we are different. Just go traveling and you'll see what I mean!

CONCLUSION

We live in times where there are great changes in political philosophy and in societies at large. These are times when the key assumptions of liberal democratic theory are being questioned and dismissed. My voice is included in the chorus of criticisms of liberal democracy's assumptions of rationalism, universalism, and individualism. I have tried to answer the call made by political philosophers such as Fraser (1997) for a credible vision of an alternative to the present order, one that addresses the need for recognition of identities as well as the need for redistribution of resources. I have offered a relational, pluralistic social political theory that moves us beyond liberal democracy. I have turned to several key political philosophers to help me show the need for change and how to encourage the development of change. Most importantly, I have turned to the students and teachers in the schools I visited to help me understand more deeply what a relational, pluralistic democracy-always-in-the-making might look like. These students and teachers and the researchers studying them taught me the themes of *shared responsibility, shared authority,* and *shared identity* for a transactional democratic theory. I have shared their stories to illustrate these themes. I have sought to keep this theory grounded in the historical, local, contingent, everyday world of schooling practices to make sure it is understandable and relevant to educators, as well as to ensure that it does not fall into the traps of essentializing, ahistoricizing, and decontextualizing theory.

I have focused on teachers and students whose stories are not often heard—minority students in American public schools whose families have historically been disenfranchised from democracy in the United States. I started this study with the realization that the three cultures with the highest drop-out rates in U.S. schools are also cultures that assume collective, communitarian values in raising their children, believing "it takes a village to raise a child." While this adage comes from Africa and was vividly modeled for me in Ghana, it also applies to Mexican American and Native American cultures. All three of these cultures embrace values that are contrary to classical liberalism's values of individuality, autonomy, choice, freedom, and competition. Their values are better represented by social democratic values of fraternity, equality, sharing, and cooperation. I started this study with a question, wondering if American classical liberal values, which shape our public school system, aren't making it even more difficult for children from these three cultural groups to succeed. From the research I read and presented in this text, the answer seems very clear: Yes, our public schools represent classical liberal values, and yes, when we insist that children adopt these values in order to succeed in school, they are presented with an impossible choice between their loved ones and the culture from which they draw their social identities, and what their schools demand of them in order to succeed.

I included Chinese American and Japanese American students in this study because they enjoy the stereotype of being "model minorities" who are doing very well in U.S. schools and yet are differing collective cultures. I wondered why they are succeeding, when they also come from cultures with collective, communitarian values, not classical liberal values, and have also experienced racism in the United States. I have been surprised to find through research and my observations that classical liberal values are not in closer agreement with Japanese and Chinese cultural values, as I originally hypothesized. I learned from talking to the Japanese Saturday School and Chinese Sunday School teachers that Japanese American and Chinese American students are struggling in American schools as well. Many of them experience the same tensions and feelings of subtraction and loss of their cultural values if they embrace the classical liberal values needed to succeed in American schools. I have been surprised to find that many Japanese and Chinese students suffer with feelings of inadequacy and depression, the very same feelings that the other students in my study suffer with as they try to find ways to digest classical liberalism without ill effect.

As I suspected, classical liberal and collective values are logically exclusive of each other; they set up binaries where we find ourselves having to choose one or the other. Each set of values has weaknesses and strengths that they mirror as opposite reflections of one another as they respond to one another's contradictions. I have suggested that there is a way out of this either/or logic by embracing a transactional assumption of selves-in-relation-with-others, which relies on a both/and logic to describe individuals and others as influencing and affecting one another. This transactional assumption also applies to the social institutions we have constructed in our various cultures: our families, religions, economies, governments, and schools, for example. I have made the case that these social institutions influence and affect one another as well; they are connected and part of one whole. Our social institutions are individuals-in-relation-to-others at a macro level (the transactional relationship on a larger scale). Just as the borders between individual selves are artificially drawn, so, too, are the borders we erect between our social institutions as we try to make sense of our world and give it meaning. These borders cannot hold up to close scrutiny, for their edges are fuzzy, appearing solid from a distance but disappearing when looked at closely. I have argued that if we try to address one social institution, such as education, while ignoring others, such as economies and families, we are doomed to failure, for it is only through addressing the transactional relationship between institutions that we will have a chance of addressing problems within social institutions and making changes.

Such a complex, interrelated description of our world may make it seem like there is no chance of ever effecting change in our social institutions. Where do we begin? What steps do we take that will start the process of change? And what hope can we ever have of seeing the changes take effect? Though the task may seem overwhelming, it is nevertheless possible to improve conditions in our education systems, but we must pause and consider the results of our actions before we act. Our actions are interconnected and our world is continually in a state of flux as actions cause reactions and affect us. We must lose our arrogance and unquestioned confidence that we know what to do to "fix things," and gain more respect for the complexity of situations. We must move more cautiously and humbly, recognizing that those at the local level who are most directly affected may understand the conditions necessary for change better than we, as outsiders, do, but we must also recognize that our outsider perspectives might be useful to insiders by contributing to the expansion of their thoughts about situations.

While it may seem impossible *to* effect changes in our social institutions and improve social conditions with the transactional description of our world that I offer, it is surely impossible *not to* effect changes in this living, breathing world. If we start with a transactional view of our world, we realize that we are continually in a state of flux. Schools that seem never to change are, in fact, always in a state of movement and change. From a transactional perspective, it is not a matter of where do we begin and how do we get started, but one of becoming aware that that we are always in process and we cannot stop. Instead, we need to worry about how we are effecting change and how our actions are affecting others.

I have argued that classical liberalism's values of individual freedom, choice, and autonomy have been spread far and wide through colonization by Euro-Western nations, such as England, France, and, more recently, the United States, which embrace those values. These values have poisoned indigenous cultures and are having the same effect on other collective cultures today. I offer a transactional view of individuals-in-relation-to-others as a powerful antidote to classical liberalism. I do not think classical liberalism will ever lead us to democracies; the exclusionary either/or logic of liberalism in fact contradicts the very idea of "democracy," which is inclusive and welcoming of others who are not like us. It is my great hope that the transactional view I offer here generates novel ways to work toward a democracy that is welcoming toward all our children.

I am deeply moved by the many administrators, teachers, and students who so generously offered me a glimpse of their worlds. I could not have completed this project without their help. I cannot forget their faces and how touched they were when they realized that I came to their schools to learn from them. I am saddened by the knowledge that I was the first to do so, to come and stay, even if only for a week. The friends I made call on me to share what I learned from them with others. The most important lesson we all need to learn is that we need one another to expand our own limited, fallible understandings of our world. It is our only chance for a democracy-someday. When we are able to respect and value one another, when we are curious about one another and seek to know more about one another, when we work on improving our communication and relational skills so we can learn from one another, when we are able to care for one another and take one another's needs into consideration, when we are able to feel generosity and empathy for one another, when we are patient and considerate of one another, when we are able to be self-reflective and learn from our mistakes and take responsibility for our actions, when we strive to fix our mistakes and apologize to one another, when we can roll up our sleeves and work hard to improve our living conditions, and when we are brave and courageous enough to act as well as persevering and resilient enough to never give up when we run into problems, then we will have a democracy. Until then, it will always be in-the-making.

Notes

Chapter 1

1. Charlene Haddock Siegfried (1996) has written about what pragmatism and feminism have to offer each other in *Pragmatism and Feminism.*

2. Other sources for beginning with an assumption of transactional relationships come from feminist scholarship in the 1980s that strove to describe how selves begin their lives in-relation-with-others, in particular, in relation with those who care for them. While there are many problems with that earlier work, Nel Noddings (1984), Sara Ruddick (1989), and Jane Flax (1983) in particular are three feminist scholars who reminded us that children do not begin their lives as individuals, that they become individuals through their relationships with their care providers. As Noddings (1984) describes the self:

> I am not naturally alone. I am naturally in relation from which I derive nourishment and guidance. When I am alone, either because I have detached myself or because circumstances have wrenched me free, I seek first and most naturally to reestablish my relatedness. My very individuality is defined in a set of relations. (p. 51)

For Noddings, we begin our lives in relation; it is an ontological basic for us. She establishes our relationality through her discussion of caring relationships, the one-caring and the one-cared-for, extending these relationships beyond the boundaries of the home and parents to include schools and teachers. Ruddick (1989) helps establish our fundamental relationality through her exploration of the maternal relationship with the child as she helps us understand that a child's spirit unfolds through the intimate relationship with another. Ruddick's focus is predominantly from the perspective of the "mother," the "person who takes on responsibility for children's lives and for whom providing child care is a significant part of her or his working life" (p. 40). She looks closely at demands that arise with mothering, demands of protecting the child from harm, helping the child to grow and flourish, and preparing the child to be socially acceptable in the society in which the mother and child reside. Flax (1983) makes the case for our fundamental relationality from the perspective of the child, relying on psychoanalytic theory to help us understand how we are literally constituted by the relationships in which we participate. For Flax, the psychological birth of the human infant takes around 3 years, and this complex process can only occur in and through social relations, in particular social relations with the infant's caregivers. For these feminist scholars, the relationality they describe is one of mutual interdependence and independence; it is a relationship of reciprocity.

3. Maxine Greene is a current philosopher of education who has also inspired me to describe democracies as always-in-the-making. Greene was influenced by Dewey as well. In her *Releasing the Imagination* (1995), she tells us she is concerned about us "becoming wide-awake to the world," and breaking free from the "cotton wool of daily life." Her goal includes the creation of a public space for this to occur through the making of a community, "a community always in the making—the community that may someday be called a democracy" (p. 6). I have written about Greene's influence on my work in *Democracies-Always-in-the-Making: Maxine Greene's Influence,* in review.

4. See for example: Chantal Mouffe's (1993) *The Return of the Political*; Mouffe's (2005) "The Limits of John Rawls's Pluralism"; Susan M. Okin's (2005) "'Forty Acres and a Mule' for Women: Rawls and Feminism"; and Michael Walzer's (August 1981) "Philosophy and Democracy" and (1983) *Spheres of Justice.*

5. One of my reviewers suggested that I do not give Dewey enough credit for his involvement in the women's suffrage movement and his support as a founding member of the NAACP. I don't deny the Dewey was active in fighting for social justice issues of his time. I would add to the reviewer's examples Dewey's support for Highlander, in Tennessee, which helped organize the Southern labor movement and, later, the civil rights movement. My criticism is with the lack of attention to racism and sexism in Dewey's democratic theory, not his way of life. I am not the only one criticizing him on these issues. See Frank Margonis's (2004) and Charlene Haddock Seigfried's (1996) contributions to this topic.

6. I maintain Barber's use of the pronoun "male" to describe human beings, for this is the term he uses. Barber published *Strong Democracy* long after the second wave of feminism in the 1960s, when sexist language was highly debated. His decision to use masculine pronouns underscores the possibility that he presents an androcentric political perspective.

7. My discussion of Dewey has been published in Thayer-Bacon, B. (2006). "Beyond Liberal Democracy: Dewey's Renascent Liberalism," *Education and Culture, 22*(2): 19–30.
Paper presentations:

a. *Beyond liberal democracy: Dewey's reticent liberalism.* Paper delivered at John Dewey Society SIG, American Educational Research Association annual conference, April 11–15, 2005, Montreal, Canada.

b. *Beyond liberal democracy: Young's deliberative democracy.* Alternative Session paper delivered at Philosophy of Education Society annual spring conference, April 21–24, 2006, Puerto Vallarta, Mexico.

c. *Beyond liberal democracy: Laclau and Mouffe's radical democracy.* Paper delivered at International Network of Philosophers of Education 10th Biennial Conference, August 3–6, 2006, St. Julians, Malta.

Chapter 2

1. Carger (1996) says that in the Latino population in the United States, there are 13.3 million Mexican Americans, 2.6 million Central Americans, 2.2 million Puerto Ricans, 1 million Cubans, and 1.4 million Caribbeans, thus placing the total Latino population at 19.5 million.

2. In the summer of 2001, I spent one week observing a Mexican school in central Mexico (*La Escuela*), and one week observing a charter school in the southwest of the United States with a population that was more than 80% Mexican American (*Los Estados Unidos*). I found the U.S. school by going through lists of charter schools in the southwest, looking for ones that had existed for at least 5 years so there was some continuity, used democratic language

in their mission statement, and described in their mission statement a recognition of the importance of including cultural awareness in their curriculum, in particular the Mexican American culture, and expressed a desire to include parents in their school community. I favored elementary schools, since my own teaching background is with elementary children, and I found that elementary schools are the best place for an observer to see most vividly children's cultures reflected in the curriculum, the school structure, and the daily practices and rituals. As children get older, high schools look more and more alike and the differences are subtler, but, at the elementary level, the differences are stronger and easier to observe.

Los Estados Unidos was a large, well-established elementary school that was more than 50% Mexican American. Also important, I was able to observe in *Los Estados Unidos* during the summer when it was in session, as it is a year-round school. I learned about *La Escuela* through a conference I attended where the founder of the school and the school's principal were keynote speakers. As they described their school's mission and history, I realized it was a strong example of a democratic approach to education and asked if I could possibly visit and observe and include it in my study. Again, the school had existed long enough to have some continuity, and it was 100% Mexican, with ages ranging from 3 to 16 years old. The age range was an added plus, as I was able to observe a wide range of students. All names have been changed in the text to protect the identity of the schools and the participants in the school communities.

3. Each year, *La Escuela* has been adding another grade level as the current students age. In 2001, the school went through 10th grade, but it now goes through 12th grade.

4. *La Escuela* had no computers in its classrooms, but a computer lab was available for all students to use as well as computers, scanners, and color laser printers in the high school print-making shop. Maria and a few of the administrators had computers and equipment that they shared with anyone who needed them (including parents and former students who would come to the school to work on projects).

5. I have presented three papers at conferences concerning Highlander Folk School:

a. *An exploration of Highlander Folk School as a radical democracy*, delivered at American Educational Studies Association annual conference, October 30–November 4, 2002, Pittsburgh, PA.

b. *An exploration of Myles Horton's caring reasoning at Highlander Folk School*, delivered at American Educational Studies Association annual conference, October 31–November 4, 2001, Miami, FL.

c. *An exploration of Myles Horton's democratic praxis: Highlander Folk School*, delivered at Southeastern Association of Educational Studies conference, March 9–11, 2001, Knoxville, TN.

Also, I have published two articles:

a. Thayer-Bacon, B. (Spring, 2004). "An exploration of Myles Horton's democratic praxis: Highlander Folk School," *Educational Foundations, 18*(2), 5–23.

b. Thayer-Bacon, B. (2002). "An exploration of Myles Horton's caring reasoning at Highlander Folk School," *Thinking: The Journal for Philosophy for Children, 16*(1), 32–41.

I rely on four sources for the biographical and historical information I present on Myles Horton's life and on Highlander Folk School:

a. Adams, Frank, with Myles Horton. (1975). *Unearthing seeds of fire: The idea of Highlander.* Winston-Salem, NC: John F. Blair.

b. Horton, Aimee I. (1971/1989). *The Highlander Folk School: A history of its major programs, 1932–1961.* Brooklyn, NY: Carlson Publishing.

    c. Horton, Myles, with Herbert and Judith Kohl. (1990). *The long haul: An autobiography.* New York: Teachers College Press.

    d. Horton, Myles, & Freire, Paulo. *We make the road by walking: Conversations on education and social change.* Philadelphia: Temple University Press.

Horton did not personally write any of these texts, but the texts record his words and stories, many of which are repeated in all the sources, and he did critically review what was published. Together they offer a full picture of Horton's life and of Highlander.

6. Maria's office was a desk to one side of a very large space with no walls. In this area were desks for three secretaries, several administrative workers, the teachers, and several computer stations, and a couch and a large round table with chairs around it. I sat to one side where I was able to watch and hear most of what went on. Much parental action took place here during the day.

7. Section 1 was presented as *Establishing shared responsibilities in a Mexican and Mexican American school.* Paper delivered at International Network of Philosophers of Education 9th Biennial Conference, August 4–7, 2004, Madrid, Spain.

Section 2 was presented as *Exploring democratic citizenship in a Mexican and Mexican American school: Varying forms of empowerment.* Paper delivered at American Educational Studies Association annual conference, October 29–November 2, 2003, Mexico City, Mexico.

Chapter 3

1. In the spring of 2002, I spent the equivalent of 1 week (1 day per week for 5 weeks) each at a high school, middle school, and elementary school in the South where the schools have a majority of African Americans. In June of 2002, I spent a week observing a K–3, 3–5, and 6–8 school system in a small village 2 hours from the capital of Ghana, Accra, in West Africa, where I was the first White woman to study their schools, or reside in their village, for that matter. Again, these schools graciously opened their doors to me and invited me to visit after I wrote to ask permission. I found the schools in Ghana with the help of a former colleague who takes his music students to Ghana to learn West African dancing and percussion. In Ghana, my life partner (Charles Bacon), son (Sam), and I had the good fortune of staying at the music school, which was also the home of one of the families in the village. While I walked to school with their children for the day, Charles and Sam stayed behind at the compound for djimbee drumming lessons. Our musician host comes to the South and performs with West African dancers and drummers from two of the schools. We have become good friends and were able to repay his generosity and kindness by hosting him in America. All names have been changed in the chapter to protect the identity of the schools and the participants in the school communities.

2. As the teachers in the JSS in Ghana went by their first names with me and by the formal title of Madam with their students, I call Fortune by her first name when I speak of her but use "Madam" when students speak to her. At River High School, the teachers go by their last names, even with one another, so I use "Ms. Lincoln" for the teacher I observed at RHS.

3. I use parentheses around the "e" of epistemology to symbolize a nontranscendent epistemology. I have written about this topic at length in *Relational "(e)pistemologies."*

4. The teachers in the West African dance and drumming class at MSS and RHS go by their first names with their students, so I give the dance teacher the first name "Lidia." At River High School, the teachers go by their last names, even with one another, so I use "Ms. Jefferson" for the teacher I observed at RHS.

5. See:
   a. Thayer-Bacon, B. (2006). Shared authority in democratic classroom communities-always-in-the-making. In K. Cooper & R. White (Eds.), *The practical critical educator: Critical inquiry and educational practice*, pp. 95–109. Amsterdam: Springer.
   b. *Hard work leads to success: Exploring democratic citizenship in an African American high school and middle school.* Paper delivered at American Educational Studies Association annual conference, November 3–November 7, 2004, Kansas City, MO.
6. Section 1 was published in: Thayer-Bacon, B. (2006). Shared authority in democratic classroom communities-always-in-the-making. In K. Cooper & R. White (Eds.), *The practical critical educator: Critical inquiry and educational practice*, pp. 95–109. Amsterdam: Springer.

Paper presentations:
   a. *Hard work leads to success: Exploring democratic citizenship in an African American high school and middle school.* Paper delivered at American Educational Studies Association annual conference, November 3–November 7, 2004, Kansas City, MO.
   b. *Shared authority: Exploring democratic citizenship in an African American elementary school.* Paper delivered at Research on Women and Education SIG, annual fall conference, October 28–30, 2004, Cleveland, OH.
   c. *Shared authority in democracies-always-in-the-making: Teaching moral lessons in an African American school.* Presented at Southeast Philosophy of Education Society annual conference, February 20–21, 2004, Tuscaloosa, AL.

Chapter 4

1. In January 2003, I spent 1 week at a primary school, upper elementary school, middle school, and high school on the Navajo Reservation, where the Native American population is over 97% (not all Navajo). These schools cautiously opened their doors to me after a contact I had spoke on my behalf. Initially, I was only able to get permission to visit the Diné Primary School. Once I was there and met people, I was given permission to visit the upper elementary, middle, and high school as well. My contact at Diné was the school counselor, Tom, a White man married to a Navajo woman who has lived at the Mesa for over 15 years. Tom had worked with a colleague of mine when she was on sabbatical at Diné for one semester, and that colleague still places students from the reservation in internships.

In the spring of 2003, I spent 1 week at an urban Native American high school in the Midwest, Young Warriors High, which is 55% Indian, and at Indian Community School (K–8), which is 100% Indian. The two schools are across the street from each other in a large Midwest city. I was advised to spend time in an urban school, as more than 50% of Native Americans now live in cities (Lobo & Peters, 2001). Initially, I was only able to get permission to visit Young Warriors High School, but once I was there and met people I was given permission to visit Indian Community School as well. I was told about Young Warriors by a (White) professor I met through my research who had lived for years on the street behind the school and had developed a long-standing, trusting relationship with them, helping them with reviews of their program and other projects. When my colleague heard about my research project, he introduced it to the school director and spoke on my behalf. All names have been changed in the text to protect the identity of the schools and the participants in the school communities.

2. Another example is Robert A. Roessel, Jr. (Spring 1999), who helped make Rough Rock school successful, and Teresa McCarty (2002), who has researched Rough Rock's literacy issues extensively.

3. I am a licensed elementary Montessori teacher who taught in an elementary Montessori classroom for 6 years. My four children attended Montessori schools from ages 3 through 12 (with a few interruptions). My goal was simple: to keep their love of learning alive. I have written extensively about my experience as a Montessori teacher in Thayer-Bacon with Bacon (1998).

4. Temperament-wise, the Navajos are low-key, not hotheads who express a lot of emotions. If colors represent their emotions, they are pastels. As Tom pointed out when I asked about this calmness, "Native Americans were shot in the United States if they were perceived as threatening—so they learned passive resistance." They still do this with one another today, teachers informed me. Even at the high school, students do not "cop an attitude" with teachers. If they don't want to do an assignment, they just quietly don't do it. The people are not pushy or loud; there's no need to be that way on the Rez. Tom told me the only pushy, loud kids they see are those born off the Rez who come there to live. "In the real world (off the Rez)," Tom said, "you have to learn how to be pushy in order to get heard. For most Native Americans, the teachers and counselors just need to remind them where they are now and that it's not necessary and they are fine. They adjust and stop being behavior problems." Tom told me they don't have kids on Ritalin and don't have big behavior problems at Diné Primary School. The week I was there, I saw only one child cry, and that was because he had to say goodbye to his parents, who lived off the Rez and were leaving him in his aunt's care so he could attend school. I watched the entire high school (800 students) have lunch together and it was the most peaceful and calm high school lunch hour I have ever observed.

5. The story of Indian boarding schools told from the U.S. government's perspective is found in Hildegard Thompson's (1975) *The Navajo's Long Walk for Education: A History of Navajo Education.*

6. As we discovered in Section 1, this same issue came up in my observations at the Navajo Reservation. Many teaching assistants on the Rez were losing their jobs because they did not have the proper credentials, even though they had years of experience teaching and had the deepest level of understanding of their indigenous culture.

7. This text puts the Native American drop-out rate at 35.8%.

8. Nicki (a male student who has been sleeping the whole time) woke up for a minute during the drumming but he laid his head back down and went back to sleep. Nicki looks Hispanic and Native American. Luke told me after class that Nicki is bipolar and his medicine makes him sleepy, so he lets him sleep. Nicki was the only one who didn't participate in the drumming.

9. For an excellent source on Indian dreams, and Black Elk's dreams in particular, see Lee Irwin, 1994.

10. Paper presentations:
a. *The role of grandmother and father in developing shared identities in a Native American urban high school.* Paper delivered at American Educational Studies Association annual conference, November 2–6, 2005, Charlottesville, VA.
b. *The role of mother and big sister in developing shared identities in a Native American urban high school.* Paper delivered at Research in Women and Education annual fall conference, October 20–22, 2005, Dayton, OH.
c. *"A street is something you walk on": Developing shared identities in a Navajo school.* Paper delivered at American Educational Studies Association annual conference, November 1–5, 2006, Spokane, WA.

Chapter 5

1. All names have been changed in the text to protect the identity of the schools and the participants in the school communities.

2. There are exceptions to this overall equality that can be found by looking at the history of the education of minority students in Japan, such as Koreans, who are not granted citizenship even today, and the *Buraku* children, who are treated as outcasts. See Okano and Tsuchiya's (1999) *Education in Contemporary Japan: Inequality and Diversity* and Schoolland's (1990) *Shogun's Ghost*.

3. There are controversies surrounding the centralized Japanese curriculum that are not addressed in their classrooms as well, such as their censored history books and lack of discussion of their role in World War II and their aggression against Korea and China that led up to World War II. Japan does not acknowledge this aggression in its history books, which continues to be a source of tension with its neighboring countries. Also, Japanese teachers at the secondary school level experience considerable pressure to help their students do well on the entrance exams that determine which high school and college will accept them.

4. Paper presentations:
a. *Hard work leads to success: Comparing Japanese and American perspectives on ability and effort.* Paper delivered at Confluent Education SIG, American Educational Research Association annual conference, April 11–15, 2005, Montreal, Canada (with C. Bacon).
b. *Exploring the teacher's role in Japan: An example of shared authority and shared responsibility.* Paper delivered at Confluent Education SIG, American Educational Research Association annual conference, March 24-28, 2008, New York (with C. Bacon).
c. *Homogeneity and diversity: Comparing Japanese and American perspectives on harmony and disagreement* (under review).

Chapter 6

1. I use "China" as shorthand to refer to the People's Republic of China. I do not include Taiwan or Hong Kong in this research, but focus solely on mainland China.

2. I spent the first week back to school after the winter break in 2005 with the 35 full-time teachers and 680 students of Canton, who graciously opened their school and classroom doors to me. In Guangzhou, China, Hongmei and I visited an upper secondary school for 3 days and a lower secondary school for 2, and spent a second week in two elementary schools. We spent the last week of May and the first week of June 2005 in these schools. All names have been changed in the text to protect the identity of the schools and the participants in the school communities.

References

Abowitz, K. K. (1999, Spring). Reclaiming community. *Educational Theory, 49*(2), 143–159.

Abowitz, K. K. (2000). Public spheres and education: Homeless, colonized, and conflicting. *Philosophical Studies in Education, 32*, 119-126.

Adams, F., with Horton, M. (1975). *Unearthing seeds of fire: The idea of Highlander.* Winston-Salem, NC: John F. Blair.

Allen, P. (1986). *The sacred hoop: Recovering the feminine in American Indian traditions.* Boston: Beacon Press.

Anderson, J. D. (1988). *The education of Blacks in the South, 1860–1935.* Chapel Hill: The University of North Carolina Press.

Asante, M. K. (1987). *The Afrocentric idea.* Philadelphia: Temple University Press.

Ashton-Warner, S. (1975). *Teacher.* London: Bantam Books.

Ayers, W., & Klonsky, M. (1994, Winter). Navigating a restless sea: The continuing struggle to achieve a decent education for African American youngsters in Chicago. *The Journal of Negro Education, 63*(1), 5–18.

Baker, S. (1995, Spring). Testing equality: The national teacher examination and the NAACP's legal campaign to equalize teachers' salaries in the South, 1936–1963. *History of Education Quarterly, 35*(1), 49–64.

Barber, B. (1984). *Strong democracy: Participatory politics for a new age.* Berkeley: University of California Press.

Between sacred mountains: Navajo stories and lessons from the land. (1982, 1994). Tucson: Sun Tracks and the University of Arizona Press.

Boler, M. (1999). *Feeling power: Emotions and education.* New York: Routledge.

Bordo, S. (1987). *The flight to objectivity.* Albany: State University of New York Press.

Bowles, S., & Gintis, H. (1977). *Schooling in capitalist America.* New York: Basic Books.

Brayboy, B. (2003). Visibility is a trap: American Indian representation in schools. In S. Books (Ed.), *Invisible children in the society and its schools* (2nd ed., pp. 35–52). Mahwah, NJ: Lawrence Erlbaum.

Brown, D. (1971). *Bury my heart at Wounded Knee: An Indian history of the American West.* New York: Bantam Books.

Butcher, R. E. (1988, Fall). "Outthinking and outflanking the owners of the world": A historiography of the African American struggle for education. *History of Education Quarterly, 28*(3), 333–366.

Carger, C. (1996). *Of borders and dreams: A Mexican-American experience of urban education.* New York: Teachers College Press.

Chen, S. (2002). *Becoming Chinese, becoming Chinese American.* Urbana: University of Illinois Press.

Choy, P., Dong, L., & Hom, M. (Eds.). (1994). *Coming man: 19th century American percep-tions of the Chinese*. Seattle: University of Washington Press.

Chun, G. H. (2000). *Of orphans and warriors: Inventing Chinese American culture and iden-tity*. New Brunswick, NJ: Rutgers University Press.

Collins, P. H. (1990). *Black feminist thought*. Boston: Unwin Hyman.

Deloria, V. Jr., & Lytle, C. M. (1984). *The nations within: The past and future of American Indian sovereignty*. New York: Pantheon Books.

Delpit, Lisa. (1995). *Other people's children: Cultural conflict in the classroom*. New York: The New Press.

Dempsey, V., & Noblit, G. (1993). The demise of caring in an African-American commu-nity: One consequence of school desegregation. *The Urban Review, 25*(1), 47–61.

Dewey, J. (1935). *Liberalism and social action*. New York: G. P. Putnam's Sons.

Dewey, J. (1939). *Freedom and culture*. New York: G. P. Putnam's Sons.

Dewey, J. (1954). *The public and its problems*. New York: Henry Holt and Company. (Origi-nal work published 1927)

Dewey, J. (1955). *Logic: The theory of inquiry*. New York: Henry Holt and Company. (Origi-nal work published 1938)

Dewey, J. (1965). *Experience and education*. New York: MacMillan. (Original work pub-lished 1938)

Dewey, J. (1996). *Democracy and education*. New York: The Free Press, MacMillan. (Origi-nal work published 1916)

Dewey, J., & Bentley, A. (1960). *Knowing and the known*. Boston: Beacon Press. (Original work published 1949)

Duran, E., & Duran, B. (1995). *Native American postcolonial psychology*. Albany: State Uni-versity of New York Press.

Ellington, L. (1992). *Education in the Japanese life-cycle: Implications for the United States*. Lewiston, NY: The Edwin Mellen Press.

Epstein, I. (Ed.). 1991. *Chinese education: Problems, policies, and prospects*. New York and London: Garland.

Finkelstein, B., Imamura, A., & Tobin, J. (1991). *Transcending stereotypes: Discovering Japa-nese culture and education*. Yarmouth, ME: Intercultural Press.

Flax, J. (1983). Political philosophy and the patriarchal unconscious: A psychoanalytic per-spective on epistemology and metaphysics. In S. Harding & M. B. Hintikka (Eds.), *Dis-covering reality* (pp. 245–281). Dordrecht, The Netherlands: D. Reidel.

Flax, J. (1990). *Thinking fragments: Psychoanalysis, feminism, and postmodernism in the con-temporary West*. Berkeley: University of California Press.

Foster, M. (1990). The politics of race: Through the eyes of African American teachers. *Journal of Education, 172*(3), 123–141.

Foster, M. (1997). *Black teachers on teaching*. New York: The New Press.

Foucault, M. (1980). *Power/Knowledge*. New York: Pantheon.

Fraser, N. (1997). *Justice interruptus: Critical reflections on the "postsocialist" condition*. New York: Routledge.

Freire, P. (1970). *Pedagogy of the oppressed*. (M. Bergman Ramos, Trans.). New York: Seabury Press.

Freire, P. (1985). *The politics of education: Culture, power, and liberation*. South Hadley, MA: Bergin and Garvey.

Fultz, M. (Spring, 1995a). African-American teachers in the South, 1890–1940: Growth, feminization, and salary discrimination. *Teachers College Record, 96*(3), 544–567.

Fultz, M. (Spring, 1995b). Teacher training and African-American education in the South, 1900–1940. *The Journal of Negro Education, 64*(2), 196–214.

Giroux, H. (1981). *Ideology, culture and the process of school.* Barcombe, England: Falmer.

Giroux, H. (1983). *Theory and resistance in education: A pedagogy for the opposition.* South Hadley, MA: Bergin and Garvey.

Giroux, H. (1988). *Schooling and the struggle for public life.* Minneapolis: University of Minnesota Press.

Giroux, H. (1992). *Border crossings.* New York: Routledge.

Giroux, H. (1997). *Pedagogy and the politics of hope.* Boulder, CO: Westview Press. (Original work published 1982)

Green, J. M. (1999). *Deep democracy: Community, diversity, and transformation.* Lanham, MD: Rowman & Littlefield.

Greene, M. (1995*). Releasing the imagination: Essays on education, the arts, and social change.* San Francisco, CA: Jossey-Bass.

Grimshaw, J. (1986). *Philosophy and feminist thinking.* Minneapolis: University of Minnesota Press.

Griswold del Castillo, R. (1984). *La familia: Chicano families in the urban southwest, 1848 to the present.* Notre Dame, IN: University of Notre Dame Press.

Habermas, J. (1984). *The theory of communicative action, I and II.* Boston: Beacon Press.

Haiducek, N. J. (1991). *Japanese education: Made in the United States.* New York: Praeger.

Haraway, D. (1988). Situated knowledges: The science question in feminism and the privilege of partial perspective. *Feminist Studies, 14*(3), 575–599.

Harding, S. (1991). *Whose science? Whose knowledge? Thinking from women's lives.* Ithaca, NY: Cornell University Press.

Hood, C. P. (2001). *Japanese education reform: Nakasone's legacy.* London: Routledge.

hooks, b. (1994). *Teaching to transgress: Education as the practice of freedom.* New York: Routledge.

hooks, b. (2003). *Teaching community: A pedagogy of hope.* New York: Routledge.

Horton, A. I. (1989). *The Highlander Folk School: A history of its major programs, 1932–1961.* Brooklyn, NY: Carlson. (Original work published 1971)

Horton, M. (1990). *The long haul: An autobiography.* (H. Kohl & J. Kohl, Eds.). New York: Teachers College Press.

Horton, M., & Freire, P. (1990). *We make the road by walking.* (B. Bell, J. Gaventa, & J. Peters, Eds.). Philadelphia, PA: Temple University Press.

Huang, J. (1997). *Chinese students and scholars in American higher education.* Westport, CT: Praeger.

Irigaray, L. (1985). *Speculum of the other woman.* (G. Gill, Trans.). Ithaca, NY: Cornell Press. (Original work published 1974)

Irwin, L. (1994). *The dream seekers: Native American visionary traditions of the Great Plains.* Norman: University of Oklahoma Press.

James, W. (1975). *The meaning of truth.* Cambridge, MA: Harvard University Press. (Original work published 1909)

James, W. (1976). *Essays in radical empiricism.* Cambridge, MA: Harvard University Press. (Original work published 1912)

James, W. (1977). *A pluralistic universe.* Cambridge, MA: Harvard University Press. (Original work published 1909)

Johnson, T., & Reed, R. (Eds.). (2002). *Historical documents in American Education* (Chapter 1.) Boston: Allyn and Bacon.

Keller, E. F. (1985). *Reflections on gender and science.* New Haven, CT: Yale University Press.

Khema, A. (1999). *Be an island: The Buddhist practice of inner peace.* Boston: Wisdom.

King, M. L. Jr. (1967). *Where do we go from here: Chaos or community?* New York: Harper and Row.

King, Y. (1989). The ecology of feminism and the feminism of ecology. In J. Plant (Ed.). *Healing the wounds: The promise of ecofeminism* (pp. 18–28). Santa Cruz, CA: New Society.

Kozol, J. (1991). *Savage inequalities.* New York: Crown Publishers.

Kozol, J. (2005). *The shame of the nation: The restoration of apartheid schooling in America.* New York: Crown.

Laclau, E., & Mouffe, C. (1985) *Hegemony and socialist strategy: Towards a radical democratic politics* (Winston Moore and Paul Cammack, Trans.). London: Verso.

Ladson-Billings, G. (1994). *The dreamkeepers: Successful teachers of African American children.* San Francisco, CA: Jossey-Bass.

Ladson-Billings, G. (2005). *Beyond the big house: African American educators on teacher education.* New York: Teachers College Press.

Levinas, E. (1994). *Outside the subject.* (Michale B. Smith, Trans.). Palo Alto, CA: Stanford University Press. (Original work published 1987, 1993)

Lewis, C. C. (1995). *Educating hearts and minds: Reflections on Japanese preschool and elementary education.* Cambridge, UK: Cambridge University Press.

Lobo, S., & Peters, K. (Eds.). (2001). *American Indians and the urban experience.* Walnut Creek, CA: Altamira Press.

Locke, J. (1960). *The second treatise on government.* Cambridge, UK: Cambridge University Press. (Original work published 1823)

Lomotey, K. (Ed.). (1990). *Going to school: The African-American experience.* Albany: State University of New York Press.

Lyotard, J. (1984). *The postmodern condition: A report on knowledge.* Minneapolis: University of Minnesota Press.

Margonis, F. (2004). The path of social amnesia and Dewey's democratic commitments. In K. Alston (Ed.), *Philosophy of Education Society 2003* (pp. 296–304). Urbana: University of Illinois Press.

Maslow, A. (1954). *Motivation and personality.* New York: Harper and Row.

McCarty, T. C. (2002). *A place to be Navajo: Rough Rock and the struggle for self-determination in indigenous schooling.* Mahwah, NJ: Lawrence Erlbaum.

McLaren, P. (2003). *Life in schools* (4th ed.). Boston: Pearson Education. (Original work published 1989)

Merchant, C. (1980). *The death of nature: Women, ecology, and the scientific revolution.* San Francisco: Harper and Row.

Montessori, M. (1976). *The discovery of the child.* New York: Ballantine Books.

Montessori, M. (1977). *The secret of childhood.* New York: Ballantine Books.

Morris, J. (1999, January). A pillar of strength: An African American school's communal bonds with families and community since Brown, *Urban Education, 33*(5), 584–605.

Morris, J. (2004, Spring). Can anything good come from Nazareth? Race, class, and African American schooling and community in the urban South and Midwest. *American Educational Research Journal, 41*(1), 69–112.

Morris, R. (1997). Educating Savages. *Quarterly Journal of Speech, 83,* 152–171.

Morris, V. G., & Morris, C. L. (2000). *Creating caring and nurturing educational environments for African American children.* Westport, CT: Bergin and Garvey.

Mouffe, C. (1993). *The return of the political.* London: Verso.

Mouffe, C. (2000). *The democratic paradox.* London: Verso.

Mouffe, C. (2005a). *On the political.* New York: Routledge.

Mouffe, C. (2005b). The limits of John Rawls's pluralism. *Politics, Philosophy & Economics, 4*(2), 221–231.

Nieto, S. (1992). *Affirming diversity: The sociopolitical context of multicultural education.* White Plains, NY: Longman.

Ning, Q. (2002). *Chinese students encounter America.* (T. K. Chu, Trans.). Seattle: University of Washington Press.

Noblit, G. W., & Dempsey, V. O. (1996). *The social construction of virtue: The moral life of schools.* Albany: State University of New York Press.

Noddings, N. (1984). *Caring: A feminine approach to ethics and moral education.* Berkeley: University of California Press.

Ogbu, J. (1991). Immigrant and involuntary minorities in comparative perspective. In M. A. Gibson & J. U. Ogbu (Eds.), *Minority status and schooling* (pp. 3–33). New York: Garland.

Okano, K., & Tsuchiya, M. (1999). *Education in contemporary Japan: Inequality and diversity.* Cambridge, UK: Cambridge University Press.

Okin, S. M. (2005). "Forty acres and a mule" for women: Rawls and feminism, *Politics, Philosophy & Economics, 4*(2), 233–248.

Pang, V. O., & Cheng, L. L. (Eds.). (1998). *Struggling to be heard: The unmet needs of Asian Pacific American children.* Albany: State University of New York Press.

Peirce, C. S. (1958). *Values in a universe of chance: Selected writings of Charles Sanders Peirce (1839-1914)* (P. P. Wiener, Ed.). Garden City, NJ: Doubleday.

Peterson, E. A. (1996, Summer). Our students, ourselves: Lessons of challenge and hope from the African American community. *New Directions for Adult and Continuing Education, 70,* 17–26.

Portales, M. (2000). *Crowding out Latinos: Mexican Americans in the public consciousness.* Philadelphia: Temple University Press.

Rawls, J. (1993). *Political liberalism.* New York: Columbia University Press.

Reyhner, J. (Ed.). (1992). *Teaching American Indian students.* Norman: University of Oklahoma Press.

Roessel, Jr., R. A. (1999, Spring). Navajo education and the future. *Journal of American Indian Education,* 14–18.

Romo, H., & Falbo, T. (1996). *Latino high school graduation: Defying the odds.* Austin: University of Texas Press.

Rorty, R. (1979). *Philosophy and the mirror of nature.* Princeton, NJ: Princeton University Press.

Rorty, R. (1998). *Achieving our country: Leftist thought in 20th century America.* Cambridge, MA: Harvard University Press.

Rousseau, J. J. (1968). *The social contract.* (M. Cranston, Trans.). Harmondsworth, UK: Penguin Books. (Original work published 1762)

Royce, J. (1916). *The hope of the great community.* New York: MacMillan.

Ruddick, S. (1989). *Maternal thinking: Toward a politics of peace.* Boston: Beacon Press.

Schoolland, K. (1990). *Shogun's ghost: The dark side of Japanese education.* New York: Bergin and Garvey.

Seigfried, C. H. (1996). *Pragmatism and feminism: Reweaving the social fabric.* Chicago: University of Chicago Press.

Senese, G. (1986, Spring). Self-determination and American Indian education: An illusion of control. *Educational Theory, 36*(2), 153–164.

Slavin, R., & Calderón, M. (Eds.). (2001). *Effective programs for Latino students.* Mahwah, NJ: Lawrence Erlbaum.

Smith, A. M. (1998). *Laclau and Mouffe: The radical democratic imaginary.* London: Routledge.

Smith, D. (1987). *The everyday world as problematic: A feminist sociology.* Boston: Northeastern University.

Smith, D. (1990). *The conceptual practices of power: A feminist sociology of knowledge.* Boston: Northeastern University.

Spring, J. (2004). *Deculturalization and the struggle for equality: A brief history of the education of dominated cultures in the U.S.* (4th ed.). New York: McGraw Hill.

Stevenson, H. W., & Stigler, J. W. (1992). *The learning gap: Why our schools are failing and what we can learn from Japanese and Chinese education.* New York: Summit Books.

Suárez-Orozco, C., & Suárez-Orozco, M. (1995). *Transformations: Immigration, family life, and achievement motivation among Latino adolescents.* Palo Alto, CA: Stanford University Press.

Thayer-Bacon, B. (2000). *Transforming critical thinking: Thinking constructively.* New York: Teachers College Press.

Thayer-Bacon, B. (2002). An exploration of Myles Horton's caring reasoning at Highlander Folk School. *Thinking: The Journal for Philosophy for Children, 16*(1), 32–41.

Thayer-Bacon, B. (2003). *Relational "(e)pistemologies."* New York: Peter Lang.

Thayer-Bacon, B., with Bacon, C. (1998). *Philosophy applied to education: Nurturing a democratic community in the classroom.* Upper Saddle River, NJ: Prentice Hall.

Thompson, H. (1975). *The Navajo's long walk for education: A history of Navajo education.* Tsaile, Navajo Nation, AZ: Navajo Community College Press.

Thompson, T. (Ed.). (1978). *The schooling of Native America.* Washington, DC: American Association of Colleges of Teacher Education.

Valdés, G. (1996). *Con respecto: Bridging the distances between culturally diverse families and schools: An ethnographic portrait.* New York: Teachers College Press.

Valenzuela, A. (1999). Subtractive schooling: U.S.–Mexican youth and the politics of caring. Albany: State University of New York Press.

Walker, V. S. (1996). *Their highest potential: An African American school community in the segregated South.* Chapel Hill: The University of North Carolina Press.

Walker, V. S. (2001, Winter). African American teaching in the South: 1940–1960. *American Educational Research Journal, 38*(4), 751–779.

Walzer, M. (1981, August). Philosophy and democracy. *Political Theory, 9*(3), 379–399.

Walzer, M. (1983). *Spheres of justice.* New York: Basic Books.

Warren, K. J. (1990, Spring). The power and the promise of ecological feminism. *Environmental Ethics, 12*(1), 125–146.

West, C. (1994). *Race matters.* New York: Vintage Books.

Wigwe, C. W. (1990). *Language, culture and society in West Africa.* Elms Court, UK: Arthur H. Stockwell.

Woodson, C. G. (1990). *The mis-education of the Negro.* Trenton, NJ: Africa World Press. (Original work published 1933)

Young, I. M. (1990a). The ideal of community and the politics of difference. In L. Nicholson (Ed.), *Feminism/Postmodernism* (pp. 300–323). New York: Routledge.

Young, I. M. (1990b). *Justice and the politics of difference.* Princeton, NJ: Princeton University Press.

Young, I. M. (2000). *Inclusion and democracy.* Oxford, UK: Oxford University Press.

Index

Abowitz, K. K., 5
Acculturation process, 51
Adams, Frank, 181–182 n. 5
Africa and African Americans, 4–5, 15, 55–82
    colonial relationships, 55, 64–65, 103, 160
    demographics of, 55–56
    Junior Secondary School (JSS, Ghana),
        56, 57–59, 64–67, 81, 157, 168
    Mountain Middle School (MMS,
        southern U.S.), 56, 72–75
    River High School (RHS, southern
        U.S.), 56, 59–63, 64, 66–72, 81
    segregation legacy and, 55–56, 75–76,
        77, 79
    West African dance and drumming
        class, 72–75
Alger, Horatio, 4
Allen, P., 66
Anderson, J. D., 55
Arthur, Chester, 130
Asante, M. K., 55
Ashton-Warner, S., 88
Authoritarianism, at Junior Secondary
    School (JSS, Ghana), 57–59, 64–67,
    68–69, 157, 168
Authority, shared. *See* Shared authority
Autonomy, 3, 19
Ayers, W., 56

Bacon, Charles, 182 n. 1, 184 n. 3
Baker, S., 56
Barber, Benjamin, 8, 13, 15, 16–20, 21, 23,
    31, 120, 132, 136, 140–142, 153, 161,
    180 n. 6

Bentley, Arthur, 3, 9
Between Sacred Mountains, 89, 90
Black Elk, 101
Boler, M., 2
Brayboy, B., 172
Brown, D., 101
Brown v. Board of Education, 56
Bush, George W., 29, 30, 87
Butcher, R. E., 55

Calderón, M., 34, 51
Canada, 159
Canton elementary school (San Francisco),
    132, 136–140, 142–143, 150
Cao, Yan, 131
Capitalism, 26
C.A.R.E. project, 5–7, 30, 32, 55, 155–178
Carger, C., 180 n. 1
Chen, Shehong, 130, 131
Cheng, L. L., 130
Child-centered approach, 63–65, 121
Chin, Frank, 131
China and Chinese Americans, 6, 130–154
    Canton elementary school (San Fran-
        cisco), 132, 136–140, 142–143, 150
    Chinese Sunday School (U.S.), 131–132
    conflict versus harmony and, 129,
        145–154
    conformity to group norms, 133–154,
        170–172
    demographics of, 130, 131
    friendships of students and, 133–143
    Guangzhou schools (China), 132, 143,
        145–152

China and Chinese Americans (*cont'd*)
    "model minority" stereotype and, 5,
        176–177
    routine rituals and freedom, 145–152,
        170–172
    student role in schools, 145–152, 170–172
Choy, P., 130
Chun, Gloria Heyung, 131
Citizenship democracy (Barber), 16–18,
    140–142, 161
Civil Rights Act of 1964, 56
Class size
    in China, 133, 163–164
    conformity to group norms, 133–154
    in Ghana, 163–164
    in Japan, 163–164
    in Mexico, 163
Class structure, 26
Clinton, Bill, 28, 125
Collectivism, 4–5. *See also* Africa and
    African Americans; China and Chinese
    Americans; Japan and Japanese Ameri-
    cans; Mexico and Mexican Americans;
    Native Americans
Collins, P. H., 80
Colonial relationships
    for Africans and African Americans, 55,
        64–65, 103, 160
    for Mexico and Mexican Americans, 51,
        55, 103, 160
    for Native Americans, 55, 83, 84, 91–93,
        101–103, 160, 164–165
Columbus, Christopher, 100–101
Communitarianism, 4–5, 23, 25, 26–27, 31,
    53. *See also* Africa and African Americans;
    China and Chinese Americans; Japan and
    Japanese Americans; Mexico and Mexican
    Americans; Native Americans
Conflict versus harmony
    China and Chinese American, 129,
        145–154
    Japan and Japanese American, 108,
        119–127, 129
    Conformity to group norms
    China and Chinese American, 133–154,
        170–172
    Japan and Japanese American, 119–127,
        170–172

Conservatism, 11
Constructivism, 26
Contract theory (Locke), 25
Cooper, K., 183 n. 5, 183 n. 6
*Creating Caring and Nurturing Educational
    Environments for African American
    Children* (Foster), 75
Critical theory, 2, 15, 20, 22–23
Cultural diversity, 18, 22, 24–25, 151, 173–175
Cultural imperialism, 151
Curriculum
    control of, 153–154, 174–175
    informal and hidden, 108, 128–129

Darwin, Charles, 11
Deconstructionism, 126
Deep democracy (Green), 142–143
Deliberative democracy (Young), 8, 20–25,
    31–32, 36, 42
Deloria, V., Jr., 83
Delpit, Lisa, 56, 75
Democracy and Education (Dewey), 9, 11–12
Democratic Paradox, The (Mouffe), 28–29,
    108, 125–127
Dempsey, V. O., 56, 76, 77, 81
Derrida, Jacques, 101, 126
Dewey, John, 2, 3, 7, 8–15, 17, 19–23, 24,
    26, 30, 31, 65, 158–159, 180 n. 3, 180 n.
    5, 180 n. 7
Differentiated solidarity (Young), 23
Diné Primary (Navajo reservation), 85–90,
    92, 104–106
Dong, L., 130
Drop-out rates, 56
Duran, Bonnie, 84, 101–103
Duran, Eduardo, 84, 101–103

Educating Hearts and Minds (Lewis), 108
Ellington, L., 107, 109, 116, 120, 124
Emancipatory authority (Giroux), 66,
    78–79, 81–82
Enlightenment, 2, 3, 18, 66
Epstein, I., 135
Essentialism, 26
Exclusion. *See* Inclusion/exclusion

Falbo, T., 43
Fallibilism (James), 17–18

About the Author

Barbara J. Thayer-Bacon is a professor of philosophy of education in the cultural studies of education program at the University of Tennessee. She has been on the faculty there since 2000, and teaches graduate courses on social foundations and philosophy of education and social philosophy and cultural diversity. She received her Ph.D. in education from Indiana University in 1991. Prior to this, she was a Montessori elementary teacher. Her primary research areas as a philosopher of education are pragmatism, feminist theory and pedagogy, and cultural studies in education. She is an active member in numerous professional organizations, including the American Educational Research Association, American Educational Studies Association, and Philosophy of Education Society, and presents papers regularly at their annual conferences. She is the author of numerous chapters in essay collections and more than 75 journal articles. She has written three previous books: *Philosophy Applied to Education: Nurturing a Democratic Community in the Classroom* (with Dr. Charles S. Bacon as contributing author), *Transforming Critical Thinking: Constructive Thinking,* and *Relational "(e)pistemologies."*